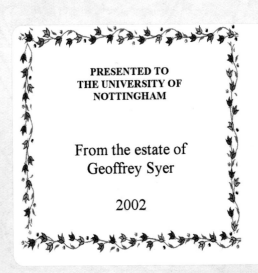

EVERYMAN'S LIBRARY
EDITED BY ERNEST RHYS

PHILOSOPHY
& THEOLOGY

BOEHME'S "SIGNATURA RERUM"
AND OTHER DISCOURSES
INTRODUCTION BY CLIFFORD BAX

HOW CHARMING IS DIVINE PHILOSOPHY

MILTON

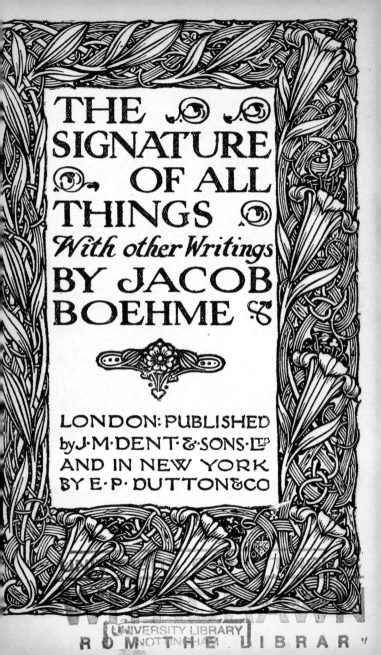

THE SIGNATURE OF ALL THINGS

With other Writings

BY JACOB BOEHME

LONDON: PUBLISHED
by J·M·DENT·&·SONS·LTD
AND IN NEW YORK
BY E·P·DUTTON&CO

INTRODUCTION [1]

*Trasumanar significa per verba
non si poria ; però l'esemplo basti
a cui esperienza grazia serba.*

THERE are few figures in history more strange and beautiful
than that of Jacob Boehme. With a few exceptions the outward events of his life were unremarkable. He was born in
1575 at the village Alt Seidenberg, two miles from Goerlitz
in Germany and close to the Bohemian border. His parents
were poor, and in childhood he was put to mind their cattle.
It was in the solitude of the fields that he first beheld a vision,
and assuredly his contemplative spirit must have been well
nourished by the continual companionship of nature.

Physically he was not robust (though he never had a sickness), and for this reason his parents, when he was fourteen,
apprenticed him to a shoemaker. Of his apprenticeship
nothing is recorded, I think, except a story about a mysterious
man who came once to the shop when the master was away,
and taking Jacob by both hands foretold to him the great
work that he should accomplish.

In 1599, when he was four-and-twenty, he became a master
shoemaker, and in the same year he married the daughter
of a butcher. The girl developed into a capable considerate
woman, and they lived together happily until Boehme died.
They had four sons and probably two daughters, but his
children do not figure prominently in the story of his life.
Already he had been visited by a sudden illumination of mind,
and in 1600 he experienced the second of those marvellous
ecstasies that gave splendour to the whole of his after-life.
This, also, was followed by a third and still more brilliant
illumination that made clear and complete much that in his
previous visions had been obscure and unrelated.

The more dramatic portion of his life begins, however, with
the publication of his first book (about 1612). At first he
called it *Morning-Glow*, but at the suggestion of a friend he

---

[1] The biographic substance of this introduction is principally drawn
from Dr. Hartmann's rare volume, and from Professor Deussen's *Preface*
to the magnificent edition of Boehme's works which has just been produced
under the enthusiastic editorship of Mr. C. J. Barker.

altered the title to that under which it has become world-famous—*Aurora*.

Now although Lutheranism had severely shaken the old orthodoxy, it had itself become, in Boehme's time, an orthodoxy just as rigid. Quite naturally the book was read by the pastor of Goerlitz, one Gregorius Richter. He was a man intolerant, conceited, violent of temper, and obtuse of intellect. He despised and feared the shoemaker. The book ruffled him into a self-righteous passion, and hurrying to the City Council he demanded that Boehme should be banished. The Council was afraid to refuse, and Boehme (like nearly all the truth-bringers) was exiled from his native town.

On the morrow, however, the Council convened again. Its members were stirred by a fine shame when it was put to them that they had banished a citizen of stainless reputation, and one, indeed, who regularly attended church. They recalled him at once, but on condition that he should write no books.

In the following year he changed his occupation. Literary work had caused his business to decline, and having sold the shop he journeyed to the larger cities of the neighbourhood (such, for example, as Prague and Dresden) selling woollen gloves; but after a while it was no longer possible for him to disobey the inner command that he should give to men his revelations, and in these last ten years he composed the unique and shining books of which we have a selection in this volume.

Gregorius Richter, as we should expect, by no means left him at peace. He was denounced from the pulpit and in his own hearing. Scurrilous treatises were flung at him, treatises full of personal abuse and ignoble sneers at his profession. "His writing," observed those who represented the Son of the carpenter, "smells overmuch of cobbler's pitch;" and again we read, "Will ye have the words of Jesus Christ or the words of a shoemaker?" The shoemaker answered them gently and with dignity, as when he declared, "Not I, the I that I am, knows these things, but God knows them in me."

In 1624 his friend Abraham von Frankenburg republished a selection of his writings under the title of *The Way to Christ*. Its radiant beauty impelled the respect of many who belonged to the orthodox church, and this very fact inflamed the Tertullians of his native town. Again they banished him on the charge of impiety, and even refused that he should say farewell to his wife and sons. He went to Dresden. There already he had found a friend in Dr. Hinkelmann. It is pleasant to record that while he was at Dresden the emperor convened a meeting of eminent divines, that Boehme was invited, and that the depth and spirituality of his thought, together with the charm and modesty with which he expressed it, were received with admiration by many and with enthusiasm by the learned doctors Gerhard and Meissner.

But at the end of the year (November 20, 1624) he died, happily and in the presence of a loving and beloved son. He had foretold the very hour of his death. So relentless were his opponents in Goerlitz that, until the intervention of the powerful Count Hannibal von Drohna, they refused a burial service, and the very priest who had attended him in death, being forced by the Council to make an oration, began by declaring that he would rather walk twenty miles than praise the gentle Boehme. The elaborate cross, too, which was put upon his tomb was torn down in anger.

We are told by Frankenburg, his friend, that he was short in stature, "worn and very plain," with "grey eyes, that lightened into a celestial blue, a low forehead, a thin beard, and an aquiline nose."

Now in the study of mysticism we soon find the essential experience of all mystics to have been identical, and that among them is no figure more representative than Jacob Boehme: so that when we read this book we are like men who from the vantage-point of one of its highest hills can see below and around them the whole expanse of a beautiful and unearthly island. If it allures us we shall then delight in exploring its verdant valleys or spirit-peopled woods or quiet starlit gardens, and all the mysterious birds and blossoms that fly or flutter within them; but if it does not seem attractive we can push off and sail for another country. By no true philalethe can mysticism be honourably ignored. It is either the noblest folly or the grandest achievement of man's mind. Alexander and Napoleon were ambitious, but their ambition dwindles to insignificance when it is compared with that of the mystic. The purpose of the mystic is the mightiest and most solemn that can ever be, for the central aim of all mysticism is to soar out of separate personality up to the very consciousness of God.

So well, indeed, had Roman Catholicism taught those who were religious the insignificance of the human soul that few among the European mystics of the Middle Ages or the Renaissance were so brilliantly conscious that they could cry out boldly with Meister Eckhardt, " I truly have need of God, but God has need of me." Often they shrank from the ultimate experience, wholly worshipping God indeed, but retaining ever a sense of separateness. Their very humility was the final veil of egotism which they dared not rend.

Jacob Boehme, the last of the great European mystics, having imagined the Spirit which pervades the universe, knew well how little was the stature of his human personality; but he had realised that God was verily within him, and he spoke with the uprightness of a divine being. Unflaggingly he counsels men (as in *The Supersensual Life*) to turn away from the worthless and separated self which hungers for honour or for bodily comfort, in order that they should rediscover within themselves " what was before nature and creature." And he means by this phrase " that light which lighteth every man who cometh into the world." It is here, he says, now and always: we have but to extricate our consciousness from all that is the effect of our time and place. We have but to quiet our own thoughts and desires, and we shall hear at once the harmonies of heaven.

The danger of such a doctrine is apparent. The true mystic may safely follow his Inward Light, but the enchanted apples are guarded by dragons and are only to be captured by the strong. Many a self-styled mystic has wasted his life in " waiting for the spark that never came: " wasted, we say, though surely not worse wasted than the thousands of lives that, for all their activity, bring nothing to the soul. It is something at least to have striven for the noblest of all ends. We must choose either safety or romance, and mysticism is the romance of religion; the mystic an explorer in the spiritual world. He does not use the instruments of intellect. He experiments. Perhaps, like the Persian Sufi poets, he thinks of God as the Great Beloved, and then, directing all his power of love to the most glorious idea that he is able to conceive, he finds that his emotion like a river has carried him into a state of soul in which he is vividly conscious of the Divine Presence. In that state he beholds the visible world as it were from within. He perceives the spiritual cause of all these material effects. He understands the essential nature of trees and flowers and mountains and the live creatures of the world. No longer does he see men by those dim lights that penetrate the dense and cloudy world of matter. He sees them as angelic toilers bowed by the burden of their own

mundane selves.   And he knows the insignificance of much
that we deem important, the deep value of much that we
count accessory, for having cleansed his vision of all personal
impediment he apprehends the true proportion of all the
elements that compose the universe.   The vast realisations
that shine within him then are by their nature not easy to
express in common terms.   Who that has loved could explain
his experience to one that had never loved?   Only those
who are near can understand, and that is why so often the
words of mystics are obscure.

Sometimes the seer will attempt to explain his illumined
state, like St. John or Jalàlu-d-din Rūmi, by the use of brilliant
symbols adapted from the material world; sometimes, like
Plotinus or Boehme, by the use of the most abstract words in
order that the mind may be led away from worldly associa-
tions: but all alike have looked upon one splendour.   By
many ways they have travelled homeward to that ideal state
in which alone the unshackled soul has perfect freedom, and
in this book, assuredly, we are communing with one who, if
any among men has ever done so, broke free from the bonds
of personality and could look upon the universe with the eyes
of God.

CLIFFORD BAX.

BIBLIOGRAPHY

WORKS.—Aurora, 1612; The Three Principles, 1619; The Threefold Life of Man, 1620; Answers to the Forty Questions of the Soul, 1620; Of the Incarnation of Christ, 1620; The Great Six Points, 1620; The Heavenly and Earthly Mystery, 1620; Of the Last Times, 1620; De Signatura Rerum, 1621; The Four Complexions, 1621; An Apology to Balthazar Tylken, 1621; Considerations upon Isaias Stiefel's Book, 1621; Of True Repentance, 1622; Of True Resignation, 1622; Of Regeneration, 1622; A Book of Predestination and Election of God, 1623; A Compendium of Repentance, 1623; Mysterium Magnum, 1623; A Table of the Principles, 1624; Of the Supersensual Life, 1624; Of the Divine Vision, 1624; Of the Two Testaments of Christ, 1624; A Discourse between a Soul Hungry and Thirsty after the Great Fountain of Life and a Soul Enlightened, 1624; An Apology against Gregory Richter, 1624; Of 177 Theosophic Questions, 1624; An Epitome of the Mysterium Magnum, 1624; The Holy Weeks, 1624; Of the Divine Revelation, 1624; Of the Errors of the Sects of Ezekiel Metts and Isaias Stiefel, 1624; Of the Last Judgment, 1624; Letters to Divers Persons, 1624. Several Treatises of Jacob Boehme, 1661, and Remainder of Books written by Jacob Boehme, 1662, Englished by J. Sparrow (a re-issue of Sparrow's translation is now in progress, 1910-12, by C. J. Barker). First collected edition of Works, Amsterdam, 1675; later editions, 6 vols., Leipzig, 1831-46; William Law's English edition, 4 vols., London, 1764-81 (the present volume follows the text of Law's edition).

BIOGRAPHIES.—Life of One Jacob Behmen, 1644; Memoirs of the Life, Death, Burial and Wonderful Writings of Jacob Behmen, by Francis Okely, 1762; Works of Jacob Behmen, translated, with a Life of the Author, by Wm. Law, 1764-72-81; His Life and Teaching, by H. L. Martensen, 1885; Life and Doctrines, by F. Hartmann, 1891; An Appreciation, by Dr. A. Whyte, 1894.

CONTENTS

SIGNATURA RERUM

SIGNATURA RERUM;

THE

SIGNATURE OF ALL THINGS.

Shewing the Sign and Signification of

The several Forms and Shapes in the Creation;

AND WHAT THE

BEGINNING, RUIN, AND CURE OF EVERYTHING IS.

IT PROCEEDS OUT OF

Eternity into Time, and again out of Time into Eternity,

AND COMPRIZES ALL MYSTERIES.

PREFACE TO THE READER

THIS book is a true mystical mirror of the highest wisdom. The best treasure that a man can attain unto in this world is true knowledge; even *the knowledge of himself*: For *man* is the great mystery of God, the *microcosm*, or the complete abridgment of the whole universe: He is the *mirandum Dei opus*, God's masterpiece, a living emblem and hieroglyphic of eternity and time; and therefore to know whence he is, and what his temporal and eternal being and well-being are, must needs be that ONE necessary thing, to which all our chief study should aim, and in comparison of which all the wealth of this world is but dross, and a loss to us.

Hence Solomon, the wisest of the kings of Israel, says: "Happy is the man that findeth wisdom, and the man that getteth understanding; for the merchandise of it is better than the merchandise of silver, and the gain thereof than fine gold; she is more precious than rubies, and all things that can be desired are not to be compared unto her."

This is that wisdom which dwells in nothing, and yet possesses all things, and the humble resigned soul is its play-fellow; this is the divine alloquy, the inspiration of the Almighty, the breath of God, the holy unction, which sanctifies the soul to be the temple of the Holy Ghost, which instructs it aright in all things, and searches τὰ βάθη τὸν Θεὸν,[1] the depths of God.

This is the precious pearl, whose beauty is more glorious, and whose virtue more sovereign than the sun: It is a never-failing comfort in all afflictions, a balsam for all sores, a panacea for all diseases, a sure antidote against all poison, and death itself; it is that joyful and assured companion and guide, which never forsakes a man, but convoys him through this valley of misery and death into the blessed paradise of perfect bliss.

If you ask, What is the way to attain to this wisdom? Behold! Christ, who is the way, the truth, and the life, tells you plainly in these words; "If any man will come after me, let him deny himself, and take up his cross daily and follow me;"[2] or as he

[1] 1 Cor. ii. 10. [2] Luke ix. 23.

3

says elsewhere, " Unless you be born again, you cannot see the kingdom of heaven: " or as St. Paul says, " If any man seemeth to be wise in this world, let him become a fool that he may be wise." [1]

Herein lies that simple childlike way to the highest wisdom, which no sharp reason or worldly learning can reach unto; nay, it is foolishness to reason, and therefore so few go the way to find it: The proud sophisters and wiselings of this world have always trampled it under foot with scorn and contempt, and have called it enthusiasm, madness, melancholy, whimsy, fancy, etc., but wisdom is justified of her children.

Indeed, every one is not fit for or capable of the knowledge of the eternal and temporal nature in its mysterious operation, neither is the proud covetous world worthy to receive a clear manifestation of it; and therefore the only wise God (who giveth wisdom to every one that asketh it aright of him) has locked up the jewel in his blessed treasury, which none can open but those that have the key; which is this, viz., " Ask, and it shall be given you; seek, and ye shall find; knock, and it shall be opened unto you: " The Father will give the Spirit to them that ask him for it.

This is the true theosophic school wherein this author learned the first rudiments and principles of wisdom, and to which we must go if we would understand his deep writings: For we must know that the sons of Hermes, who have commenced in the high school of true magic and theosophy, have always spoken their hidden wisdom in a mystery; and have so couched it under shadows and figures, parables and similies, that none can understand their obscure, yet clear writings, but those who have had admittance into the same school, and have tasted of the Feast of Pentecost.

And this does not seem at all strange to the children of divine Mercury; for the mysteries of philosophy, divinity, and theosophy must not be profaned, and laid open to the view of the outward astral reason, which turns all to its selfish pride, covetousness, envy, wrath, and cunning hypocrisy; and therefore a parabolical or magical phrase or dialect is the best and plainest habit and dress that mysteries can have to travel in up and down this wicked world: And thus parable have a double and different respect and use; for as they conceal and hide secrets from the rude and vulgar sort, who are not able or

[1] 1 Cor. iii. 13.

patient to bear anything but what suits with their common conceits and opinions, so likewise they sweetly lead the mind of the true searcher into the depths of wisdom's council. They are as the cloudy pillar of Moses; they have a dark part, and they have a light part; they are dark to the Egyptians, the pharisaical sons of sophistry, but light to the true Israel, the children of the mystery.

And therefore whoever will be nurtured and trained up by Sophia, and learn to understand and speak the language of wisdom, must be born again of and in the Word of Wisdom, Christ Jesus, the Immortal Seed: The divine essence which God breathed into his paradisical soul must be revived, and he must become one again with that which he was in God before he was a creature, and then his Eternal Spirit may enter into that which is within the veil, and see not only the literal, but the moral, allegorical, and anagogical meaning of the wise and their dark sayings: He then will be fit to enter, not only into Solomon's porch, the outer court of natural philosophy, sense and reason, but likewise into the inward court of holy and spiritual exercises, in divine understanding and knowledge; and so he may step into the most inward and holiest place of theosophical mysteries, into which none are admitted to come, but those who have received the high and holy unction.

I will now endeavour briefly to hint to the reader what this book contains, though in it the spirit of wisdom cannot be delineated with pen and ink, no more than a sound can be painted, or the wind grasped in the hollow of the hand: But know, that in it he deciphers and represents in a lively manner the Signature of all Things, and gives you the contents of eternity and time, and glances at all mysteries.

Herein the author sets forth fundamentally the birth, sympathy, and antipathy of all beings; how all beings originally arise out of one eternal mystery, and how that same mystery begets itself in itself from eternity to eternity; and likewise how all things, which take their original out of this eternal mystery, may be changed into evil, and again out of evil into good; with a clear and manifest demonstration how man has turned himself out of the good into the evil, and how his transmutation is again out of the evil into the good: Moreover, herein is declared the outward cure of the body; how the outward life may be freed from sickness by its likeness or assimulate, and be again introduced into its first essence; where also, by way of parable and similitude, the Philosopher's Stone is with great life described for the temporal cure; and along with it the holy Corner Stone, Christ alone, for the everlasting cure, regeneration, and perfect restitution of all the true, faithful, eternal souls. In a word, his intent is to let you know the inward power and property by the outward sign; for nature has given marks and notes to everything, whereby it may be known; and this is the Language of Nature, which signifies for what everything is good and profitable: And herein lies the mystery, or central science of the high philosophical work in the true spagiric art, which consummates the cure, not only for the body, but for the soul.

But let the reader know that the sharp speculation of his own reason will never pry into the depth of this book, but rather bring him into a maze of doubtful notions, wherein he will bewilder himself, and think the author's phrase tedious and strange; and therefore the understanding lies only in the manifestation of that Spirit, which in the Day of Pentecost gave forth the true sense and meaning of all languages in one: Now if that Spirit rules and dwells in you, then you may understand this author in the deepest ground, according to your creaturely constellation, both in the eternal and temporal nature; but if not, these things will be but as a relation of trifles and chimeras to you. And therefore if you be of a saturnine property, dull and dark, shut up in the house of Luna, soar not too high with your censure and scorn, or with a critical speculation of your outward reason, lest you fall indeed into the deep abyss of darkness; but wait patiently, till the divine Sol shall shine again in your dark and selfish Saturn, and give you some beams and glimpses of his eternal light, and then your angry Mars will be changed into pure love-zeal, and your prating, pharisaical and hypocritical Mercury into a meek, mild, and Christian speaking of God's works and wonders in the dispensation of his wisdom; and your doubtful, unsettled Jupiter will be turned into a plerophory, or most full assurance of true joy and saving comfort in your religion; your earthly Venus into heavenly love, and your eclipsed mutable Luna into the pure, perfect, and crystalline streams of light, life, and glory.

But the proud scorner that will take no warning is of Lucifer's regiment, who saw the mystery of God's kingdom to stand in meekness, simplicity, and deep humility, and therefore out of his pride would aspire to be above the divine love, and harmony of obedience to God's will, and so fell into the abyss of the dark world, into the outmost darkness of the first principle, which we call Hell, where he and his legions are captives; from which the Almighty God of Love deliver us.

I will end with the words of the author at the conclusion of the book, where he says thus; " I have faithfully, with all true admonition, represented to the reader what the Lord of all beings has given me; he may behold himself in this looking-glass [1] within and without, and so he shall find what and who he is: Every reader, be he good or bad, will find his profit and benefit therein: It is a very clear gate of the great mystery of all beings: By glosses, commentaries, curiosity and self-wit, none shall be able to reach or apprehend it in his own ground; but it may very well meet and embrace the true *seeker*, and create him much profit and joy; yea be helpful to him in all natural things, provided he applies himself to it aright, and seeks in the fear of God, seeing it is now a time of seeking; for a lily blossoms upon the mountains and valleys in all the ends of the earth: ' He that seeketh findeth.' " And so I commend the reader to the grace and love of Jesus Christ, in whom are hidden all the treasures of wisdom and knowledge.

[1] Mirror.

JACOB BOEHME

SIGNATURA RERUM
THE SIGNATURE OF ALL THINGS

CHAPTER I

HOW THAT ALL WHATEVER IS SPOKEN OF GOD WITHOUT THE
KNOWLEDGE OF THE SIGNATURE IS DUMB AND WITHOUT
UNDERSTANDING; AND THAT IN THE MIND OF MAN THE
SIGNATURE LIES VERY EXACTLY COMPOSED ACCORDING TO
THE ESSENCE OF ALL ESSENCES [1]

1. ALL whatever is spoken, written, or taught of God, without
the knowledge of the signature is dumb and void of understanding; for it proceeds only from an historical conjecture,
from the mouth of another, wherein the spirit without knowledge
is dumb; but if the spirit opens to him the *signature*, then he
understands the speech of another; and further, he understands
how the spirit has manifested and revealed itself (out of the
essence through the principle) in the sound with the voice.
For though I see one to speak, teach, preach, and write of God,
and though I hear and read the same, yet this is not sufficient
for me to understand him; but if his sound and spirit out of
his signature and similitude enter into my own similitude, and
imprint his similitude into mine, then I may understand him
really and fundamentally, be it either spoken or written, if he
has the hammer that can strike my bell.

2. By this we know, that all human properties proceed from
one; that they all have but one only root and mother; otherwise
one man could not understand another in the sound, for with
the sound or speech the form notes and imprints itself into the
similitude of another; a like tone or sound catches and moves
another, and in the sound the spirit imprints its own similitude,
which it has conceived in the essence, and brought to form in
the principle.

[1] Being of all beings.

3. So that in the word may be understood in what the spirit has conceived,[1] either in good or evil; and with this signature he enters into another man's form, and awakens also in the other such a form in the signature; so that both forms mutually assimilate together in one form, and then there is one comprehension, one will, one spirit, and also one understanding.

4. And then secondly we understand, that the signature or form is no spirit, but the receptacle, container, or cabinet of the spirit, wherein it lies; for the signature stands in the essence, and is as a lute that liest still, and is indeed a dumb thing that is neither heard or understood; but if it be played upon, then its form is understood, in what form and tune it stands, and according to what note it is set. Thus likewise the signature of nature in its form is a dumb essence; it is as a prepared instrument of music, upon which the will's spirit plays; what strings he touches, they sound according to their property.

5. In the human mind the signature lies most artificially composed, according to the essence of all essences; and man wants nothing but the wise master that can strike his instrument, which is the true spirit of the high might of eternity; if that be quickened in man, that it stirs and acts in the centre of the mind, then it plays on the instrument of the human form, and even then the form is uttered [2] with the sound in the word: As his instrument was set in the time of his incarnation,[3] so it sounds, and so is his knowledge; the inward manifests itself in the sound of the word, for that is the mind's natural knowledge of itself.

6. Man has indeed all the forms of all the three worlds lying in him; for he is a complete image of God, or of the Being of all beings; only the order is placed in him at his incarnation; for there are three work-masters in him which prepare his form [or signature], viz. the threefold fiat, according to the three worlds; and they are in contest about the form, and the form is figured according to the contest; which of the masters holds the predominant rule, and obtains it in the essence, according to that his instrument is tuned, and the other lie hid, and come behind with their sound, as it plainly shews itself.

7. So soon as man is born into this world, his spirit plays upon his instrument, so that his innate genuine form [or signature] in good or evil is seen by his words and conversation; for as his instrument sounds, accordingly the senses and thoughts

---

[1] Or, formed itself; or originally put forth itself.
[2] Proceeds from the mouth.   [3] Or conception.

proceed from the essence of the mind, and so the external spirit of the will is carried in its behaviour, as is to be seen both in men and beasts; that there is a great difference in the procreation, that one brother and sister does not as the other.

8. Further we are to know, that though one fiat thus keeps the upper hand, and figures the form according to itself, that yet the other two give their sound, if their instrument be but played upon; as it is seen that many a man, and also many a beast, though it is very much inclined either to good or evil, yet it is moved either to evil or good by a contrary tune, and often lets its inbred signature [or figure] fall, when the contrary tune is played upon his hidden lute or form: As we see that an evil man is often moved by a good man to repent of and cease from his iniquity, when the good man touches and strikes his hidden instrument with his meek and loving spirit.

9. And thus also it happens to the good man, that when the wicked man strikes his hidden instrument with the spirit of his wrath, that then the form of anger is stirred up also in the good man, and the one is set against the other, that so one might be the cure and healer of the other. For as the vital signature, that is, as the form of life is figured in the time of the fiat at the conception, even so is its natural spirit; for it takes its rise out of the essence of all the three principles, and such a will it acts and manifests out of its property.

10. But now the will may be broken; for when a stronger comes, and raises his inward signature with his introduced sound and will's spirit, then its upper dominion loses the power, right, and authority; which we see in the powerful influence of the sun, how that by its strength it qualifies a bitter and sour fruit, turning it into a sweetness and pleasantness; in like manner how a good man corrupts among evil company, and also how that a good herb cannot sufficiently shew its real genuine virtue in a bad soil; for in the good man the hidden evil instrument is awakened, and in the herb a contrary essence is received from the earth; so that often the good is changed into an evil, and the evil into a good.

11. And now observe, as it stands in the power and predominance of the quality, so it is signed and marked externally in its outward form, signature, or figure; man in his speech, will, and behaviour, also with the form of the members which he has, and must use to that signature, his inward form is noted in the form of his face;[1] and thus also is a beast, an herb, and

---

[1] His look, or physiognomy.

the trees; everything as it is inwardly [in its innate virtue and quality] so it is outwardly signed; and though it falls out, that often a thing is changed from evil into good, and from good into evil, yet it has its external character, that the good or evil [that is, the change] may be known.

12. For man is known herein by his daily practice, also by his course and discourse; for the upper instrument, which is most strongly drawn, is always played upon: Thus also it is with a beast that is wild, but when it is overawed and tamed, and brought to another property, it does not easily shew its first innate form, unless it be stirred up, and then it breaks forth, and appears above all other forms.

13. Thus it is likewise with the herbs of the earth; if an herb be transplanted out of a bad soil into a good, then it soon gets a stronger body, and a more pleasant smell and power, and shews the inward essence externally; and there is nothing that is created or born in nature, but it also manifests its internal form externally, for the internal continually labours or works itself forth to manifestation: As we know it in the power and form of this world, how the one only essence has manifested itself with the external birth in the desire of the similitude, how it has manifested itself in so many forms and shapes, which we see and know in the stars and elements, likewise in the living creatures, and also in the trees and herbs.

14. Therefore the greatest understanding lies in the signature, wherein man (viz. the image of the greatest virtue) may not only learn to know himself, but therein also he may learn to know the essence of all essences; for by the external form of all creatures, by their instigation, inclination and desire, also by their sound, voice, and speech which they utter, the hidden spirit is known; for nature has given to everything its language according to its essence and form, for out of the essence the language or sound arises, and the fiat of that essence forms the quality of the essence in the voice or virtue which it sends forth, to the animals in the sound, and to the essentials [1] in smell, virtue, and form.

15. Everything has its mouth to manifestation; and this is the language of nature, whence everything speaks out of its property, and continually manifests, declares, and sets forth itself for what it is good or profitable; for each thing manifests its mother, which thus gives the essence and the will to the form.

---

[1] Vegetables.

CHAPTER II

OF THE OPPOSITION AND COMBAT IN THE ESSENCE OF ALL
ESSENCES, WHEREBY THE GROUND OF THE ANTIPATHY AND
SYMPATHY IN NATURE MAY BE SEEN, AND ALSO THE COR-
RUPTION AND CURE OF EACH THING

1. SEEING then there are so many and divers forms, that the
one always produces and affords out of its property a will
different in one from another, we herein understand the contrariety and combat in the Being of all beings, how that one
does oppose, poison, and kill another, that is, overcome its
essence, and the spirit of the essence, and introduces it into
another form, whence sickness and pains arise, when one essence
destroys another.

2. And then we understand herein the cure, how the one
heals another, and brings it to health; and if this were not, there
were no nature, but an eternal stillness, and no will; for the
contrary will makes the motion, and the original of the seeking,
that the opposite sound seeks the rest, and yet in the seeking it
only elevates and more enkindles itself.

3. And we are to understand how the cure of each thing
consists in the assimulate; for in the assimulate arises the
satisfaction of the will, viz. its highest joy; for each thing
desires a will of its likeness, and by the contrary will it is dis-
comfited;[1] but if it obtains a will of its likeness, it rejoices in
the assimulate, and therein falls into rest, and the enmity is
turned into joy.

4. For the eternal nature has produced nothing in its desire,
except a likeness out of itself; and if there were not an everlasting mixing, there would be an eternal peace in nature, but
so nature would not be revealed and made manifest, in the
combat it becomes manifest; so that each thing elevates itself,
and would get out of the combat into the still rest, and so it
runs to and fro, and thereby only awakens and stirs up the
combat.

5. And we find clearly in the light of nature, that there is no
better help and remedy for this opposition, and that it has no

[1] Made sick.

13

higher cure than the liberty, that is, the light of nature, which is the desire of the spirit.

6. And then we find, that the essence cannot be better remedied than with the assimulate; for the essence is a being, and its desire is after being: Now every taste desires only its like, and if it obtains it, then its hunger is satisfied, appeased and eased, and it ceases to hunger, and rejoices in itself, whereby the sickness falls into a rest in itself; for the hunger of the contrariety ceases to work.

7. Seeing now that man's life consists in three principles, viz. in a threefold essence, and has also a threefold spirit out of the property of each essence, viz. first, according to the eternal nature, according to the fire's property; and secondly, according to the property of the eternal light and divine essentiality; and thirdly, according to the property of the outward world: Thereupon we are to consider the property of this threefold spirit, and also of this threefold essence and will; how each spirit with its essence introduces itself into strife and sickness, and what its cure and remedy is.

8. We understand that without nature there is an eternal stillness and rest, viz. the Nothing; and then we understand that an eternal will arises in the nothing, to introduce the nothing into something, that the will might find, feel, and behold itself.

9. For in the nothing the will would not be manifest to itself, wherefore we know that the will seeks itself, and finds itself in itself, and its seeking is a desire, and its finding is the essence of the desire, wherein the will finds itself.

10. It finds nothing except only the property of the hunger, which is itself, which it draws into itself, that is, draws itself into itself, and finds itself in itself; and its attraction into itself makes an overshadowing or darkness in it, which is not in the liberty, viz. in the nothing; for the will of the liberty overshadows itself with the essence of the desire, for the desire makes essence and not the will.

11. Now that the will must be in darkness is its contrariety, and it conceives in itself another will to go out from the darkness again into the liberty, viz. into the nothing, and yet it cannot reach the liberty from without itself, for the desire goes outwards, and causes source and darkness; therefore the will (understand the reconceived will) must enter inwards, and yet there is no separation.

12. For in itself before the desire is the liberty, viz. the

nothing, and the will may not be a nothing, for it desires to manifest in the nothing; and yet no manifestation can be effected, except only through the essence of the desire; and the more the reconceived will desires manifestation, the more strongly and eagerly the desire draws into itself, and makes in itself three forms, viz. the desire, which is astringent, and makes hardness, for it is an enclosing, when coldness arises, and the attraction causes compunction,[1] and stirring in the hardness, an enmity against the attracted hardness; the attraction is the second form, and a cause of motion and life, and stirs itself in the astringency and hardness, which the hardness, viz. the enclosing,[2] cannot endure, and therefore it attracts more eagerly to hold the compunction, and yet the compunction is thereby only the stronger.

13. Thus the compunction willeth upwards, and whirls cross-ways, and yet cannot effect it, for the hardness, viz. the desire stays and detains it, and therefore it stands like a triangle, and transverted orb, which (seeing it cannot remove from the place) becomes wheeling, whence arises the mixture in the desire, viz. the essence, or multiplicity of the desire; for the turning makes a continual confusion and contrition, whence the anguish, viz. the pain, the third form (or sting of sense) arises.

14. But seeing the desire, viz. the astringency becomes only the more strong thereby (for from the stirring arises the wrath and nature, viz. the motion), the first will to the desire is made wholly austere and a hunger, for it is in a hard compunctive dry essence, and also cannot get rid and quit of it, for itself makes the essence, and likewise possesses it, for thus it finds itself now out of nothing in the something,[3] and the something is yet its contrary will, for it is an unquietness, and the free-will is a stillness.

15. This is now the original of enmity, that nature opposes the free-will, and a thing is at enmity in itself; and here we understand the centre of nature with three forms, in the original, viz. in the first principle, it is Spirit; in the second it is Love, and in the third principle Essence; and these three forms are called in the third principle Sulphur, Mercury, and Sal.

16. Understand it thus: Sul is in the first principle the free-will, or the lubet in the nothing to something, it is in the liberty without nature; Phur is the desire of the free lubet, and makes in itself, in the Phur, viz. in the desire, an essence, and this

---

[1] Or sting.   [2] Contraction, or constringency.
[3] Love and anger, father and son.

essence is austere by reason of the attraction, and introduces itself into three forms (as is above mentioned) and so forward into the fourth form, viz. into the fire; in the Phur the original of the eternal and also external nature is understood, for the hardness is a mother of the sharpness of all essences, and a preserver of all essences; out of the Sul, viz. out of the lubet of the liberty, the dark anguish becomes a shining light; and in the third principle, viz. in the outward kingdom, Sul is the oil of nature, wherein the life burns, and everything grows.

17. But now the Phur, viz. the desire, is not divided from Sul; it is one word, one original also, and one essence, but it severs itself into two properties, viz. into joy and sorrow, light and darkness; for it makes two worlds, viz. a dark fire-world in the austereness, and a light fire-world in the lubet of the liberty; for the lubet of the liberty is the only cause that the fire shines, for the original fire is dark and black, for in the shining of the fire in the original the Deity is understood, and in the dark fire, viz. in the anguish-source, the original of nature is understood, and herein we do further understand the cure.

18. The source is the cure of the free lubet, viz. of the still eternity; for the stillness finds itself alive therein, it brings itself through the anguish-source into life, viz. into the kingdom of joy, namely that the nothing is become an eternal life, and has found itself, which cannot be in the stillness.

19. Secondly, we find that the Sul, viz. the lubet of the liberty, is the curer of the desire, viz. of the anxious nature: for the lustre of the liberty does again (from the enkindled fire out of nature) shine in the dark anguish, and fills or satiates the anguish with the liberty, whereby the wrath extinguishes, and the turning orb stands still, and instead of the turning a sound is caused in the essence.

20. This is now the form of the spiritual life, and of the essential life; Sul is the original of the joyful life, and Phur is the original of the essential life; the lubet is before and without nature, which is the true Sul; and the spirit is made manifest in nature, viz. through the source, and that in a twofold form, viz. according to the lubet of the liberty in a source of joy, and according to the anxious desire's lubet; according to the astringency, compunctive, bitter, and envious from the compunction, and according to the anguish of the wheel wholly murderous and hateful; and each property dwells in itself, and yet they are in one another; herein God's love and anger are understood, they dwell in each other; and the one apprehends

not the other, and yet the one is the curer of the other; understand through imagination, for the eternal is magical.

21. The second form in nature, in eternity is the Orb with the compunctive bitter essences: for there arises the essence, understand with the perturbation; for the nothing is still without motion, but the perturbation makes the nothing active: but in the third principle, viz. in the dominion in the essence, and source of the outward world, the form is called Mercury, which is opposite, odious, and poisonful, and the cause of life and stirring, also the cause of the senses: Where one glance [1] may conceive itself in the infinity, and then also immerse itself into it, where out of one only the abyssal, unsearchable, and infinite multiplicity may arise.

22. This form is the unquietness, and yet the seeker of rest; and with its seeking it causes unquietness, it makes itself its own enemy; its cure is twofold, for its desire is also twofold, viz. according to the lubet of the liberty, according to the stillness and meekness; and then also in the hunger according to the rising of unquietness, and the finding of itself; the root desires only joy with the first will, and yet it cannot obtain it, except through the opposite source, for no joy can arise in the still nothing; it must arise only through motion and elevation that the nothing finds itself.

23. Now that which is found desires to enter again into the will of the still nothing, that it may have peace and rest therein; and the nothing is its cure; and the wrath and poison is the remedy of the seeker and finder, that is their life which they find, an example whereof we have in the poisonous gall, whence in the life arises joy and sorrow, wherein we also understand a twofold will, viz. one to the wrathful fire and anxious painful life to the original of nature, and one to the light-life, viz. to the joy of nature; this takes its original out of the eternal nothing.

24. The first will's cure is the lubet of the liberty, if it obtains that, then it makes triumphant joy in itself; and the wrath in the hungry desire is the curer and helper of the other will, viz. the will of nature; and herein God's love and anger are understood, and also how evil and good are in the centre of each life, and how no joy could arise without sorrow, and how one is the curer of the other.

25. And here we understand the third will (which takes its original out of both these, viz. out of such an essence, viz. out

[1] Thought or sparkle of the will.

of the mother), viz. the spirit, which has both these properties in it, and is a son of the properties and also a lord of the same; for in him consists the power, he may awaken which he pleases; the properties lie in the essence, and are as a well-constituted life, or as an instrument with many strings,[1] which stand still; and the spirit, viz. the egress is the real life, he may play upon the instrument as he pleases, in evil or good, according to love or anger; and as he plays, and as the instrument sounds, so is it received of its contra-tenor, viz. of the assimilate.

26. If the tune of love be played, viz. the liberty's desire, then is the sound received of the same liberty and love-lubet; for it is its pleasing relish, and agreeable to its will's desire; one similar lubet takes another.

27. And thus likewise is it to be understood of the enmity and contrary will; if the instrument be struck according to the desire to nature, viz. in the wrath, anger, and bitter falsehood, then the same contrary sound and wrathful desire receives it; for it is of its property, and a satiating of its hunger, wherein we understand the desire of the light, and also of the dark world; a twofold source and property.

28. The desire of the liberty is meek, easy, and pleasant, and it is called good;[2] and the desire to nature makes itself in itself dark, dry, hungry, and wrathful, which is called God's anger, and the dark world, viz. the first principle; and the light world is the second principle.

29. And we are to understand, that it is no divided essence, but one holds the other hidden or closed up in it, and the one is the beginning and cause of the other, also its healing and cure; that which is awaked and stirred up, that gets dominion, and manifests itself externally with its character, and makes a form and signature according to its will in the external after itself. A similitude whereof we see in an enraged man or beast; though the outward man and beast are not in the inward world, yet the outward nature has even the same forms; for it[3] arises originally from the inward,[4] and stands upon the inward root.

30. The third form is the anxiousness which arises in nature from the first and second form, and is the upholder or preserver of the first and second; it is in itself the sharp fiat; and the second form has the Verbum, viz. the property to the word, and it consists in three properties, and makes out of herself with the three the fourth, viz. the fire; in the external birth, viz. in the third principle, it is called Sal, or salt, according to its matter;

---

[1] Or voices.   [2] Or God.   [3] Nature.   [4] World.

but in its spirit it has many forms; for it is the fire-root, the great anguish, it arises betwixt and out of the astringency and bitterness in the austere attraction; it is the essentiality of that which is attracted, viz. the corporality, or comprehensibility; from Sulphur it is of a brimstone nature, and from Mercury a blaze or flash; it is in itself painful, viz. a sharpness of dying, and that from the sharp attraction of the astringency: It has a twofold fire, one cold, another hot; the cold arises from the astringency, from the sharp attraction, and is a dark black fire; and the hot arises from the driving forth the compunction [1] in the anguish in the desire after the liberty, and the liberty is its enkindler, and the raging compunction is the cold's fire's awakener.[2]

31. These three forms are in one another as one, and yet they are but one; but they sever themselves through the original into many forms, and yet they have but one mother, viz. the desiring will to manifestation, which is called the father of nature, and of the Being of all beings.

32. Now we are to consider the hunger of the anxiety, or the salt-spirit, and then also its satiating or fulfilling: The anguish has in it two wills, from the original of the first will out of the liberty to the manifestation of itself; viz. the first will is to nature, and the other reconceived will is the son of the first, which goes out of the manifestation again into itself into the liberty; for it is become an eternal life in nature, and yet possesses not nature essentially, but dwells in itself, and penetrates nature as a transparent shining, and the first will goes outwards,[3] for it is the desire of manifestation; it seeks itself out of itself, and yet amasses the desire in itself; it desires to educe the internal out of itself.

33. Thus it has two properties; with the seeking in itself it makes the centre of nature: For it is like a poison, a will of dreadful aspiring, like a lightning and thunder-clap; for this desire desires only anguish, and to be horrible, to find itself in itself, out of the nothing in the something; and the second form proceeds forth as a flagrat, or produces sound out of itself; for it is not the desire of the first will to continue in the horrible death, but only thus to educe itself out of the nothing, and to find itself.

34. And we understand by the centre in itself, with the aspiring wrathfulness, with the wrathful will to nature, the

---

[1] Or sting of instigation.   [2] Raiser, enkindler, or inflamer.
[3] Or out of itself.

dark world, and with the egress out of itself to manifestation, the outward world; and with the second will out of the first, which enters again into the liberty, we understand the light world, or the kingdom of joy, or the true Deity.

35. The desire of the dark world is after the manifestation, viz. after the outward world, to attract and draw the same essentiality into it, and thereby to satisfy its wrathful hunger; and the desire of the outward world is after the essence or life, which arises from the pain and anguish.

36. Its desire in itself is the wonder of eternity, a mystery, or mirror, or what is comprehended of the first will to nature.

37. The outward world's desire is Sulphur, Mercury, and Sal; for such an essence it is in itself, viz. a hunger after itself, and is also its own satisfying; for Sul desires Phur, and Phur desires Mercury, and both these desire Sal; for Sal is their son, which they hatch in their desire, and afterwards becomes their habitation, and also food.

38. Each desire desires only the essentiality of salt according to its property; for salt is diverse; one part is sharpness of cold, and one part sharpness of heat; also one part brimstone; and one part salniter from Mercury.

39. These properties are in one another as one, but they sever themselves, each dwelling in itself; for they are of a different essence, and when one enters into another, then there is enmity, and a flagrat. A similitude whereof we may apprehend in thunder and lightning, which comes to pass when the great Anguish, viz. the mother of all salts, understand the third form of nature, impresses itself; which comes to pass from the aspect of the sun, which stirs up the hot fire's form, so that it is penetrative, as the property of the fire is; and when it reaches the salniter, then it enkindles itself; and the salniter is in itself the great flagrat in Mercury, viz. the flash, or compunction, which enters into the coldness, so also into the cold sharpness of the salt-spirit; this coldness is exceedingly dismayed at the flash of the fire, and in a trice wraps or folds up itself in itself, whence arises the thunder-clap (or the tempestuous flash, which gives a stroke in the flagrat) and the flagrat goes downwards, for it is heavy by reason of the coldness, and the sal-nitrous spirit is light by reason of the fire, which [spirit] carries the thunder or sound sideways, as is to be heard in tempests and thunder; presently thereupon comes the wind or spirit out of all the four forms one against another, for they are all four enkindled in the penetrating flagrat; whereupon follows hail and rain; the

hail folds itself together in the coldness, in the property of the cold salt-spirit; for the wrath attracts to itself, and turns the water to ice, and the water arises from the meekness, viz. from the desire of the light, for it is the essentiality of the meekness; this the cold salt-spirit congeals into drops, and distils it upon the earth, for before the congelation it is only as a mist, or steam, or as a vapour, or damp.

40. Thus we see this ground very exactly and properly in thunder and lightning; for the flash, or lightning, or ethereal blaze, goes always before, for it is the enkindled salniter; thereupon follows the stroke in the flagrat of the coldness; as you see, as soon as the stroke is given the astringent chamber is opened, and a cool wind follows, and oftentimes whirling and wheeling; for the forms of nature are awakened, and are as a turning wheel, and so they carry their spirit the wind.

CHAPTER III

OF THE GRAND MYSTERY OF ALL BEINGS

1. COURTEOUS reader, observe the meaning right; we understand not by this description a beginning of the Deity, but we shew you the manifestation of the Deity through nature; for God is without beginning, and has an eternal beginning, and an eternal end, which he is himself, and the nature of the inward world is in the like essence from eternity.

2. We give you to understand this of the divine essence; without nature God is a mystery,[1] understand in the nothing, for without nature is the nothing, which is an eye of eternity, an abyssal eye, that stands or sees in the nothing, for it is the abyss; and this same eye is a will, understand a longing after manifestation, to find the nothing; but now there is nothing before the will, where it might find something, where it might have a place to rest, therefore it enters into itself, and finds itself through nature.

3. And we understand in the mystery without nature in the first will two forms; one to nature, to the manifestation of the wonder-eye; and the second form is produced out of the first, which is a desire after virtue and power, and is the first will's son, its desire of joyfulness. And understand us thus; the desire is egressive, and that which proceeds is the spirit of the will and desire, for it is a moving, and the desire makes a form [2] in the spirit, viz. formings of the infinity of the mystery.

4. And this form [or likeness] is the eternal wisdom of the Deity; and we understand herein the Trinity of the only Deity, whose ground we must not know, how the first will arises in the abyss from eternity, which is called Father; only we know the eternal birth, and distinguish the Deity, viz. what purely and merely concerns the Deity, or the good, from nature, and shew you the arcanum of the greatest secret mystery; namely, how the abyss, or the Deity, manifests itself with this eternal generation; for God is a spirit, and as subtle as a thought or will, and nature is his corporeal essence, understand the eternal nature; and the outward nature of this visible comprehensible [3] world is a manifestation or external birth of the inward spirit

---

[1] Mysterium.   [2] Similitude, likeness, or signature.   [3] Palpable.

and essence in evil and good, that is, a representation, resemblance, and typical similitude of the dark fire and light world.

5. And as we have shewn you concerning the original of thunder and lightning with the tempestuous stroke; so likewise the inward nature of the inward world is, and stands in the generation: For the outward birth takes its original from the inward; the inward birth is unapprehensible to the creature, but the outward is apprehensible to it; yet each property apprehends its mother from whence it is brought forth.

6. As the soul comprehends the inward eternal nature, and the spirit of the soul, viz. the precious image according to God, comprehends [1] the birth of the angelical light-world, and the sidereal and elemental spirit comprehends the birth and property of the stars and elements; every eye sees into its mother from whence it was brought forth.

7. Therefore we will set down the generation of all essences out of all mothers and beginnings, how one generation proceeds from another, and how one is the cause of another, and this we will do from the eyesight of all the three mothers.

8. Let none account it impossible, seeing man is a likeness according to and in God, an image of the Being of all beings; and yet it stands not in the power of the creature, but in the might of God; for the sight and science of all essences consist alone in the clearest light.

9. We have made mention before how the external birth, viz. the essence of this world, consists in three things, viz. in Sulphur, Mercury, and Sal: Now we must set down and declare what it is, seeing that all things arise from one original, and then how its inward separation is effected, that out of one beginning many beginnings are produced; this is now to be understood, as is before mentioned, concerning the centre of all essences.

10. For Sulphur in the eternal beginning consists in two forms, and so also in the outward beginning of this world: viz. in the internal the first form, viz. the Sul consists [2] in the eternal liberty; it is the lubet of the eternal abyss, viz. a will or an original to the desire; and the other original is the desire, which is the first motion, viz. an hunger to the something; and in this same hunger is the eternal beginning to the pregnant nature,[3] and it is called Sulphur, viz. a conception of the liberty, viz. of the good, and a conception or comprehension of the desire, viz. of the austere attraction in the desire.

[1] Or apprehends, or conceives.   [2] Or stands.
[3] Or to the nature of the pregnatrix

11. Sul in the internal is God, and Phur is the nature; for it makes a spirit of the nature of brimstone, as is to be seen externally in the property of brimstone; for its substance is a dry constringent matter, and is of a painful anxious fiery property, forcing itself forth; it attracts eagerly and hardly into itself, and parches up as a dry hunger, and its painful property does eagerly and anxiously force itself forth: The cause and original is this, because it stands in two beginnings, viz. in the property of the desire, which is an attraction; and in the property of the light or liberty, which is driving forth, or pressing to the manifestation through the desire of nature.

12. The desire, viz. the attraction makes hardness, and is the cause of the fire, and the lubet is a cause of the lustre or light of the fire: Sul is light, and Phur makes fire, yet it cannot be reduced alone in Sulphur to fire and light, but in Mercury, and at last in Sal, which is the real body, but not of the brimstone, but of the essence and water: And so understand, that in the first desire, which arises in the lubet of the liberty, all things are, and are made substantial and essential, from whence the creation of this world is proceeded; and we find herein the property of the earth, so likewise of all metals and stones, and also of the astrum,[1] and the original of the elements, all out of one only mother, which is the lubet and the desire, from whence all things proceeded and still proceed.

13. For Mercury is generated in Sulphur: It is the severing, viz. of light and darkness from one another, the breaking wheel, and cause of the various division or multiplicity: it separates the dark essentiality from the essentiality of the light, viz. the metals from the gross, astringent, dark, stony, and earthly property; for the property of the desire gives and makes dark essence, and the property of the free lubet makes light essence, viz. metals, and all of the same kind and resemblance.

14. Mercury has in the beginning of his birth three properties, viz. the *trembling* in the austereness, and *anguish* from the hard impressing of the astringent hard desire, and the *expulsion* of the multiplicity, viz. the essential life; for the desire attracts very hard to itself, and the attraction makes the motion, or sting of trembling [or horrible compunction], and that which is impressed is the anguish; but if the liberty be therein comprehended, it refuses it, and there arises the original of enmity, and the severing, that one form separates from another, and a twofold will arises.

[1] Stars.

15. For the lubet of the liberty does again set its desire into the stillness, viz. into the nothing, and forces again out of the darkness of the desire's austereness into itself, viz. into the liberty, without the wrath of the enmity; and so it has only sharpened itself in the austere impression in Mercury, that it is a moving feeling life, and that its liberty is sharpened so that it becomes a lustre, which is, and causes a kingdom of joy in the liberty; and so understand us, that the spirit's dominion, viz. the spirit and the essence [1] do thus separate.

16. The essence remains in the impression, and becomes material; that is not God, but gold, or any other metal, according to the property of the first conception in the Sulphur, or stone, or earth, out of the desire's own peculiar property, all according to the first sude [2] or seething in Mercury; for no metal can be generated without salniter, which is the flagrat in Mercury; which also becomes material in the astringent impression, and divides itself in the separation, one part into brimstone, another into salniter, and a third into a salt sharpness; whereas yet there cannot be any corporeal essence in all these, but only the spirit of the essence; the essence proceeds wholly out of the death through mortification, which is effected in the great anguish of the impressure, where there is a dying source, which is the mercurial life, where the salnitral flagrat arises as an opening, displaying flash: For the liberty, viz. the property of the eternal lubet, does there separate itself, [3] and yet the attracted essence out of the lubet of the liberty continues all along in the comprehension of the attraction in the astringent austere dark anguish: Now if the wrath enters so vehemently into itself as to raise up the salnitral flagrat, then it apprehends the essentiality of the free lubet in itself, from whence arises the flagrat; for the wrath there apprehends the meekness, which is even as if water were poured into fire, which gives a flagrat; and then the wrath of the great anguish dies, and with the flagrat the joy ascends, and the flagrat is out of mercury, or out of the anguish of death, and becomes also material, but by reason of the liberty it changes itself into white, which is salniter: Now if the fire, viz. the horrible anxious sharpness, does again come into it, then the salniter is dismayed, and gives a repulse; [4] for the first property [which was] before the death is again enkindled with the brimstone spirit; a sufficient resemblance of

---

[1] Or substance.
[2] Boiling.
[3] Or separates itself in itself.
[4] Report, clash.

which you have in gunpowder, which is the matter of these properties.

17. Further, we are to know the dying with the enkindling of the fire, all which is done in the flagrat; for it is a flagrat to death, and to life; one part immerses itself into the property of death, viz. into the wrath of the austere desire; and the other part, which is from the lubet or love-essentiality, arises up in the kingdom of joy: But seeing there happens also a mortifying in the free materia (though it is no mortifying, but a redeeming from the wrath, for the materia of the liberty will be free from the wrath), thereupon this materia falls [1] downwards, which is water; and it is not of the property of the wrath, but the wrath holds it captive in itself; but they are separated from one another in the essence and source; the wrath's essence gives earth and stones, and the essence of the liberty is water, which arises with the enkindling of the fire through the mortification out of the meekness of the light.

18. But seeing this water does also separate itself in the salnitral flagrat, and before the salniter was all mutually enwrapt together, thereupon it obtains different properties in the separation, and there is a diversity of water; and this various diversity of properties gives in each property also a bodily or corporeal essence, all according to the first separation of mercury in sulphur, for in the mortification in the salnitral flagrat two things are effected and come forth, viz. a life, and a body of the life; understand an essential, and a lifeless senseless body, whose materia is mortified in the flagrat: Thus there is a diversity of water, and a diversity of the life, and a diversity of the body,[2] or of the materia; as each body is, so is also its essential spirit.

19. Now we must consider this from the first original; as (1) from the lubet of the liberty; and (2) from the desire to nature, or the manifestation of the abyss.

20. First, in the salnitral flagrat there is produced through the anxious mortification a sulphureous water from the anguish, which affords a brimstone, as we plainly see, and all whatever is of the like sort and resemblance.

21. Secondly, there is generated from the astringent, austere, attractive property, which draws in to itself, a salt water; its materia is salt; if it be again impressed through the fire or heat, then it turns into salt; and all whatever is sharp and attractive, be it either in herbs or trees, proceeds from thence; for there is

---

[1] Sinks.   [2] Corpus.

as much diversity of brimstone and salt, as there is variety of taste and fire to be found in all creatures, herbs, and trees; also all whatever lives and grows has brimstone and salt; for the saltish property attracts, and preserves the body;[1] and the brimstone has in it the oil or light, wherein the free lubet to manifestation consists, whence the growth arises.

22. Thirdly, there is brought forth through the salnitral flagrat out of the property of the bitter compunctive attraction, in the first impression in the spirit, an earthly property of water; its materia is earth; for the same arises from the dark essentiality, where the darkness impresses itself in the first desire, wherein the darkness arises, as is before mentioned: Thus it begets out of its property in the impression a mist, smoaky steam, or vapour, which the flagrat in the salniter apprehends, and its essence is dismayed or dies, and falls downwards; this is the materia of the earth, though the earth is not of one only sort, but has in it all whatever became corporeal in the flagrat, all which springs through the death of the earth, according as it was wrapt and driven together in the creation into a lump, as we plainly see.

23. Further, we are to consider of the highest arcanum, viz. of the heavenly essentiality, and then of the precious stones and metals, from whence they all take their rise and original; seeing that all things come out of one mother, which is the lubet and desire of eternity to its own manifestation.

24. Now concerning the incorruptible essence of corporality, the same arises also in the first desire to nature, yet in the impression of the free lubet, and goes all along through all the forms even into the highest sharpness, where it retires again into itself, as a life out of the fire: The eternal fire is magical, and a spirit, and dies not; the liberty is its enkindler, but the eternal nature is its sharpness; this same essence loses the wrath's property in the light; it is in the same fire as a dying, yet there is no dying, but an entrance into another source, viz. out of a painful desire into a love-desire; it yields also spirit and essence from the fire-spirit, and the essence of meekness from the light.

25. For that which dies to the fire, or sinks through death, that is divine essence; and it is effected likewise through the salnitral flagrat of the divine joyfulness, where the property trembles in the joy of meekness, and immerses itself through the death of the fire, which is called God's anger, and quenches it,

[1] Corpus.

so that God dwells in a meek light; and the first property to the enkindling of the light is fire, and wrath of the eternal nature, and makes [1] the dark world.

26. The properties of the first mother in the lubet and desire do also divide themselves in the salnitral flagrat of joyfulness into distinct parts, as is to be seen in this outward world; it yields also water, but of a very sovereign essence, and it resembles only a spirit of a pleasant lovely desire: This is the water of which Christ told us that he would " give us to drink," and "whosoever should drink the same, it should spring up in him to a fountain of eternal life."

27. It retains also in the flagrat of the disclosure the fiery property which is called heaven, in which the wonders of the divine kingdom of joy are known and manifest; and in the watery property [it retains] the pleasant spring, or paradise; for in the fiery [property] the eternal element arises, and it is the real essence of the divine corporality, wherein consists all whatever may be known in God, as is sufficiently and in order cleared at large in our other writings of the *Divine revelation*, treating of the *Divine wisdom*, and of the *Divine eternal abyssal birth :* And now we will turn us to the essence of the outward world, viz. to the manifestation of the eternal, viz. to metals, herbs, and trees; so also to men and beasts.

28. We see that the metals have another manner of body than the living creatures, or are otherwise than the earth and stones are: Now reason asks, How is the original of everything, seeing that in the beginning all arose out of one mother, and yet the eternity has no temporal beginning? Here we must again consider the mother of the first pregnatrix, where, and how one essence separates itself from another, viz. the inchoative from the eternal, time from eternity, and yet they stand mutually in each other, but are severed into two principles, viz. into the kingdom of God, and of this world; and yet all is God's: But seeing Christ calls the devil " a prince of this world," and we also are able to declare how far, and in what he is a prince, and that this world is not his own,[2] but he is the poorest creature in this world, and also not at all in this world; now therefore look upon the first ground, upon the mother which has thus generated all creatures.

29. So also as to the earth, stones, and all metals, the earth's property, consists in a spiritual Sulphur, Mercury, and Sal, and all whatever has had beginning is arisen in and out of her

---

[1] Gives, or affords.   [2] Or propriety.

impression, and inchoatively thereupon it came forth with the first form of the mother, viz. with the astringent attraction, through the fiat into a creatural being, and affords a diversity of essence and spirit, according to the first property of the separation.

30. As first, the high spirits, which were created out of the free lubet in the desire, in the fire's property, viz. out of the centre of all essences, had in them the properties of both the eternal worlds; but those which after their corporising [or being made creaturely] remained with their desire in the property of the free lubet, and introduced their will out of the fire into the light, they became angels; and the other, which introduced their desire again into the centre (viz. into the austere properties), became devils, viz. outcasts from the free lubet out of the light, as is mentioned in other writings.

31. Therefore the devils have neither the kingdom of God, nor the kingdom of this world in possession; for in the beginning of the creation this world was created out of both the inward properties, whereupon the devil has now only the wrath's part in possession, the other profits him nothing; and thus he is in the world, and also not in the world, for he has but one part thereof in possession, from the other he is cast out.

32. After the creation of the highest spirits, God created this visible world with the stars and elements as an external birth out of the mother of all essences; all which proceeded out of the eternal beginning, and took a temporal beginning: For here we are to consider, that the eternal pregnatrix moved itself, and enkindled its own form [or similitude], where then the one became corporeal in the other; but afterwards God created the earth, which we are thus to consider of.

33. The first desire to nature impresses itself, and introduces itself with the impression into three forms, viz. into Sulphur, Mercury, and Sal, and in the impression all become rising and moving, which is not in the still nothing, and so forces itself into the highest anguish, even to [1] the salnitral flagrat, where then is the original of the fire: Thus the source whirls in itself, as a boiling of water upon the fire: for the austere desire is attractive, and the fiery is expulsive, which is a sulphur; and the astringent attraction is a wrathful sting [or compunction], viz. a contrition; and yet it is held by the austereness, that it cannot move away, whereupon it is painful, and causes pain, as if it were seething, which yet is only spirit without essence,

[1] Or until.

which comes to pass in Mercury, and is Mercury's own form.

34. And there is the separation of two wills, viz. one remains, and is the very anxious essence, seeing it originally arises from the desire; the other, which arises out of the lubet of the liberty, retires back again into itself into the liberty, and yet there is no parting or dividing from one another, but thus it goes one with another all along through the enkindling of the fire through the salnitral flagrat, where with the enkindling of the fire the death is effected in the wrath of the fire, where the source dies, and yet there is no death, but a likeness of death; and yet the real, eternal, and temporal death is in that manner, even where the liberty apprehends itself in itself, and the death or flagrat falls down into the liberty as impotent, and freely resigns itself; and the spirit, viz. the source (understand the very sharp, fiery, anxious source), becomes material, and retains only an essential working, like to an impotent desire; and in the enkindling of the fire in the salnitral flagrat each property separates itself in itself, and the whole materia is particularised, viz. to metals, stones, and earth.

35. The highest metal,[1] as gold, arises from the liberty, which is comprised all along in the flagrat in the astringent impression; and it is not free from the materia of the rest, for all is comprised or wrapt up together; but seeing the liberty with the Sul, or light's property, is comprised or comprehended therein also, thereupon Sul is expulsive to the manifestation of itself, as it is the property of the liberty so to be: Hence it comes that metals grow, and not the gross hard stones, which are too hard comprised in the impression out of the wrathful essentiality, and have too little Sul in them.

36. But concerning the precious stones, with their radiant lustre and great virtue, the same have their original in the flash of the fire, where life and death separate; as when one part by reason of the dark essentiality descends, and the other by reason of the liberty ascends, and yet all is brought into essence in the flagrat; so that the same flash or glance becomes also material in the flagrat; and therefore they are hard, and of a blinking glance, like an eye; for so also is the original of the eye or sight in the womb,[2] when the life enkindles; all according to the right of eternity.

37. And therefore they are of so great power, efficacy, and virtue, in that they are so nigh to the Deity, and bear the

---

[1] Or the highest or chiefest of the metals.   [2] Body.

incorporated names of the divine power in them; as also gold is nigh to the divine essentiality, or heavenly corporality: If man could open [or disclose] the dead body, and reduce it to a flying [1] moving spirit, which only can be effected through the divine motion, then it should be seen what it could be, which no reason believes or understands without divine sight [or vision].

38. Further, we are also to consider of the other metals and minerals, which in like manner do thus take their original; but in the salnitral flagrat each property is separated; as we see that the property of the fire and light is different, and all from the first impression; where before the impression the lubet and desire of the liberty stand mutually in each other, as a *chaos*, a complexion of great wonders, where all colours, powers, and virtues are contained in this only CHAOS, or wonder-eye; which CHAOS is God himself, viz. the Being of all beings, who thus manifests himself in particular beings with the eyes of eternity; each materia is an essence according to the spirit from whence it was generated; and if it be enkindled in the fire, it yields likewise such a light as the spirit is in the essence.

39. And thus also we are to consider of the metals; what kind of spirit each of them has, such a glance and lustre it yields, and also such a body [2] it has.

40. As the mind acts and moves the thoughts and senses from the highest to the lowest, and comprehends and commands by the thoughts from the highest to the lowest; so the eternal mind has manifested itself from the highest majesty, even to the lowest [meanest, or outermost thing], viz. to the greatest darkness; and this world, with the sun, stars, and elements, and with every creaturely being, is nothing else but a manifestation of the eternity of the eternal will and mind; and as it was in the beginning, so it still stands in its seething and vegetation,[3] and so it still puts forward to light and darkness, to evil and good. And all things consist in these first three forms, viz. in Sulphur, Mercury, and Sal, as one degree in order after another; for so likewise are the quires of the spirits, as also of the stars, trees, herbs, and of all kinds whatever which have been, and are; so also are the inward heavenly quires with their distinction.

---

[1] Liquid. [2] Corpus. [3] Boiling, growing, and waxing.

CHAPTER IV

OF THE BIRTH OF THE STARS, AND FOUR ELEMENTS IN THE METALLINE AND CREATURELY PROPERTY

1. As it is before mentioned, all things proceed out of one only mother, and separate themselves into two essences, according to the right of eternity, viz. into a mortal and an immortal, into life and death, into spirit and body; the spirit is the life, and the body is the death, viz. a house of the spirit: As the holy Trinity stands in the birth, so also is the external birth: There is likewise essence and spirit in heaven; a figure of which we see in this outward world, where there are four elements, and yet there is but one only element, which separates itself into four properties, viz. into fire, air, water, and earth, as is above mentioned.

2. For so we are to consider of the creation of this world, that the whole essence of eternity has moved itself in the place [1] of this world, and the whole form was enkindled and stirred, and that in the desire to manifestation; and there the generation divided itself in the flagrat of the enkindled fire into four parts, viz. into fire, water, and earth, and the air is its moving egressive [2] spirit; as is to be considered in Sulphur, which consists in these four things.

3. In like manner also the astrum is thus generated out of the first mother; and all put together is only one body, and it all takes its rise from the inward spirit; as a hand or foot grows forth from the inward centre, and has already its form in the centre, viz. in the first operation, and so only grows into a form as the spirit is.

4. The first mother of all things, viz. the lubet with the desire, does especially introduce itself into seven forms, and yet continues steadfast in three only, but manifests itself in seven forms. [3]

5. The first form is astringent, viz. an austere attraction, which is a cause of coldness and salt, and all corporality.

[1] Loco.   [2] Outgoing, breathing.
[3] Or in a sevenfold form.

6. The second form is the compunction,[1] viz. the drawing or motion, and causes the feeling, also pricking, aking, tormenting; the affection [2] of bitterness, enmity and friendliness, joy and sorrow.

7. The third form is the great anguish in the impression, which causes two wills, viz. one to the fire, where the will of the free lubet falls down to the wrath in the fire, and again goes into itself, and makes a lustre in the fire's sharpness.

8. Now the fourth form is the fire itself, viz. the first principle in the life, with which the dark and light world do separate; also in this flagrat all material separations are effected, and the corporality and multiplication begin according to the property of the first eternal mind, viz. according to the essentiality a mortal [ens], and according to the free source a living [ens].

9. The fifth form is now the second desire, which is effected after the separation, and that according to two properties; viz. one according to the lubet of the liberty out of the light, which is the highest love-desire; and the other according to the fire's lubet, which leads its life of its essence in the love in the light, from whence the joyfulness and every true life arises.

10. The love gives essence; for it is expressive, and yielding, viz. itself; for God gives himself to every essence; and the fire is receptive; for it needs essence in its wrathful hunger, else it extinguishes; and then the lustre of the light would go out, and the desire of love would cease, for the fire makes the light desiring, viz. of the joyfulness; for if the fire dies, the light waxes dark, and love turns into anguish, as may be conceived of in the devils.

11. The sixth form arises from the turning wheel before the fire, where the multiplication of the essence arises out of the property of Mercurius in the salnitral flagrat; with the enkindling of the fire one form is introduced into another; and if now the love-desire penetrates all the forms, then all the forms grow very desirous the one after the other, for the dear lovely child Venus is in all.

12. Here begin the taste, smell, hearing, seeing, feeling, and speaking; for the light opens another principle of another source, and fills all; and here springs up the life in death, viz. the love in the anger, and the light shines in the darkness; here the bridegroom embraces his bride, and God himself resists his anger, viz. the wrath of nature; and in this form all speeches, understanding, and senses arise, and the true real life of all

[1] Or sting.   [2] Stirring up, or moving.

creatures; so also the life in the vegetables, viz. trees and herbs, in each thing according to its property.

13. The seventh form arises from all the other, and is the body, mansion-house, or food of the other, and it is thus effected; when the other forms taste each other in their mutual penetration in the love-desire, then in each form there is an hunger or desire after the love, viz. after the light; now each hunger or desire is reaching forth after the thing it desires, and eagerly attracts the property of the thing desired; and thus out of two one essence is made, viz. out of the hunger, and that which the hunger desires; for this hunger does not stand in death, it does not any more enclose itself up in death, unless it be too great, and the imagination in the hunger be too great, and the hunger cannot obtain that same thing, then it choaks; as many times a child is so choaked or smothered in the mother's womb, if this form be enkindled in another form to eat of some external thing, whereupon the mother grows so ardent in longing, and if she cannot get it, the child also cannot get it; now it choaks in the hunger, or else a member is spoiled, from whence the hunger arose.

14. The first hunger in the centre before the fire is a spiritual hunger, which makes the dark world; and the hunger of the free lubet makes the light world; both which are only spirit, till they pass both together through the enkindling of the fire, where then they are mortified to the spirit, and are a likeness of the first spirit, viz. a manifestation of the incomprehensible spirit, which is called God in love and anger, in a twofold source: Thus each stands undivided in itself, viz. God in the time, and the time in God, and the one is not the other, but they come from one eternal original; thus the temporal spirit's hunger gives a temporal body, and the eternal spirit's hunger affords an eternal body, and are both mutually in each other, and yet are distinct.[1]

15. The seven forms make them a body according to their hunger out of their own property; therefore all whatever the spirit has in all properties lies in the body.

16. Further we are to know, that there is a separation made in the creation of this world; for this is to be seen in the sun and stars; so likewise in all creatures; also in metals, stones, and earths; for this same is the manifestation of God.

17. We see in the firmament seven planets, and in the earth seven metals which are fixed, and also seven planets only which

[1] The one is not the other.

are fixed in their property; the rest are minerals, and so of the stars: And as the planetary orb has its predominant stamp or influence, so is also the birth of each thing.

18. As the Deity, viz. the divine light, is the centre of all life; so also in the manifestation of God, viz. in the figure, the sun is the centre of all life; in the highest life the highest things have taken their beginning, and so forward successively one from another to the lowest: In every external thing there are two properties; one from time, the other from eternity; the first property of time is manifest; and the other is hidden, yet it sets forth a likeness after itself in each thing. *His Body*

19. Whatever has its beginning out of the lubet of the liberty stands with the root in an heavenly property, and with the body in an earthly; but the eternal stands in time, and manifests itself with time.

20. Sulphur is on one part in the internal heavenly, and as to the body earthly, yet puts forth an heavenly likeness according to the eternal out of itself, which is fixed and stedfast; as is to be seen in gold, and is much more to be understood in the human body, if it were not corrupted in the desire in Mercury; for the spiritual or heavenly man consists in Sulphur, and in Mercury the corporeal, viz. the similitude of the divine [man]; so also the metalline property in Sulphur is the noblest, most excellent, and highest, for it is the highest spirit.

21. Understand it thus: In the heavenly being there is also a property of a seething,[1] when the liberty is apprehended and enkindled in the highest desire, wherein the joyfulness arises; this is effected in the heavenly Sulphur, where it is made essential in the heavenly Mercury, viz. in the eternal word, which is a spiritual essence.

22. But if the same spirituality longs to manifest itself in a similitude, both according to the property of the spirit, and the essentiality too, according to the Trinity of the Deity, according to the mortal and immortal essence, then that image is represented in the stars and elements; and lastly it is set forth in man, who is a lively image of the whole essence according to the divine and outward world; also the inward and outward worlds are represented with the metals in a mortal image, as a resemblance and similitude of the living heavenly essentiality.

23. The beginning is in Sulphur; for Sul is the lubet of the light, or the liberty, which longs to manifestation, and it cannot otherwise be effected but through fire: In Phur arises the desire,

[1] Boiling, or decoction.

viz. an austere attraction, which makes the dark earthly property, and the austereness of the spirit, viz. the fiery essence: In this austereness arises Saturn, which is the thing impressed; and Mercury is the desire of the hunger, and the rager, raver, and breaker; and Mars is the wrath in the hunger, a cause of anger; these three are the property of Phur, viz. of the free lubet's desire.

24. The free lubet's property begets the essence in the three fore-mentioned forms, viz. in Saturn, Mercury, and Mars; for it gives itself in to each property, and the property in the hunger of Mercury makes it a corporeal form; but if the free lubet turns also to an hunger in the austere desiring, then it makes also three forms according to itself, viz. Jupiter, who is the understanding of the lubet; and Venus, which is the desire of the lubet; and Luna, which is the body of the lubet; and according to the property of the light it makes Sol; all this is spirit; but now in every spirit's hunger there is also an essence, both according to the mortal and immortal *ens*, a fixed, and unfixed; a figure according to the heavenly, and a figure according to the earthly [being, or property].

25. In the saturnine property the desire of the free lubet makes (according to Saturn's own property) lead, and according to the watery [property] in Saturn, salt; and according to the mortal and earthly [property] in Saturn, stones, and earth, and all whatever is of that sort and semblance.

26. But according to the liberty, or according to the free desire's own property (in that it yields up itself to Saturn, viz. to the desire), it makes in Saturn gold, according to the desire of the light, where the spirit and body separate; the spirit of its desire is Sol, and the body is gold, understand, the golden body is in Saturn according to the property of the free desire, and not according to Saturn's property; his property in himself is lead, salt, and earth; but he keeps the golden child shut up in himself as a black raven, not in his gray form, but in a darkish cast: He is a great lord, but his dominion, by reason of the golden child which he has in his bowels, stands not in his own power: He is not father of the child, but Mercury is he which forms [1] the child; but he puts his morning mantle upon it, that he can have no joy with the golden child; he corporises the fair child; for he is its fiat or creator, and hides and covers it close under his mantle: He cannot give it the body from his own property, for it (understand the golden body) is the essence of

[1] Or fashions.

the free desire in the highest degree of corporality in the fixed death, where yet there is no death, but an enclosing, and in the similitude a representation of the divine heavenly essentiality.

27. Mercurius is the master-workman [1] of this child, which Saturn hides; when he gets it into his hunger, he casts off his black cloak, and rejoices in it; but he is too malignant in his fire-wrath,[2] he devours the child, and turns it wholly to his own property: When he is most sharply hungry in the fire, then Sol must be given him (it is his wife) that his hunger may be appeased; and then when he is satisfied, he labours in the materia of the child with his own hunger or fire,[3] and fills up his sufficed desire out of Sol's property, which he before had eaten, and nourishes the child till it gets upon it all the four elements with the constellation, and he grows exceeding pregnant with the child, and then it belongs [or is fit for] a strange fire, and yet not strange, an earnest fire; and then the father gives it the soul, viz. the fire-spirit; and its first mother, which Mercury did eat down in its hunger, which was fixed and perfect, [gives] the soul's-spirit, viz. the light-life: Then the death [4] arises, and the child is born, and becomes afterwards its own, and a child of the liberty, and cares no more for its work-master: It is better than its father, but not better than its mother, in whose seed it lay, before the father wrought in it; it bruises the head of its father's fiery essence, viz. of the serpent, and passes freely through death in the fire: Dost thou understand nothing here? Then thou art not born to the highest knowledge of the spagirical science.

28. Further, we are to consider of the degrees, what the liberty, viz. the eternal lubet, gives to the hunger of the other forms in Sulphur, in the property of the other planets; the form of the birth is as a turning wheel,[5] which Mercury causes in the Sulphur.

29. The birth of the highest degree turns round (viz. the desire), for this world is round, so also the birth; when the liberty has given its highest lubet (as a golden hunger) to Saturn, and placed Mercury for work-master, then it betakes itself into itself, into its desire, according to the property of meekness; for the first conception to the golden child is effected according to

---

[1] Or faber.
[2] In a strange fire, and yet not strange; when the cloak is laid aside, it needs only its own fire.
[3] Here must be its own fire only from within and from without.
[4] And it is the tincture which tinctures the body.
[5] Or rotation.

the property of joyfulness; but this out of goodness and meekness resigns itself to Luna; for it is a pleasant demission by reason of the meekness, which Mercury apprehends and works therein also; this body is silver, and comes from the first impression, where the yellow and white separate in the fire, viz. the colours of the virtue; then Luna arises out of the yellow and turns into white, by reason of the divine meekness; and because its original is from Sol's colour, therefore it has a perpetual hunger after Sol, and receives the sun's lustre into it, puts it on [1] and shines with it.

30. Now as the superior is, so is likewise the inferior (namely metals), therefore silver is the next degree to gold; and as gold is generated, so is also silver: Venus clothes it, which Mercury cannot endure, seeing he is the master-worker, and he gives his garment also; but the silver has neither the property of Venus nor Mercury, for it retains the property of its mother, viz. the meekness in the liberty, and is hatched, as the gold by reason of the sun: The moon has an heavenly property, but in reference to its own proper form from the property of the desire, it is of a very earthly property, it is a cabinet and keeper of the earthly and heavenly essence: In like manner as the outward body of man, which before the Fall in Adam was comparable to silver, but when he died in the lubet then the earthly property only lived in him, and therefore he continually hungers after Sol's glance [and glory], he would fain take again his splendour with Luna from the sun, but he gets only an earthly lunar lustre, wherein he acts and exercises pride, unless he be born again out of Sol's splendour, that is, out of God's power in the heavenly Mercurius; and so he becomes again the golden silver-child in divine essentiality, only covered and clothed this life-time with the earthly moon, that is, with earthly flesh.

31. Saturn also is the house of silver, he is likewise the cause of the first conception, but he turns his desire only upon the golden child, and leaves the silver its garment, and takes it into his stony earthly property, and lets Mercury hatch it.

32. The desire of the free lubet is fixed and steadfast, as concerning the property of the desire only, which brings its will again from the body into the combat in the senses, and makes Jupiter, that is on the orb [2] upwards under Saturn, under the saturnine power; its metal is tin, and it is the third degree; for the lubet of the liberty in the desire proceeds forth into the desire of the austereness, and so it gives itself into the fiat.

[1] Draws it to itself.   [2] Wheel, or sphere.

33. We must understand it thus; the lubet of the liberty goes forth out of itself, as a plant, and makes one degree after another in order, but Mercury makes the sphere, for he is the work-master: And as the eternal birth is in itself in the heavenly Mercury, viz. in the eternal word in the Father's generation; so likewise with the motion of the Father it came into a creaturely being, and so proceeds in its order, as may be seen in the wheel of the planets; for the order is just so placed as man is in his order.

34. First there is in him the true golden divine man, which is the likeness of God: Next there is in him the man of heavenly essentiality, viz. the inward holy body, generated from the fire and light in the tincture, which is like to the pure silver if it were not corrupted. Thirdly, there is in him the elemental man from the pure element resembling Jupiter. Fourthly, the mercurial, which is the growing or paradisical [man]. Fifthly, the martial, from the fire, viz. the soulish [man], according to the Father's property. Sixthly, the venerine [man], according to the outward desire, and the water's property. Seventhly, the solar, according to the sun's property, viz. according to the outward world, as a seer and knower of the wonders of God: And yet it is but the one only man; yet is both in the inward and outward world. Thus likewise is the similitude [or form] of the seven metals; with one property according to the inward world, and with another visible and palpable property according to the outward world.

35. From Jupiter the sphere turns round, and out of the separation Mercury proceeds forth with a broken metal, according to his spirit's property; externally quicksilver, and internally he is a paradisical working; he is in his spiritual property the distinguisher (or articulator) of the words, voices, and speeches. It is written, "God hath made all things by his word:" The heavenly eternal Mercurius is his word, which the Father expresses in the enkindling of his light, and the expressed is his wisdom; and the word is the worker, framer, and maker of the formings in the expressed wisdom. Now what the inward Mercurius does internally in God's power, that likewise the outward Mercurius effects in the outward power in the created essence: He is God's instrument, wherewith he works extrinsically to death and to life; in each thing according to its property he builds, and breaks down.

36. According to Saturn's property he builds, and according to his own property he distinguishes and dissipates [1] the hardness

---

[1] Attenuates, destroys.

in Saturn, viz. the enclosed, and opens it to life: He opens the colours, and makes forms and shapes, and carries in him an heavenly, and also an earthly property; in the earthly he carries out of the first desire to nature, viz. out of Saturn, Mars, viz. the wrathfulness of the impression; for he is his soul, wherein Mercury lives; he gives him the fiery essence, and stands under Jupiter in the order upwards on the sphere; for he carries the fire-spirit in Sulphur into all planets, and forms and gives to each thing its source, and true spirit of life.

37. Mars in the first impression is the great anguish, and causes the love-will of the liberty to separate from him; and that which is separated is called God; and the anguish, or fire-source, is called God's anger, viz. the wrath of the eternal nature: And as internally God's love separates from God's anger, that is, from the wrathful property of the eternal nature, viz. heaven from hell, God from the devil; so also it is effected in the birth of the outward nature.

38. Love proceeds out of the wrath, and is an humility, or submission: Thus likewise it came in the creation into order; therefore Venus stands in the sphere on the line of Mars under the sun, for so is the separation in nature; and so one proceeds forth from another: Its metal is copper, the original whereof is this, that the love is a desire, and desires only light and joy; for the materia is made out of the desire's property: But if the love-desire shall come to be corporeal in the impression, then it must resign itself to the wrathful fiat, viz. to the desire of Mars in the fire, or in the fiery property; for the saturnine property takes all into its might, and makes it corporeal.

39. Therefore the metal of Venus is so nearly related to gold, by reason of her own property from the liberty, but Mars makes it too wrathful; and because it separates itself out of Mars's fire, it retains a great part of the property of Mars in it.

40. Mars's metal is iron, for he is the wrath in Sulphur, in which the fire enkindles, and arises; his original with the materia is in the austereness of the desire: copper separates itself in the generation out of iron, for it arises from the will of Venus, and they differ as body and soul; for Mars is the fire-soul of Venus, and makes Venus corporeal; otherwise Venus, as to her own property, gives only water in the mortification in the salnitral flagrat; for her fire is only a pleasant shining, smile, or love-fire, as she is alone void of other mixture; and therefore she cannot produce any corporeal essence from her own power and ability, which is hard and tough; she is only the

mother [1] to her child without a creaturely soul; Mars is her soul, and Saturn makes her body.

41. The spirit of Sol may tincture Mars and Venus, and change them into the highest metalline perfection, viz. into gold; which cannot so easily be effected in silver, unless it be reduced into the first materia, where Saturn, Mars, and Mercury are together in the Sulphur, and then it can be done: Venus receives its toughness from Saturn, and its redness from Mars as the fire.

42. Now the desire of Venus is only eager, and longing after Sol, as after her first mother, from whence she springs forth in her birth in the first original; for the love comes forth originally from God, and so it is likewise in the external birth in the figure: The desire of Venus goes into Sol, into the sun, and receives in its desire the property of the sun, and shines from Sol; she has a very peculiar shining and lustre above all the planets and stars, which she receives from her mother; and in her mother's power consists her joy, viz. the pleasant twinkling smiling aspect which she has in her; she is in her own property (as she is purely alone without the property of the other planets) a real daughter of the sun (understand in Sulphur, where all is wrapt together), therefore she stands next under the sun, as a child of the sun; not that the sun did generate that star, for he is likewise created with her, but in the Sulphur without the creation, merely in the generation, it is so, both in the heavenly and earthly [being, or principle].

43. For God the Father generates the love through his heart; now the sun, by way of similitude, betokens his heart; for it is a figure in the outward world according to the eternal heart of God, which gives strength and virtue to every life and essence.

44. And understand it right; all things proceed from the word and heart of God (which is the divine Sulphur) in the birth of the Holy Trinity, and manifest themselves in and through the proceeded (or egressed) essence, which is God's wisdom; and they again do eagerly force and press out of the egress, in and towards his heart and power, and vehemently long after it, as Paul saith, all creatures groan and pant with us to be delivered from vanity.

45. So also does the outward essence in the outward birth of metals, planets, stars, and creatures; each thing longs after its centre, viz. after its first mother, whence it proceeded, viz. after the sun in Sulphur, for it is the tincture of all essences: Whatever the first desire with the impression in Saturn makes evil

[1] Woman, wife.

in the wrath of Mars, that the sun turns again into good. As the divine sun tinctures the anger or wrath of God, so that the wrathful property of God's anger is changed into a joyfulness; so likewise the outward sun tinctures the outward Sulphur, viz. Saturn and Mars, that there is a pleasant temperature, viz. a growth, springing, and blooming in all metals and creatures; therefore the sun is the centre, which reason will not believe; understand, in the planetary orb, and in all vegetables and animals.

CHAPTER V

1. ALL life and motion, with understanding, reason, and senses, both in animals and vegetables, consist originally in Sulphur, viz. in nature's desire, and in the lubet's desire of the liberty.

2. In nature's desire arises the death and enclosing, and in the desire of the liberty arises the opening and the life; for the liberty's desire tinctures the desire of the dark nature, so that the wrathful mother foregoes her own right, and freely resigns to the liberty's desire, and so the life grows in death, for there is no life without light; but if the light goes out in the essence of the Sulphur, then it is an eternal death, which no man can revive, unless God moves himself in the lubet-desire in the same death; for death can receive no life into it, unless the first desire, viz. the free lubet's desire, manifests itself in the desire to nature, wherein the enclosing and death are generated.

3. Therefore when man died in the Sulphur, none could have made him alive again, unless the free lubet, viz. the desire to the eternal life did again enter into his Phur, viz. into the birth of the nature of the human property, and moved the enclosed death, viz. the centre of nature, and gave itself again into the centre, viz. into the soul-like property, and into the soul's essentiality and corporality; and this was so brought to pass.

4. We know that the right Sulphur is a generation of all spirituality and corporality; so far as concerns its first original, where it is heavenly, it is the generation of the essence of all essences: For all, whatever eternity and time is in itself, has, and is able to effect, lies in this birth: But now as to the kingdom of this world it is earthly, viz. a figure of the eternal; for in it the time and creature consist, and all whatever is visible and invisible.

5. Now man, and every life also, as to the kingdom of this world, was created and generated out of the outward Sulphur; man out of the inward and outward [Sulphur], and the outward creature only out of the outward; for man is an image and likeness of God, and the other creatures are as a similitude

43

according to the figuration in the internal generation in God's wisdom, viz. in the expressed or procreated heavenly essence, according to both eternal principles.

6. But now man was created good and perfect, according to and out of all the three worlds, as an image of the Deity, in whom God dwelled; and he was even that essence what God is, according to eternity and time in all the three worlds; but he was a creature with a beginning, as to the creature, and died through the lubet [1] as to the heavenly and divine essence: For the inward lubet, which was generated in the centre, viz. in the fire, wherein stood the life in the divine essentiality, that is, that which enkindled the essence of the divine meekness, wherein the joyfulness or the angelical form consists; that (I say) turned itself from the inward lubet of the liberty and eternity into the time, viz. into the external birth, into the planetary property, [it departed] out of the pure divine element into the four elements: Thus the inward divine essentiality, or inward corporality did no longer retain any leader or life: And this was the death; for the soul's fire proceeding from the Father's property turned itself away from the Son's property, in which alone the divine life consists.

7. Thus the property of the soul remained naked only with its will in the outward Sulphur, and the inward disappeared, and continued steadfast in the eternal unchangeableness, [2] as in an eternal nothing, wherein there was no more any effecting [or working efficacy to bring to pass].

8. Thus man with his outward body lived barely and merely to the time; the precious gold of the heavenly corporality, which tinctured the outward body, was disappeared, and so the outward body stood barely and alone in the life of nature's desire, viz. in the soul's fiery property; understand in the form and property of Mars, viz. in the wrath of God, which is the wrath in Sulphur, viz. the property of God's anger and the dark world: But seeing the outward body was created out of the time, therefore the time, viz. the constellation with the four elements, presently obtained the dominion in him; and the divine property, viz. the desire of the Deity (which ruled and tinctured time, so that there was a holy life in the creature out of the time), was vanished; its own peculiar love in the divine desire was turned to water, and it became blind and dead in the will and desire of God; and the soul must help itself with the sun's light.

[1] Lust.   [2] Or immobility.

9. But seeing that time has beginning and end, and the will with the desire has given up itself to the temporal leader, therefore the dominion of time destroys its own contrived spirit, and so the body also dies and passes away; and this is that which God said to Adam, that " he should not eat of the tree, or plant, of the knowledge of good and evil," of both properties, lest he died;[1] as it also came to pass, he died in the Sulphur; the Sul in the kingdom of God, viz. the lubet of the divine liberty, out of which the light of God shines, and in which the divine love, viz. the love-fire burns [disappeared and withdrew from him].

10. Now there was no remedy for him, unless God's desire entered again into his dead Sulphur, that is, into his Sul, which was dead, viz. into the dead [or mortified] essentiality, and again enkindled it with the love-fire; which came to pass in Christ: And there the heavenly body, wherein God's light shines, did again arise. But if this must be effected, then the love-desire must again enter into the desire of the enkindled anger, and quench and overcome the anger with the love; the divine water must enter again into the soul's burning fire, and quench the wrathful death in the astringent fiat, viz. in the desire to nature, that the love-desire, which desires God, might be again enkindled in the soul.

11. For man's happiness[2] consists in this, that he has in him a true desire[3] after God, for out of the desire springs forth the love; that is, when the desire receives the meekness of God into itself, then the desire immerses itself in the meekness, and becomes essential; and this is the heavenly or divine essentiality, or corporality; and therein the soul's spirit (which lay shut up in the anger, viz. in death) does again arise in the love of God; for the love tinctures the death and darkness, that it is again capable of the divine sunshine.

12. And as this is done in man, so likewise it is in the transmutation of metals: The Sulphur is shut up in Saturn, viz. in the death, and yet there is no death, but a vegetative life; and the outward Mercury is the life thereof.[4] Now if the metalline body shall come to the highest perfection, then it must die unto the external dominator,[5] viz. to the elements, and come again into such a Sulphur as it was, when as yet it had not the four elements on it, but lay only in the element in unity.[6]

---

[1] Or he should die.   [2] Salvation.
[3] An upright, full, and unfeigned desire.
[4] Or therein.   [5] Leader.   [6] In one.

13. But now none can reduce it into such a body, but he only who has generated; he that has given it the four elements, he alone can take them away; and he that at first made it corporeal, he must bring it to himself, and transchange it in himself into another body; and this is the Sulphur, which has Mercurius as its chief faber in itself. He must again take it out of dark Saturn's bowels in the fiat, and introduce it into his own, and with his own fire separate the four elements from it, and reduce it into one; as God at the last day will in the enkindling of his own fire separate the essence of the four elements from the pure element, that the eternal corporality in the pure element may arise [1] and spring forth: And as in the death of man the four elements separate from the true man (who is the element of God) and the heavenly body remains only in itself; so it goes in the transmutation of metals.

PROCESS

14. The body lies shut up in a disesteemed form in Saturn, not wholly in Saturn's property, in a dark colour, marked with Mercurius its father, and Sol its mother, clothed with Saturn, and manifest with the life of Mars; but its mother is not outwardly manifest and known on it, unless its faber be enraged with its own iniquity; which yet cannot be, unless an alienate be applied, whereby its propriate is enraged; and then (if his anger be set on a fire or fury) he becomes so very hungry and thirsty, and yet can find no refreshment in itself; then it seizes on its faber who has made it, and fights against its creator, as the earthly wicked man does against God, so long till he devours and consumes himself, as a fiery [pestilent] poison consumes the body, unless you remedy, stay, and allay its hunger; yet there is none that can still this horrible hunger, but God himself who has made him; and if he assists not in due time, then the hunger in the wrath consumes the body, and puts it into the eternal darkness.

15. This hunger desires nothing but the mercy of God, that he might be freed from the anguish of hell; but this he cannot obtain of himself, for he is shut up in the anger of God; and his dear mother, which nursed him in the beginning, is also shut up in death: But if God shews his grace, and gives him again of his love, then the anger is dismayed at the love;[2] and this is a flagrat of great joy: For he again tastes the sweetness

---

[1] Begin.   [2] Or in the divine love.

of his dear mother, and then he knows full well that he has been so vile and wicked, and repents of his iniquity, and will turn and mortify the old Adam, and cast it away from him.

16. So the artist takes him presently away with the old Adam from the strange anger, and lays him in a soft bed; for the old Adam is sick, and will die; and then his own faber in the old Adam is in the love of God,[1] which destroyed the anger, and will make a young child, and rejoices in the child; and the old Adam grows sick, and weak, wholly dark, and swarthish, and dies; and the four elements go out [2] from him with their colours: So the faber gives him even leave to go, and continually labours on the new body, which shall arise from death; and none sees his labour, for he works in the dark.

17. But the artist takes no care about the work,[3] but gives the faber his own food, till he sees that a vegetative life appears in the dark death with a new colour out of the black; and then, when the new man is ready, the artist comes, and brings the soul, and gives it the faber; at which the faber is dismayed that another life comes into him; and he puts the soul into the new body, and it goes inwardly in the anger: Thus the new man arises in great power and glory from death, and bruises the head of the old serpent in the anger of God, and passes through the anger, and the anger can do him no harm at all.

> Whoe'er thou art, that to this work art born,
> A chosen work thou hast, howe'er the world may scorn.

[1] Or upon the love of God.   [2] Depart.   [3] Labour.

CHAPTER VI

1. ALL life, growth, and instigation consist in two things, viz. in the lubet, and then in the desire; the lubet is a free will, and as a nothing in comparison to nature; but the desire is as a hunger: In the desire arises the moving spirit, viz. the natural, and in the lubet the supernatural, which yet is nature's,[1] but not out of its own property, but out of [or from] the property of the desire.

2. The desire is the instigation of the essence, viz. an hunger, and the lubet is the hunger's essence,[2] which it takes into itself; for the desire is only an hungry will, and it is the natural spirit in its forms; but the lubet is out of the liberty: For God is without desire as concerning his own essence, inasmuch as he is called God; for he needs nothing. All is his, and he himself is all.

3. But he has a lubet-will, and he himself is the will, to manifest himself in the lubet; yet in the lubet which is free, without affection, no manifestation can be effected, for it is void of desire; it is as if it were nothing in respect of nature, and yet it is all; but not according to the desire, viz. according to nature, but according to the satisfying of nature it is the satisfying of the hungry desire, viz. of nature; it freely and willingly gives itself into the hunger of nature; for it is a spirit without essence and desire, wholly free as a nothing; but the desire makes it essential [or materialises] in itself, and that according to two properties, viz. one according to the eternal liberty, which is free from the source; and the other according to the desire, which gives a vegetative life, viz. a growing, or a giving forth of itself.

4. The free essence is, and gives an oil, and the desire's property gives a life of the oil; the oil is a light, and the desire's property gives to the light the essence, viz. the fiery property, so that the light shines, as is to be seen in the fire and light,

[1] Of or belonging to nature. [2] Being, materia, or food.

48

and the free lubet remains yet a free will in itself, but gives its meekness, viz. a free resignation into the desire, that it comes to essence and lustre: Its will is only good, it has no other desire but only to be good, meek, and pleasant; there is also no other possibility therein; for it [1] is as a nothing, wherein no disturbance or source can be, but it is the meekness itself.

5. But seeing it cannot be a nothing, by reason that it is a cause and beginning of the desire, therefore it gives itself freely, as the sunshine freely gives itself into every property; and the desire conceives [or takes] this free lubet, viz. the lustre or shining of the abyss of eternity into itself, and makes it in itself into essence according to its property; so much property as is in the desire, so much also there is of essence: And we are to consider, that when the free lubet gives in itself into the hunger of the desire, that the desire then makes out of the free lubet's property a similitude according to the liberty, which is as if it were nothing, and yet is; this is a water and oil.

6. But seeing the desire, that is, the hunger, is filled with the free lubet, it makes its own property in the essence of the liberty also into essence; its essence is water, and the essence of the free lubet is an oil. Thus a twofold property arises in one only spirit, viz. a fiery [property] according to the property of the desire, and a joyful or lucid property according to the liberty.

7. The fiery gives [2] in its essence, viz. in its water a sharpness from the austere desire, which is saltish, or a salt; and from the fiery anguish a brimstone, from whence in the *impression* and creation of the world, are made stones, earth, and metals; so also the elements and stars, all according to the forms in the desire; and the oleous property gives its meekness, viz. a love-lubet, wherein the fiery is impressed with the desire, and makes corporality: And the oleous gives itself out in its meekness, and makes the vegetable life, viz. a springing and growing in the fiery impression, whereinto the fire must give its essence and instigation, viz. the vehement compunction [3] in the attraction of the desire, which is the separator in the corporality, viz. the distinguisher, carver, and cause of the essence and multiplicity [or variety].

8. Philosophers have called this form Mercurius, from the anxious inciting sphere, which is the cause of all life and motion, and a faber in the oily and watery property.

---

[1] Understand the free will.
[2] Affords, produces, or makes.   [3] Or raging sting.

9. Thus we are to search and find out the great mystery, how there is an oil, brimstone, and salt in everything, and how they arise; for God has made all things out of nothing, and that same nothing is himself, viz. a love-lubet dwelling in itself, wherein there is no affection: But now the love-lubet would not be manifest, if it remained one in the stillness without essence, and there would be no joy or moving therein, but an eternal stillness.

10. But seeing[1] he introduces himself into essence through the desire, his eternal stillness becomes an essence and working power, and that with two properties, viz. in an oil, in which the working power is a good spirit according to the property of the love-lubet, which resists the desire's wrath in the brimstone, salt, and poisonful Mercury, and appeases and heals his poisonful hunger with the pleasant meekness; that which Mercury destroys with the raging sphere[2] of his own property, that the lubet of the love-oil does again heal: And thus there is good and evil in each life, and yet there is no evil in anything, unless the good, viz. the love-oil famishes in its own lubet, which falls out in the forms of the impression of the hunger of the desire.

11. That is, if the hunger-spirit does in its own forms too much impress itself [long, or imagine] after itself, and too eagerly hunger after its own manifestation, it cannot take the free lubet, which appeases its hunger, into itself; for nature's property must be sincerely bent and inclined to the free lubet's property, viz. to God's love-*ens*, and wholly direct its hunger after love; and then the hunger receives the love into itself, and makes the same essential in itself, and is no longer a famished dark hunger, which rages in itself, and raves as a poisonful Mercury; but the hunger becomes a love-desire, which is called God's nature, and the hungry fiery [desire] is called God's anger; and in the outward nature it is called a fire, but in the inward world's property, where the desire does act with energy in the property of the free lubet, this desire is called the divine desire, wherein the fiery love burns, and from whence the joyfulness proceeds; for the free lubet does therefore give itself into the austere desire, that it may bring forth a fiery love, viz. a joyfulness, which could not be in the still lubet; for where there is a stillness there is no joy, or motion.

12. Now the free lubet, viz. God's property, manifests itself through the fiery property, and the fiery property makes the free lubet's essence, viz. the oil which arises in the impression

[1] Or when.   [2] Or furious wheel.

of the desire into a light or lustre; for the austere desire gives the anxious darting flash, viz. a sulphureous spirit, and the meekness of the oil gives its love into it, and dispels that which was drawn into it, viz. the darkness, and manifests the eternal liberty, viz. the nothing, and this is now the seeing.

13. For when the fire-splendour tastes the sweetness of the light, then the fire's desire reaches after the meekness, and the meekness of the free lubet is as a nothing wholly incomprehensible: Now the hunger of the desire comprehends its own essence and devours it, and makes it to nothing; this is the darkness, which is the hunger's essence, which the fiery hunger devours through the property of the light, or free lubet: As we see, that as soon as the light shines it deprives the darkness of its power; therefore God is a Lord over all beings, for he is the eternal Power and Light: A similitude whereof we see in the sun, that it is lord of the darkness and of all essences, and rules whatever grows, lives, and moves in this world.

14. Further, we are to consider of the manifold salts, how they take their rise in the original, and separate into many properties. In the original of the impression, viz. in the verbum fiat, a twofold salt does arise: The first is spiritual, and gives the sharpness in the essence of the free lubet; it is a severising, or a sharpness of the powers: The other salt is the sharpness of the impression, according to the property of the astringent austerity which is the anguish in the impression, that is, brimstone, and the essential property is water.

15. The water is the senseless mortal property of the salt; and the sulphureous, which is from the anguish, is the property of the quick salt; for it has the sting of motion, viz. the Mercury in it, which makes life's form, and yet the brimstone is not the salt, but it is the anguish in the impression, which also comes to be corporeal.

16. The salt is the sharpness in brimstone as to the astringency; the salt causes the anguish to be corporeal; and so salt dwells in the brimstone, and is the brimstone's sharpness, and preserves the brimstone in the corporeal essence, and also the spirit of the brimstone, that it falls not to dust: The salt impresses the powers of the anguish, and the impressed life is the mercurial life; the same is the life of the anguish, viz. of the brimstone, and separates the materia according to the forms to nature, and the materia of the free lubet into two essences, viz. into a watery and oily, and then into a corporeal.

17. The corporeal is twofold; both according to the darkness

and the light: According to the property of the austere desire it makes in the watery [property] a sand, or stony nature, from whence the stones have their original; understand out of the sulphureous, viz. out of the brimstone's water.

18. The other property, as to [1] the mortification in the salnitral flagrat, is the common running water; the other corporeal [water] is the metalline body from the free lubet's property in the impressed form; and from the watery property (where the brimstone is in the water) it produces trees, herbs, and all whatever grows in the earthly property, viz. in the mortified or dead substantiality, which yet has a life without sense,[2] viz. a vegetative.

19. The oily property is also twofold according to the impression; viz. one part forces again into the liberty to be free from the wrath of the impression, which is the good spirit, viz. the light in the oil; the other part yields itself into the anguish of the brimstone, and remains in the corporality, and unites and applies itself in each thing, according to the salt-property of the thing; as in a fiery salt, it is fiery; in a bitter salt, it is bitter; in an astringent, astringent, etc.

20. The first property according to the light is sweet in all things, and the other property of the oil is according to the form, viz. the taste of the thing, let it be either sweet, sour, astringent, sharp, or bitter, or how it will; as it is to be found out and known in herbs: In some it is a bitter poison, and in some again a healing of the poison; but if the poisonful property be broken by Mercury in the oil of meekness, then the love of the light inclines itself also into the oil, for the original of both is from one will, but it is altered in the impression: As the devil, when he was an angel, changed himself into a poisonous devilish property, and Adam out of an heavenly into an earthly [property].

21. Whatever grows, lives, and moves in this world, consists in Sulphur, and Mercury is the life in Sulphur, and the salt is the corporeal being of Mercury's hunger, though the body is manifold; according as the property of the brimstone and salt is, according to the same property is also the ingrafted oil, which springs up all along in the power; for the oil makes the power [or virtual influence] in each thing. In the oil of the impression, viz. in the impressed oil, is the other oil, viz. the spiritual, which gives us light, but it has another principle; it receives no other source into it but the lubet of love; it is divine essentiality: Therefore God's own essence is nigh unto all things, but not

---

[1] According to, or after.   [2] Dumb.

essentially in all things; it has another principle, and yet inclines itself to all things; as far as the thing has anything of the divine property in it, it receives virtue from the divine property, be it either a vegetable or animal; for there are herbs and trees, and also creatures to be found, in which something of the divine power is couched, with which in the magical cure the false magic, viz. the corrupt evil oil can be resisted, and changed into a good oil.

22. All sharpness of taste is salt, let it be whatever it will in this world, nothing excepted; and all smell proceeds from the brimstone, and Mercury is the distinguisher in all motion [or affection], both in the smell, power, and taste; but I understand by my Mercury the sphere of the birth of all essences, as is before mentioned; not a dead Mercury, but a living one, viz. the strongest, according to the property of the dry poison, etc.

23. Now it behoves the artist and physician to know these things, else he cannot cure any sickness or disease, unless he hits on it by chance, if he knows not wherewith the oil is poisoned in the body, and what kind of hunger Mercury has in the sickness, and after what he hungers; for if he may obtain [1] the salt according to the property of his hunger (after which he is desirous) with such an oil as he fain would have, then is the sickness over very soon; for he turns his oil again into the property of the love of the light, whereupon the life begins again to shine bright.

24. For every disease in the body is nothing else but a corruption or poisoning of the oil, from which the life's-light burns or shines; for when the light of the life shines or burns clear in the oil, it expels and drives away all poisonful influences and operations, as the day expels the night.

25. For if the oil, out of which the life burns, be infected [or inflamed] with a poisonful Mercury or salt, let it be done either from the constellation, or salt of meat, viz. from a contrary source, whereby a loathing [or nauseous detestation] arises in the oil, which the oil would always spew out, which Mercury helps; then Mercury eagerly troubles and perplexes itself in the sulphureous fire more and more, and continually labours to drive forth the abominate, but does only inflame itself in itself in this austere endeavour, and more and more enkindles its inward form, whereupon the oil grows more dark and poisonful, until at last the oil becomes wholly waterish and earthly, and then the light, and also the fire, extinguishes, and Mercury

[1] Can but get.

with the sulphureous spirit departs from it, as when a candle is put out; thus Mercury passes out with the sulphureous spirit in death's baneful steam,[1] until he also be famished; for a time he may help himself in the sidereal body, which passes along with it; but when Mercury in the spirit of the great world has consumed and starved its property, then is the temporal life wholly gone; for as soon as the light of the vital oil extinguishes, the elemental body falls down into putrefaction, viz. into the fiat, from whence it came to be; and then this time ends in the creature, which is the death, dying, or departure; and from thence there is no deliverance or return, unless the heavenly divine Mercury does once more move itself in him, which yet cannot be, except there has been a good property of the oil in him, viz. from the divine essentiality: In this property, which is capable of the divine essentiality, the light does only enkindle itself again.

26. For the divine essentiality, or this heavenly Mercury, changes the dead oil again into his, and becomes its life; for the outward Mercury, which has ruled the life, returns not again, it has only been for a time a mirror of the eternal, but he is changed into another source; for being suffocated, he passes again into the mystery, from whence he at first proceeded in the creation of the world, and the body also goes into the same mystery.

27. Thus it remains, and belongs yet to another motion of the Deity, viz. to a separating, where the evil, wherein the death was, shall be separated from the good, and the verbum fiat shall restore and bring forth that which has fallen into it in death.

28. The physician is to know, that in the strongest Mercury, which is most poisonful, the highest tincture lies, but not in Mercury's own property, which must be broken;[2] for his own property, even from the centre, is the anxious poisonful life: But he has another property in him, viz. an oil from the light, whereby he is so strong and potent, which is his food and preservation; if this may be separated from him, it becomes a tincturing and mighty enkindling of all obscured lives, viz. of all diseases and sicknesses; for in this oil lies the joyful life, and it is an hunger after life, viz. that it might enkindle the weak, and lift it up on high.

29. In a toad, viper, or adder, or the like poisonful beasts, worms, or insects, the highest tincture is to be found, if they are reduced into an oily substance, and the wrath of Mercury

---

[1] Sting.   [2] Or taken from him.

separated from them; for all life, both external and internal, consists in poison and light, as we understand, that the wrath and anger-fire of God is a cause of the divine joyfulness: The like also we are to know is externally; for all life that is void of the poisonful Mercury is mort, and an abominate,[1] and accounted as dead.

30. Now Mercury is an enkindler of the fire, and every moving life consists in the fire; and though some creatures dwell in the water, yet fire is their life, viz. the poison-gall, wherein Mercury manages the life; but the water in the gall is a poison, wherein an oil is hid, in which the life in Mercury does burn and shine; of which thou hast a similitude: If in a creature there be a strong poisonful Mercury, of a dry quality, that creature is strong, bold, courageous, and potent, which has also a clear oil in it; for the fiery property of the Mercury consumes the waterish, but if its fat be enkindled, it yields a clear light; much more would it be, if the watery property were separated from the oleous.

[1] Or loathsomeness.

CHAPTER VII

HOW ADAM IN PARADISE, AND HOW LUCIFER WAS A FAIR ANGEL,
AND HOW THEY WERE CORRUPTED AND SPOILED THROUGH
IMAGINATION AND PRIDE

PROCESS

1. WE will give an occasion of consideration to the earnest
searcher and seeker, and if he apprehends our meaning he shall
indeed be able to find the noble philosopher's stone, but so that
he be chosen thereto by God, and his life also stands in the
heavenly Mercury, otherwise we are a mystery to him; and we
will represent it to him in similitudes, in the most manifest,
and yet mystical manner.

2. When Adam was created in paradise, the heavenly Mercury
did then lead him; his life burned in a pure oil, therefore his
eyes were heavenly; and his understanding did excel nature, for
his light shined in the oil of the divine essentiality; the external
waterish property was not manifest in his oil; he was *iliastrich*,
that is, angelical, and became in the Fall *cogastrish*, that is, the
watery nature in the mortal property was manifest in his oil,
and penetrated, so that the mercury in him became an anxious
poison, which before in his oil was an exaltation of joyfulness.

3. For the salnitral flagrat in the impression in the coldness,
viz. according to the saturnine property, was thereby elevated,
and got the dominion, as a cold poison, which arises in the
impression of death, from whence the darkness was generated in
the oil, and Adam died to the divine light; to which the devil
persuaded[1] him by[2] the serpent, that is, by the essence and
property of the serpent; for the kingdom of wrath, and also the
outward kingdom was manifest in the serpent; for it was more
subtle than any beast of the field, and this subtlety Eve desired;
for the serpent persuaded her that her eyes should be opened,
and she should be as God, and know good and evil.

4. Which also was the will of the devil, that he would know
evil: And in the enkindling to the knowledge in Mercury he
became corrupt and dark; for he entered with the imagination,

[1] Or led.　　　　　　　　　　[2] Or through.

according to his condition, knowledge, and desire, into the fiery byss; and Adam, according to his knowledge and desire, went into the cold byss into the impression, into the procreated watery property in the salniter, where both kingdoms stand separated: He desired to prove and taste the watery mercury, in which is the mortal poison; and Lucifer [desired] the fiery Mercury, which gives strength and might; from whence his pride arose, viz. out of the fiery Mercury: But both, viz. Lucifer, and also Adam, lost the oil of the meekness of the divine essentiality.

5. Now we are to consider of the serpent, which deceived Adam with its craft; how it was, and what its subtlety was after which Adam and Eve did imagine; why they did eat of the forbidden tree which was evil and good, and how they did eat death thereby; and what their salvation and restoration is naturally and properly; what evil and good are, what the property of the eternal life, and then the property of eternal death is; what the cure is, whereby the sickness introduced by Adam, and its death, may be healed, and restored both to the temporal and eternal life.

6. Let the reader attend to the sense and meaning; for we have not the ability to give this into his hands; that only belongs to God; but the gates shall stand open for him, if he will enter in; if not, flattery [1] avails him not.

7. The devil was a fair angel, and the serpent the subtle beast, and man the likeness of the Deity; now all three were corrupted [2] by imagination and pride, and got the curse of God for their false lust [or cunning].

8. All whatever is eternal proceeds originally from one ground, as angels and souls; but the serpent is not out of the eternal ground, but out of the beginning, as we have before given you to understand, how with the enkindling of the fire in the salnitral flagrat two kingdoms separate, viz. eternity and time; and how the eternity dwells in the time, but yet only in itself; but yet so nigh to the time, as fire and light which are in one another, and yet make two kingdoms; or as darkness and light dwell in each other, and the one is not the other. The like we are to consider of the inchoative poisonful mercury in the devil, and in man, and in the serpent also; how an oil corrupts, and yet the essence or being of God is not hereby at all corrupted, but enters into itself, viz. into the nothing; and the creaturely mercury, which arises, or is begotten with the beginning of the

---

[1] Or the riddle.   [2] Spoiled, undone.

creature in the creature, goes out of itself,[1] that is, out of the eternal into time, viz. into the beginning of the creature; it desires its own self, that is, the beginning; and will be its own, or of a selfish property, and forsakes the eternity, into which it should be wholly confined, and resigned with its desire, and bring its hunger thereinto; and then its poison-source would not be manifest.

9. For whatever hungers after the eternal nothing, viz. after the quiet meek liberty of God, that is not manifest to itself, but it is manifest in the still liberty, viz. in God; for as the hunger is, such is also the essence in the hunger; each hunger or desire makes itself an essence according to the property of the hunger or desire.

10. Thus the devil makes [or causes] in himself his darkness; for he went with his desire into himself, into the property of the centre to the desire, and forsook the eternity, viz. the nothing, that is, the lubet of love; so that he enkindled himself in his poisonful mercury, that is, in the forms to life in himself, and became an anxious fire-source in the darkness; as wood that is burnt to a coal, which only glows, and has no more any true light in it, also no oil or water; so it went with him. Now in his own property, viz. in his life's forms, there springs forth nothing but a stinging envious property, where one form hates and annoys the other, and yet they so beget each other.

11. And so was the serpent likewise, yet not by its own aspiring haughtiness; but when God said; Let all sorts of beasts come forth, each according to his property [or kind], then came forth beasts out of every property of nature, as it was manifest in the separation, when God moved himself to the creation; for the devil would domineer over the love and meekness of God, and put his desire also into the anger,[2] that is, into the austere might, where the poison-life arises, viz. into the fiat of the wrathful property, out of which form are proceeded vipers, serpents, toads, and other venomous worms; not that the devil has made them, that he cannot; only as the desire was in the impression of the fiat, such also was the creature in the evil and good.

12. For in the impression of the fiat, in the original of the outward Mercury, viz. of the life, which is manifest to itself internally, was the separation, where God and the world separate, viz. God inwardly,[3] the world outwardly,[4] as a simili-

---

[1] Or outwards.

[2] Or set his desire upon the anger.

[3] Text, into himself.

[4] Out of itself.

tude of the abyss, or a looking-glass of eternity; even there the inward wrath, from whence God is called an angry zealous God, and a consuming fire, manifested itself externally in figures, as in a similitude of the inward birth in the centre; like as the eternal lubet, which he is himself, stirs up [awakens] and causes the desire to the nature of the eternal manifestation, and gives in itself into the desire, and turns the wrath of the desire into joyfulness.

13. Thus it is also with the serpent's craft: [1] In the highest Mercury is the highest sharpest proof of all things; the more poisonful a thing is, the more sharply it proves a thing; for the sharpest [2] taste and smell consists in the great poison, viz. in a dying source.

14. And the eternal light is generated [3] out of the Father's sharpness, that it attains the shining, and goes forth with its own source through the sharpness out of the anguish-source again into the liberty, viz. into the nothing, where the light, by reason of the fire's-source and property, becomes also a desire, which is the desire of the divine love and joyfulness; in which desire Mercurius, the eternal word, or the understanding of eternity, or deity, is rightly considered and named: And this efflux from the fire (understand from the eternal magical spiritual fire) is a procreation, viz. of the word of the power, colours, and virtue: And this desire of the same mercury, or word, does also modelise [4] the power into its own desire, and makes it essential; which is the meekness and the love, which quenches the wrath of the Eternal Father, viz. of the eternal nature's desire with love, and changes it into joyfulness, where the name of God has its original from eternity. This immassed essentiality causes [5] two properties, viz. one oleous, which is heavenly essence, a cause of the shining of the light; and also a powerful [property] from the motion of the eternal impression, or desire of the Father after the birth of the Son; from whence the divine air (as the power through the shining of the light) proceeds forth out of this love-fire, which is the Spirit of God.

15. In like manner know this, that the eternal love (understand the essence, viz. the heavenly essentiality) has given itself forth into the creation with the verbum fiat, to set [6] the Father's anger, viz. the form of the eternal nature, into the highest joyfulness, and to set forth the likeness of the eternal

---

[1] Or wit, or subtlety.   [2] Quickest, keenest.
[3] Or begets itself.   [4] Or form, or immass.
[5] Affords, yields, produces   [6] Bring, turn, or sublime.

generation; and where the nature of the wrath was most elevated through the fiat, there also the desire did most incline itself towards the liberty, to be free from the wrath, and to bring it into the kingdom of joy,[1] from whence the great and deep knowledge is arisen, and also the most precious and highest tincture; understand the desire of the wrathful hunger received that into itself after which it hungered,[2] viz. the liberty; for all things were created good in the beginning; also the devil was good while he was an angel; so also the serpent [was good in its creation before the curse].

16. But seeing the devil went into the highest fire's desire, God departed from him, as a light that is put out, or extinguished in a candle; and afterwards he lived according to his own desire.

17. But seeing he knew that there was such a tincture in the serpent, and the serpent being created out of the beginning of time, therefore he insinuated [3] with his desire into the serpent, and took possession of the serpent's tincture, and wrought forth his desire through the serpent against man, to introduce him to long after the serpent's property: For the serpent's tincture was from both originals, viz. out of the deadly mercury from the dying in the fire, viz. from the coldness in the impression; and then also from the wrathful [fiery property in the impression]. The cold impression is earthly, which arises from the wrath, viz. from the dying in the wrath, in the impression; and the fiery [impression] arises from the quick poison of mercury, in which property the spirit's life consists.

18. Thus Adam and Eve were infected with the devil's desire through the serpent, viz. through the earthly, deadly property of the serpent; and also [through] the wrathful poisonful living property of God's wrath according to the devil's own property; and was inflamed in his divine oil, that is, in the heavenly essentiality.

19. Even then the divine light, which shined out of the divine body of the heavenly essentiality, was extinct to him; for the curse seized upon the soul. Now God's cursing is a withdrawing,[4] viz. the divine power, which was in the body, departed into its own principle; and his holy oil (wherein the power of God dwelt, and had made a kingdom of joy, viz. the paradise) became a poison.

20. For the earthly part according to the mortifying of the

---

[1] Or joyfulness.　　　　　　　　[2] Or receives that which it hungers after.
[3] Crept.　　　　　　　　　　　　[4] Or is a banishing.

water, viz. the cogastrish property, was manifest; and forthwith mercury, viz. the coldness in the death's property, got the dominion, whereas before he was as it were swallowed up in the divine power: Thus Adam died unto God, and lived to death; here it was necessary that God should regenerate him; and therefore the serpent was cursed, because it had served, and willingly obeyed the devil.

21. Thus we understand what lies hid in the greatest anguish, viz. in the strongest mercury, viz. an oil, which cures and tinctures all diseases; but the cold poison, viz. the death's source must be done away, and put into a fiery [property] which is desirous of the light; for God created all things good in the beginning, but through his cursing or withdrawing the evil came in: For when God's love-desire dwelt in the outward world's-source, and penetrated it, as the sun the water, or the fire an iron, then the outward world was a paradise, and the divine essence sprang forth and budded through the earthly, the eternal life through the mortal; but when God cursed it for man's sake, the mortal [life [1]] was manifest in man, and also in the fruit of which man should eat, which property before was only manifest in the " tree of the knowledge of good and evil," on which Adam and his wife were tempted, whether their desire would enter into the eternity, viz. into God's essence, or into the essence of time, into the living or mortal oil, in which source the soul's spirit would live, that is, burn.

22. Thus by God's curse, or withdrawing, the heavenly body was shut up, and the anger-source set open, and so [the heavenly body] lies still shut up: But seeing man by the eternal mercury, that is, by the word of divine power, was in one part formed out of eternity into body and soul, none could disclose [2] the poison-death, and destroy the mortal mercury, and change it again into the light's-source, viz. into the source of the divine joyfulness, but only the very divine Mercury, viz. the power and the word of life itself: For the serpent's poisonful earthly property was manifest and stirred up in man; therefore when God's word did pity the corruption of man, and did again embrace him,[3] he said, " The seed of the woman shall bruise the serpent's head," and thou (understand the serpent's poison or fire) shalt sting him in the heel.

23. Herein now lies the philosopher's stone, [to know] how the seed of the woman bruises the serpent's head, which is done in the spirit and essence temporally and eternally; the sting of

[1] Part or property.　　[2] Open, or exclude.　　[3] Or took his part.

the serpent is God's anger-fire, and the woman's seed is God's
love-fire, which must be again awakened, and illustrate[1] the
anger, and deprive the wrath of its might, and put it into the
divine joyfulness, and then the dead soul, which lay immersed in
God's curse, does arise: When the poisonful Mercury, which
resembles God's anger, is tinctured with love, then the death's
anguish in Mercury is changed into the highest joyfulness and
desire of love, which does again make a love-essence in itself,
viz. an heavenly body out of the earthly: When Mercury is
changed into an heavenly source, it desires no longer [or more]
the earthly mortal life; [it desires] not the four elements, but
only the one, wherein the four are contained, as it were swallowed up; as the light holds the darkness swallowed up in itself,
and yet the darkness is in it, but not manifest in the light; as
God dwells in time, and the time comprehends him not, unless
it be translated and wrapped up into eternity, that the divine
light does again shine in its source, and then the time is manifest
with its wonders[2] in the eternity.

24. In this manner also is the process of the wise men with
the precious stone: There is no nearer consideration of the same
than to consider [and know] how the eternal word, viz. the
heavenly divine Mercury in the divine power, is become man,
and has slain death, and the anger in man, viz. changed the
Mercury into the divine joyfulness, whereby the human Mercury,
which before lay shut up in God's anger, viz. in the source of
death, does with its new enkindled desire, which now is called
faith in the Holy Ghost, attract divine essentiality, viz. Christ's
body to itself, and sets itself in divine power and light above
the anger of God, and the poison of the serpent, and bruise the
head of the anger, viz. the poison of death with the life of divine
joyfulness: That is, the anger was master, but in the light it
became a servant, which now must be a cause of the joyfulness,
as it is most plain, clear, and manifestly made known and shewn
to us in the mercurial life.

25. Now observe the process, and meditate on it, ye dear
children of wisdom, and then you shall have enough temporally
and eternally;[3] do not as Babel does, which amuses and comforts
itself with the philosopher's stone, and boasts of it, but keeps only
a gross mason's stone shut up in poison and death, instead of
the precious philosopher's stone:[4] What is it for Babel to have
the stone, when it lies wholly shut up in Babel? It is as if a

---

[1] Shine through, irradiate.   [2] Or works and effects.
[3] Here and for ever.   [4] Or noble stone of the wise men.

lord bestowed a country upon me, which indeed was mine, but I could not take possession of it, and remained still a poor man notwithstanding, and yet I boasted of the dominion, and so had the name, and not the power: Even thus it goes with Babel about the precious stone of the new-birth in Christ Jesus.

26. In the sweet name, Jesus Christ, the whole process is contained, what, and how the new-birth is out of death into life, which is very clearly understood in the language of nature: For the name Jesus is the property of the free lubet of eternity, which yields itself into the pregnant centre, viz. into the Father's property, and figures itself in the centre in the Father's property, viz. in the Father's fire, to a word of eternal power.

27. Understand, the Father, viz. the Father's fiery forms, do figure [shape] this divine voice essentially in itself in the lubet of the liberty; that is, the Father's fiery property makes itself in the divine essence of the eternal love to a mercury of joyfulness; for the Father's property is the fire-source, and the Son's, viz. the eternal lubet's property, is the love-source; and yet also there would be no desire of love, if the Father's fire did not enkindle it, and make it movable, viz. desirous; from the fire arises the desire.

28. The Father of all essences begets this holy desire through his fire-source, which is now his heart of love, which gives in his fire the shining lustre and splendour; even there the wrath in the fire's property dies from eternity to eternity, and is changed into a love-desire.

29. Thus observe it; the free lubet's property is here in the fire's property called Christ, which signifies in the language of nature a potent champion,[1] depriving the wrath of its power, a shining of the light in the darkness, a transmutation, where the love-lubet rules over the fire-lubet, viz. over the wrath, the light over the darkness: Here the seed of the woman (understand of the free lubet, in which there is no source) bruises the head of the wrath of the eternal nature, viz. of the eternal desire; for the fire's property is rightly called the head, for it is the cause of the eternal life; and the liberty, viz. the free lubet, or the nothing, is rightly called *the woman ;* for in the nothing, viz. in the liberty of all source,[2] consists the birth of the Holy Trinity of the Deity.

30. Now the fire gives life, and the free lubet gives essence into the life, and in the essence is the birth, where the Father, viz. the eternal ground, begets his essence, viz. his heart out

---

[1] One that breaks through irresistibly.　　[2] Or void of all source.

of the abyss in himself, that is, out of the abyss in himself into a byss; the Son is [1] the Father's byss: Thus the Father remains in himself, as touching his own property only, the byss of the eternal nature; and the Son remains in the Father, the byss of the power and kingdom of joy; a resemblance whereof you see in the fire and light: And thus the Son tinctures the Father with the liberty, viz. with the nothing; and the Father tinctures (the Son) the nothing, that there is an eternal life therein, and no more a nothing, but a sound or voice of the manifestation of the eternity.

31. Thus, dear philosophers, observe here the ground how you should tincture; seek not the Son without the Father to tincture therewith: It must be one body; [2] the serpent-bruiser lies therein beforehand; for the seed of the woman has not bruised the serpent's head without the humanity, but in the humanity: The source of the divine lubet (understand of the love) manifested itself through a resurrection [3] in the human essence, and became manifest in the human life, and tinctured the wrath of death with the blood of the divine tincture, and there the wrath of death was changed into a source of divine love and joyfulness: Thus the love bruised the head of the anger and the oleous poison in Mercury, and deprived the wrath of its dominion, and sublimed the wrath into the highest joyfulness; even there the anger, and the astringent cold death, were made open shew of [4] in a fiery love: Then it was said, " Death, where is thy sting? Hell, where is thy victory? God be thanked who has given us victory."

32. Now it behoves the wise seeker to consider the whole process with the humanity of Christ from his opening in the womb of his mother Mary, even to his resurrection and ascension; and so he may well find the Feast of Pentecost with the joyful spirit, wherewith he may tincture, cure, and heal whatever is broken and destroyed: We declare it in the ground of truth, as we have highly known it; for the rose in the time of the lily shall blossom in May when the winter is past,[5] for blindness to the wicked, and for light to the seeing.

33. God be for ever praised, who has granted us eyes to see through the poisonful heart of the basilisk, and see the day of restitution of all whatever Adam lost.

---

[1] Or becomes.   [2] Corpus.
[3] Or awakening, or stirring itself up.
[4] Or victoriously triumphed over.
[5] Or the blooming spring of the paradisical new-birth in man.

34. Now we will come to the process of Christ, and go with him out of eternity into time, and out of time into eternity, and bring again the wonders of time into eternity, and openly set forth the pearl, for honour unto Christ, and scorn to the devil; he that sleeps is blind, but he that wakes sees what the May [1] brings.

35. Christ said, " Seek, and you shall find; knock, and it shall be opened unto you: " You know that Christ signifies in a parable concerning the wounded Samaritan, that he fell among murtherers, who beat him and wounded him, and pulled off his clothes, and went away, and left him half dead, till the Samaritan came, and took pity on him, dressed him, and poured oil into his wounds, and brought him into the inn: This is a manifest and lively representation of the corruption of man in paradise, and also of the corruption of the earth in the curse of God, when paradise departed from it.

36. Now wilt thou be a magus? Then thou must become the Samaritan, otherwise thou canst not heal the wounded and decayed; for the body which thou must heal is half dead, and sorely wounded; also its right garment is torn off, so that it is very hard for thee to know the man whom thou wilt heal, unless thou hast the eyes and will of the Samaritan, and seekest nothing else thereby but to restore the loss of the wounded.

37. Now consider! The eternal word manifested itself in Adam with divine living essentiality, with the heavenly Mercury, but when the soul's-fire in Adam, by the infection of the devil, poisoned the will's spirit in Adam, and introduced it through the property of the serpent into earthly deadly lust, then the heavenly Mercury of the heavenly essence withdrew, that is, the soul's will departed from it with its desire, and introduced its hunger into the earthly mortal essence, viz. into the property of the cold Mercury, which had made stones and earth. Adam's spirit would prove this [Mercury], and have the knowledge in evil and good, and so this Mercury of the four elements immediately drew him into its poison, and effectually wrought in him, and robbed him of the divine property, stung, and wounded him with heat and cold, and made him half dead, and stripped him of his angelical rayment, viz. the garment in the pure element, where the heavenly source penetrates the four elements, and tinctured them in Adam's body: Then he needed no other garment, for heat and cold were as it were swallowed up in him; as the day holds the night swallowed up in itself, and yet the

[1] Or pleasant spring.

night dwells in the day, but it is not manifest: Thus it went
with man when the property and source of the night seized on
him, then it domineered in him; and thus it went also with the
earth when God cursed it.

38. Now wilt thou be a magus? Then thou must understand
how to change the night again into the day; for the source of
the night, viz. of the darkness, is the anguish-source of death;
and the source of the day, viz. of the light, is the life, and the
lustre in the life; now Christ has again enkindled this shining
in the humanity, and quickened man again in himself: Now
if thou wilt tincture, then thou must change that which is shut
up, and closed in the death of the night again into the day, for
the day is the tincture, and yet the day and night lie in each
other as one essence.

39. Now says reason, How may I begin to do it?[1] Look
upon the process, how God began with the humanity, when he
would tincture the same.

40. Christ came into this world in the shut-up human form,
and brought into the enclosed fortress of death the tincture of
life, viz. the Deity; he came into the world as a pilgrim in our
poor form; he became ours, that he might tincture us in himself:
But what did he do? Did he live in joy? Did he behave and
carry himself as a lord? No; he entered into death, and died,
and put away the night's-source in him through us: But how
did he do it? He assumed the essence of our soul and body
unto the divine essence, and quickened our essence with the
divine, that our essence entered again with its will and desire into
the divine essence, and then the heavenly fiat was moved again
in the humanity; for the humanity inclined itself again into the
liberty, viz. into the free lubet of the Deity.

41. This being done, the man Christ was tempted forty days,
so long as the first Adam was alone in paradise, and was
tempted: Then the outward earthly food was taken from him,
and the humanity must eat with its desire of God's essence;
there was represented unto him all whatever the first Adam had
amused himself in, and whereinto he imagined, and wherein he
was captivated, as in the death of the night. This the devil,
being a prince of this world, now represented unto him in the
property of death, as he had represented it to Adam through
the serpent, whereon Adam and his wife did amuse themselves,
and entered thereinto with the imagination.

42. Now behold! What did Christ do when he was to undergo

[1] Or what shall I first do to effect it?

the combat of this trial, when the human essence was to enter
again with its desire into the Deity, and eat of God's bread,
that is, of the divine essentiality? He went to Jordan, and was
baptized of John. With what? With the water in Jordan,
and with the water in the word of life, viz. the divine essence,
which must tincture our mortal essence in the outward humanity
of Christ, from whence the divine hunger arose in the human
essence, that he desired to eat of God's bread: Therefore the
Spirit of God took him and carried him into the wilderness, and
there the Father's property in the wrath did oppose him through
the prince in the wrath; and there God's bread, and also the
bread of God's anger according to the death's desire, was
tendered to him; now it was tried, whether the soul, which was
generated and created out of the Father's property, would after
this tincturation of baptism enter again into the love-desire,
viz. into the nothing out of all source.

43. What is hereby intimated to the magus? A mystery is
hinted to him: If he will do wonders with Christ, and tincture
the corrupt body to the new-birth, he must first be baptized,
and then he gets an hunger after God's bread, and this hunger
has in it the verbum fiat, viz. the *archeus* [1] to the new generation, that is, the Mercury: But I do not speak here of a priest's
baptism; the artist must understand it magically; God and
man must first come together ere thou baptizest, as it came to
pass in Christ: The Deity first entered into the humanity, but
the humanity could not presently comprehend it, till it was
quickened through baptism, and the hunger, viz. the dead
Mercury in the human essence, was again stirred up in the
heavenly part.

44. And here began again the human eating; viz. the Mercury
received again divine property and will; and then the inward
Mercury (understand man's property) did eat in the taste of the
divine word of God's essence: And the four elemental properties did eat of the night's property so long, till the human
Mercury sublimed its life, and changed the four elements into
one: And the life tinctured death, which was done on the cross:
Then the four elements departed from him; that is, he died to
time, viz. to the night, that is, to the four elements, and arose
in the pure element, and lived to eternity.

45. The magus must keep and observe this process also with
his alchymy. Dost thou ask how? I will not put it into thy
mouth by reason of the wicked, who is not worthy of it: Observe

[1] Work-master, or faber.

only the baptism, that thou baptizest the dead Mercury, which lies in the heavenly essentiality, enclosed and shut up in impotency with its own baptism, [and mark] of what essence he is in a thing; [1] but thou must have this divine water, and also the earthly; for the earthly Mercury cannot else receive the divine [Being] except the divine Mercury receives of its power, whereupon it stirs and hungers: Then the heavenly [Mercury] seeks, but yet finds not divine essence about it for its food; thereupon it brings its will through the desire of death into itself, viz. into the verbum fiat, which has made and produced it, and sets its hunger upon the same; whereupon the divine essence inclines itself to it, and will become joyfulness in him; even then arises the beginning of the new body out of the divine essentiality, which the desire nourishes and brings up; and when the new life is born, viz. the day, then the four elements die: And then the new body is shut up in the dark death, and on the third day it rises again from death; for the night is swallowed up in the grave, and the morning rises.

46. If thou didst understand this, then hadst thou the pearl: But my intent and purpose is otherwise; I will shew thee Christ along with it, and also this pearl; therefore none shall find it but he that loves Christ.

47. Thou sayest, Tell me the baptism? and I have already told it thee. Every hunger is a desire after its property; now if thou givest again the property of death to the hunger of death, then death encreases; but if thou givest him heavenly property, then death receives it not, for hell is against heaven; therefore thou must give death and the anger of God to death, and in this anger give him heavenly essence, viz. the baptism, and so the baptism will swallow up the death into itself, and then the anger dies in the death through the baptism, but not presently; thou must first keep the process of Christ, and suffer the baptized to preach, that is, appear in his divine form and colours; exceedingly persecute and plague him, and give him no rest; for so the right Mercury becomes working and active; and when he has shewn all his wonders through the old Adam, then thou must cast the old and new man into God's great anger, and slay the old man, ventilate him, and hang him naked [2] on the cross, and again take him thence, and lay him into the putrefaction, viz. into the grave.

48. And then Christ will arise from death, and appear; but

[1] Or whose essence is in everything.
[2] Or openly.   Text, in the air.

only his own know him: He walks about in heavenly form, and sometimes in his own [form which he had here] until the Feast of Pentecost, for now here is tried in him the highest perfection, whether he will persist in the angel's form, and eat only of the divine essence; and then comes the Holy Ghost, and proceeds with his power out of the whole corpus, viz. out of the body and soul, which then tinctures the dead and broken being; as it may be seen in the Day of Pentecost, where Saint Peter tinctured three thousand souls at once with his heavenly Mercury, and delivered them out of death.

49. Dear seekers, herein lies the pearl; had you the universal, then you could also tincture as Saint Peter did, but your covetous death withholds you and shuts you up; for you seek only covetousness and temporal honour in the pleasure of the flesh, to generate yourselves in the night's property; therefore the pearl hides itself from you; yet the day shall again appear when the wrathful anger of God is fulfilled, satisfied and appeased in the blood of the saints, and turned to a love-life; and the time is near.

Process

50. Every creature keeps in its generation and propagation to its own kind; the male to the female, and the female to the male: Now God said to Adam and Eve after the Fall, " The seed of the woman shall bruise the serpent's head; " he said not [the seed] of the man: Herein lies the baptism of nature: The male has the fire-spirit, and the female the water-spirit to the tincture; now the Mercury is a fire-life, and makes himself a body according to his hunger and desire; now the chief of the work is in the beginning to give the fire-hunger a love-virgin out of its kind for its consort, that so his wrathful hunger may be changed into a love, and then they sleep together in their own marriage bed: Now the devil is an enemy of this wedlock, who soon comes with a strange desire, and tempts these married people, but dares not lay an hand of violence on them, but only afflicts and plagues them with a false strange desire; now if they yield their desire to his will, and his desire overcomes them, then they become enemies to one another, and bring forth a false child; for Christ said, " An evil tree bringeth forth evil fruits, and a good tree good fruits."

51. Therefore the artist must beware, and keep himself from such anger, and yet must prepare a cross for this married couple;

for he is their foe and friend, that so they both in their marriage bed of love might lift up their desire to God, and so with their desire God's essence may be pregnant in their desire, and then in their copulation they shall beget such a child, which they [1] (understand the mother, viz. the female) shall nourish in their belly, till it be ripe.

52. In the meantime let the mother take heed she bear no love to any other besides her consort, and also not imagine after strange things, else she will imprint a spot or mark on the child; she must continue simply in one love, till the child be perfect as to its body, which comes to pass in the fourth month; yet according as the parents are of one or other property, so strife and contrariety will arise in the essence in the child, when the child is to receive its soul's life.

53. But when the essence is in its wresting combat, the artist must assist the soulish, viz. the fiery property, till the soul's spirit attains its life, then he appears in the woman's form and lustre: Now the artist supposes that he has the child that is born, but there belongs a further time to it, till the soul grows strong, and then it appears and shews itself in its red and white coat.

54. But there is yet a wonderful process behind; when the soul's life is born, then the new soul casts away the vegetable life of the parents (which is propagated and inherited to the body from the parents' *vegitta*, wherein the body of the child congealed [2] and grew till the time of the soul), and the life of the four elements dies, and the life in the one element arises; the child is hidden in the dark death, and the artist supposes it to be dead, but he must have patience till the child be born.

THE PECULIAR PROCESS IN THE SHAPING OF THE MAGICAL CHILD

55. The course of Christ upon the earth is a real type how the new child is nourished in the mother's womb after its conception, as is before mentioned, and attains a vegetable life, and grows up to the time of its right soul's and spirit's life; and how the child arises from the parents' essence; and how in the enkindling of its right, viz. of its own life, it casts away the parents' **vegitta** and working; and how a new plant, viz. a new peculiar operation, does now arise according to the new enkindled spirit's property, whereby the child is more noble than its parents, understand as to its outward life.

[1] Or she shall.   [2] Curdled.

56. But perhaps some rude clownish sophister might meet with this treatise, and draw a strange understanding from it, in that I write of a soul in the vegetative life; but let him know that we do not understand the image of God, which was formed into a likeness according to God [to be] in metals, stones, and herbs; but we understand the magical soul, how the eternity, viz. the Deity, imprints and pourtrays itself into its likeness, according to the model of its wisdom in all things, and how God fills all in all; we understand the *summum bonum*, the good treasure which lies hidden in the outward world's essence as a paradise.

57. When Christ in his childhood grew up in human and divine property till he was twelve years old, he went with his mother Mary to the feast at Jerusalem, and went into the Temple among the Scribes, asked them, and hearkened to them, and gave answer to the questions of the teachers; but when his parents returned home, supposing him to be among the company, he remained purposely behind among the doctors, and followed not the intent of his parents, but the divine will, till they came back again, and sought him; and then his mother said to him, " My son, why hast thou dealt so with us? Lo! thy father and I have been seeking thee sorrowing. Then he said unto them, How is it that you have sought me? wist ye not that I must be about my Father's business? And he went home with them, and was subject unto them."

58. In this figure we have the type of the wills of the inward and outward world, how they are in one another, and against one another, and yet are but one: Even as in Christ there were two kingdoms manifest; one which was wrought unto God's will, and broke the outward world's will of its parents, in that Christ tarried behind contrary to the will of his parents, at which they were troubled, which the divine will in Christ knew well enough; and the other kingdom, viz. of his parents' will, broke the divine will, that he went home with them, and was obedient to them according to their will.

59. This figure shews the magus, that he shall find two wills in his purpose, which he thinks to carry on; one will not be obedient and subject unto him, viz. the divine will; and yet if its own peculiar external will shall rightly apply itself thereunto, and only seek the dear child Jesus with Mary, with desire and earnest sorrow, and not earthly pleasure of the flesh, then the divine will will be obedient to him, and go home with him, and be used according to his good pleasure.

60. Secondly, it shews him the twofold working and will in all things; and if he will be a magus, and according to his will turn the will and essence of the good property out of the inward into the outward, then he must be first capable of the inward, viz. of the divine will, otherwise he cannot change the inward will into the outward; as Christ was not obedient to the external will of his mother till she sought him with grief and sorrow of heart, and turned her will into God's will, and wrestled in his compassion with God's will, as Jacob the whole night, till the Lord blessed him, and God said unto him, Thou hast wrestled with God and man, and hast overcome, or got the victory.

61. Also let the magus know, that he need not go about to implant the right will to perfection from without into his purpose; it is already in all things; only he must introduce a divine desirous will according to the thing's property into that thing which he takes in hand, which wrestles with the divine will as Jacob, and blesses the will introduced to God's will, that the divine will yields itself freely into the hunger, or inclines itself to the desire, and makes the imperfect will (which earnestly presses into his compassion) perfect, and then it is rightly said, Thou hast wrestled with God, and hast overcome; then thy purpose obtains a transformed body, which is heavenly and earthly.

62. Observe it! It is the first beginning to baptism, and so you are fit and prepared to the baptism, and not otherwise, else you baptize only with the water of the outward world; but the true magus baptizes with the outward and inward water: If he has a right divine desire in him, then God's will in his baptism is the first glimmering tinder in Mercury, so that the life enkindles death, viz. the Mercury shut up in death, and he gets divine desire; even then Mercury begins to hunger after divine essence, and does his first miracle, and turns the water into wine, as Christ did after his baptism: This is the first tincturation in the dead corpus in the power of baptism, that the vegitta, or working energetical life, obtains another property, viz. an hunger of love, wherewith she embraces her bridegroom, viz. the fire-source, that he is enkindled in her love, and changes his cold deadly wrath and will into a fiery love-will: Then the mortal water turns into wine (a sharpness of a fire and water-taste), out of which at last comes an oil to another baptism, after the manner and disposition of the artist, viz. according as he intends and begins; after the magus has joined the virgin and young man together, then Christ, viz. the bridegroom,

is led with his bride into the desert, and tempted of the devil.

63. Here is the trial whereby the artist is proved by God what he seeks with his baptism; for here is the proof in paradise to try whether the bridegroom be not too bad; for the virgin casts her love upon him, and invites him; if he receives it with desire, and gives his will thereinto, then she gives him her heart and will wholly: This is the heavenly tincture, which gives itself into the enkindled anger of God (viz. into the curse of the earth when God cursed it), that is, into the Mercury enclosed in death, which is the bridegroom, for the seed of the woman, viz. the heavenly tincture, must bruise the head of the serpent, viz. the poisonful Mercury, in the property of death, and change his poison into wine, and then the virgin receives the seed of the bridegroom, and not before.

64. The desert is the earthly outward body, where Mercury is tempted; when the devil appears to Mercury, and plagues him, and assaults him in his fiery essence, then must the virgin come to help him, and give him her love: Now if the Mercury eats of the virgin-like love, that is, of God's bread, then he may stand before the devil; and at last the angels come to him, and serve him; the illuminated magus will well understand what is meant by the devil.

65. Hereby let the magus in the temptation (seeing the whole marriage stands in the devil's temptation) have a careful eye upon his purpose; and if the angels do not appear in forty days' space, then is his purpose in vain; therefore let him look, that he suffer not too fierce a devil to tempt, and also not too weak, lest Mercury become light, and desire to continue in his own poisonful death's property, and devour the baptism as a wolf, and the old one remains.

66. As soon as he espies the forms of angels, let him bring Christ out of the desert, and let the bridegroom eat again his own food, and dismiss the devil, that he may no longer plague him, and then Christ will do many wonders and signs, at which the artist will wonder and rejoice: Then he has nothing to do, the bride is in the bridegroom, they are already married,[1] he need only make their bed ready, they will warm it well enough themselves; the bridegroom embraces the bride, and the bride the bridegroom; and this is their food and pastime till they beget a child.

67. But if the artist will needs be so diligent as to warm the

---

[1] Or in wedlock.

married couple's bed, then let him have a care he do not anger and enrage them in their love; what he begins he must go on with; only the bridegroom is wonderful: He has continually two wills, viz. an earthly hunger after God's anger, and an hunger after his bride; therefore he must always have his own earthly food given him, but not into his belly, but magically, that so he may satisfy only his own will's-hunger; his food is his mother that begets him, as it is before mentioned.

68. In brief, the whole work which men speak so much and wonderfully of consists in two things, in an heavenly and in an earthly; the heavenly must make the earthly in it to an heavenly: The eternity must make time in it to eternity: The artist seeks paradise; if he finds it, he has the great treasure upon the earth: But one dead man does not raise another; the artist must be living, if he will say to the mountain, Arise, and cast thyself into the sea.

69. When the incarnation of the child begins, then first of all Saturn takes it, and then it is dark and disesteemed, and is contemned and derided, that such a mystery should lie hid in such a mean form; there Christ walks in a poor simple form upon the earth, as a pilgrim, and has not so much room and propriety in Saturn as to lay his head: He goes as a stranger, as if he were not there at home.

70. After this the moon takes it, and then the heavenly and earthly properties are mixed,[1] and the vegetative life arises, and then the artist rejoices; but he is yet in danger.

71. After the moon Jupiter takes it, who makes an understanding in Mercury, viz. a pleasant habitation, and gives him its good will; and in Jupiter his enclosed life, viz. Mercury is quickened, who takes it with its orb, and forces it into the highest anguish: And then Mars apprehends it, and gives the fire-soul to Mercury; and in the flagrat of Mars the highest life enkindles itself, and separates itself into two essences, viz. out of the love into a body, and out of the fire into a spirit; then the life of love in the fiery flagrat sinks downwards, and appears beautiful, but it is Venus, a woman: Then the artist supposes that he has the treasure, but the hungry Mercury devours Venus, and the child turns to a black raven; then Mars afflicts Mercury in himself, till he grows faint, and yields himself to death: Then the four elements depart from him, and the sun receives the child into its property, and sets it forth in a virgin-like body in the pure element; for in the property of Mars the light is

[1] Blended.

enkindled, and the right life is born, and stands in the pure element; no anger nor death can destroy it.

72. It seems strange in the eyes of reason, that God has kept such a process with the restoring of man in Christ, that he appeared in such a poor disesteemed form in the human property, and was reviled, mocked, scorned, scourged, crucified and slain; and that he was buried, and rose again out of the grave, and walked forty days upon the earth before he entered into his invisible kingdom. Reason is so blind, that it understands nothing of the eternal birth, it knows nothing of paradise, how Adam was in paradise, and how he fell, and what the curse of the earth is: If it understood this, the whole process were manifest to it: As the eternal birth is in itself, so is also the process with the restoration after the Fall, and so likewise is the process of the wise men with their philosopher's stone, there is not the least tittle of difference betwixt them; for all things originally arise out of the eternal birth, and all must have one restoration in one and the same manner.

73. Therefore if the magus will seek paradise in the curse of the earth, and find it, then must he first walk in the person of Christ; God must be manifest in him, understand in the internal man, that he may have the magical sight: He must deal with his purpose as the world did with Christ, and then he may find paradise, wherein is no death.

74. But if he be not in this birth of restoration, and walks not himself in the way wherein Christ walked upon the earth, if he steps not forth into the will and spirit of Christ, then let him give over and leave off his seeking; he finds nothing but death, and the curse of God. I tell him plainly and faithfully, for the pearl of which I write is paradisical, which God does not cast before swine, but gives it to his children for their play and delight.

75. And though much might be mentioned here, that even reason might obtain open eyes, yet it is not to be done; for the wicked would grow worse, and more full of pride; therefore seeing he is not worthy of paradise, and also cannot enter thereinto, no heavenly jewel shall be given him: And therefore God hides it, and permits him to whom he reveals it, to speak of it no otherwise than magically; therefore no one attains it, unless he himself be a magus in Christ, unless paradise be manifest in his internal man; and then he may find, if he be born to it, and chosen by God.

CHAPTER VIII

1. LET the reader but consider what before is written concerning the centre of the generation of all essences, and then he
may easily proceed here: All whatever is corporeal, let it be
either spirit or body, consists in a sulphureous property; the
spirit in such a spiritual property, and the body out of the spirit
in such a corporeal property.

2. For all things are risen from the eternal spirit, as a likeness
of the eternal; the invisible essence, which is God and the
eternity, has in its own desire introduced itself into a visible
essence, and manifested itself in a time, so that he is as a life
in the time, and the time is in him as it were dead; [1] as a master
that makes his work with an instrument, and the instrument is
mute to the master, and yet it is the making, the master only
guides it; even so are all things confined into limit, measure, and
weight, according to the eternal generation; and they run on
in their operation and generation according to the right and
property of eternity.

3. And God has appointed over this great work only one
master and protector, which can alone manage the work, which
is his officer,[2] viz. the soul of the great world, wherein all things
lie; [and] he has appointed a type of its likeness as the reason
over this officer, which represents to the officer what he is to
do and make; and this is the understanding, viz. God's own
dominion wherewith he rules the officer: Now the understanding
shews to the officer what the property of each thing is, how the
separation and degrees proceed from each other; for all things
are contained [3] in the sulphureous body, and Mercury is Sulphur's life, and the salt is the impression, that preserves the
body [4] from falling to ashes, so that the spirit is known in a
palpable essence.

[1] Dumb, senseless, mute. [2] Governor.
[3] Lie. [4] Corpus.

76

4. The property of Mercury is in Sulphur, as the boiling of a water; Sulphur is the water wherein Mercury seethes, and produces continually two forms out of the water; viz. one oleous, living, from the liberty of the divine power's property; and one mortal from the dissolution in the fire in the salnitral flagrat.

5. The oily is in stones and metals, herbs, trees, beasts, and men; and the mortal [property] is in the earth, in the water, in the fire and air; likewise the oleous property is in these four forms (viz. in the earth, water, fire, and air) as a spirit or life, and these four properties are as a dead body, in which the oil is a light or life, from whence the desire, viz. the growth, arises as a springing out of the dead property, which is the vegetative life, a springing, budding, and growing out of death.

6. But now the oily property could not be a life, if it were not in the anguish of death; the anguish makes it to pullulate or move, in that its will is to fly from, and press out of the anguish, and forces itself eagerly forwards, from whence the growth arises: Thus must death be a cause of the life, that the life may be stirring [or active], and therefore Mercury is the true moving life.

7. In the mortal property he is evil, and is called the life of death, of hell, and the anger of God; and in the oily property he is good, from the efficacy of the meekness and liberty of God; and he is the officer's faber, whereby the officer distinguishes the degrees in the vegetative life, [separating] the living [being] from the mortal, the heavenly essentiality from the dead or earthly, and appoints it into two kingdoms; viz. the good in the oleous [property] into a heavenly [being], viz. into a light, and the mortal [part] into the darkness.

8. These two kingdoms are in continual combat one with another, and there is an incessant wrestling in them; as water boiling on the fire; each boils in its property, viz. the oily in joy and meekness, and the mortal in the anguish of darkness, and yet one is the cause of the other: The light is the death, and deadly destruction of the darkness, viz. of the anguish; for in the light the anguish has no strength, but it changes it into the exultation of joyfulness, and the cause of joy, else there would be no joy; for the meekness is like a stillness, but the source of anguish sublimes it, and turns into a pleasant laughter: So also the anguish, viz. the darkness, is the death and destruction of the oily property; for if it gets the upper hand in the oleous property, it takes possession of the corpus,[1] and turns the oil

[1] Or body.

into a poisonful source, viz. into a dark spirit, or body wholly earthly, as Adam was when he imagined into the evil.

9. And yet we do not acknowledge that the oleous property takes any poison-source into itself; but Mercury, viz. the fire-life, insinuates itself into the anguish, and poisons the essence of time, which the outward Mercury itself makes in its own desire, that is, he departs from the inward oleous essence, and then the internal [being] remains immoveable in itself, and the essence and spirit of time do separate from the essence and spirit of eternity, and yet there is no parting [or dividing], but both principles remain in one essence; whereas there are two essences, but the one comprehends not the other, as eternity does not comprehend time: For thus also Adam and Eve died; the soul's Mercury departed with its imagination from the essence of eternity into the essence of time, viz. into the anguish-source, and then the essence of eternity lost its leader, which Christ restored again by the divine word, or Mercury; so that the essence of eternity, which in Adam was forsaken by the soul's Mercury, obtained the life again.

10. And thus we know that the essence of eternity lies hid in the anxious Mercury, as in the fortress of death; and our writing and teaching are to shew how a man may bring the poisonful Mercury with its desire so far, as to enter with its desire again into the essence of eternity, viz. into the enclosed, and reassume the essence of eternity for a body, and with the same tincture the essence of time, and reconcile them in one, that the whole corpus of the inward and outward world may be only one, that so there may be only one will in the spirit, viz. a love-hunger; and this hunger does then make to itself only one essence, and then every spirit eats of its [own] essence or body, so that afterwards no evil will can arise any more therein.

11. Thus we understand, that joy and sorrow, love and enmity, do originally arise through imagination and longing; for in the inclination [or earnest desire] towards God, viz. the free love, the kingdom of joy arises in the midst of the anguish of death; and if the desire departs out of the free love into the anguish of death, viz. into the source of darkness, then is the desire filled with the source of death, and so Mercury works effectually in the source of death.

12. Thus we declare with a true ground, that there is nothing so bad, but there lies a good therein, but the badness is not capable of the good; also there lies in the most poisonful Mercury, the greatest pearl and jewel; if his poisonful will may

be introduced into the same,[1] then he himself manifests the pearl; for he changes himself; as is to be seen in the earth, where Mercury seeks its pearl, and turns it in the ore [2] to gold, and to other metals, according as the Sulphur is in each place.

13. For there is a continual combat [3] in the earth; the eternity travels with longing through time to be free from vanity, and in its longing it gives itself to Mercury, as to its life and faber; and when Mercury obtains it in his hunger, he becomes joyful, and makes this free lubet corporeal in him, and there arises gold and silver, together with other metals and good herbs, all according to the powerful efficacy of each place; As the boiling [4] is in each place, so likewise is the metal, all according to the property of the seven forms of nature; that form which is chief in a place, according to the same property grows a metal, also herbs and trees.

14. Here the physicians must observe, that they learn distinctly to know what kind of property is the strongest in each thing with which they would cure; if they do not know it, they will oftentimes give their patients death: Also they must know, that they are to understand, and very exactly know the property of the patient, which of the properties among the seven forms of nature is the Mercury in Sulphur; for such a salt he also makes: Now if the physician gives him a contrary salt, Mercury is only thereby the more vehemently enraged, and made more venomous; but if he may obtain his own salt according to his own property (after which he hungers) then he [5] rejoices, and readily quits the poison-source in the fire of Mars. But the right physician has another cure, he first brings his Mercury with which he will cure out of death's anguish into the liberty: He may well cure,[6] the other is dangerous and uncertain; if he happens to cure, it is by chance, and very inconstant, and cannot cure any disease fundamentally; for the outward Mercury is shut up, it can reach no further than into the four elements, into the mortal essence; it is able to do nothing in the sidereal body: But if it be turned and introduced into the love, as is before mentioned, then it touches [7] the very root and ground, and renews it even to the divine power in the second principle.

15. We have an excellent resemblance of this in the blooming earth on the herbs; for in the earth Mercury is earthly and

---

[1] Or if his poison-will be brought into the moving spirit of love.
[2] Gross stone.   [3] Wrestling.   [4] Or seething.   [5] The Mercury.
[6] Or such a physician has true skill to cure.   [7] Or seizes on.

venomous; but when the sun tinctures him, then he reaches after the sun's power, after its light, and brings it into his hungry fiery Mars-desire, into his salt, viz. into his corporeal essence, viz. into Sulphur, which is his mother, and wheels it about with its rotation in the essence, as if he also boiled; and then the liberty, viz. the highest power, reaches after its property, viz. after the solar property, and apprehends Mercury also along with it.

16. Now when Mercury tastes the heavenly Being in itself, it grows exceeding desirous after the power of love, and draws the same into its desire, whereupon it changes itself, and its salt, so also its mother, the Sulphur, into a pleasant source; and now if the liberty be so introduced into a moving life with Mercury, then it is very full of joy, and springs up in its joy, as a light from the fire, and puts forth through the Sulphur-spirit in the salt: Thus is the growing of the root, and from thence the root gets such a pleasant smell and taste; for in the original the salt's sharpness in the first impression from Saturn is a sharpness of death's anguish, and here it is turned to a pleasant power; for all taste in herbs is salt.

17. Thus understand us further about the root in the earth; when the inward power of the liberty in Mercury's property, which now is changed, does thus force itself forth to the manifestation of the Deity, then the sun's power does eagerly press towards the divine power, and inclines itself with great desire to the highest heavenly tincture, and draws it with its desire to it; viz. out of the earthly body into a solar: Thus the sun draws the power out of the root in the earth, and the joyful Mercury ascends up along with it, and continually draws the sun's power from above into itself, and from beneath it draws its mother viz. the Sulphur, to itself: And here all the seven forms of nature arise in joyfulness in the combat, each will be uppermost; for so it is in the taste, viz. in the generation of nature; and what form in nature gets to be the chiefest, according to the same taste is the salt in Sulphur, and such an herb grows out of the earth, let it be what it will; though now everything springs from its mother, yet all things have so taken their original, and do still take it; for just so is the right of eternity.

18. Now we are to consider of the stalk: When the herb or sprig looks out of the earth, it comes up at first below with a white form, then further more upwards with a brownish [colour], and above with a green colour: This is now its signature, [shewing] what kind of form is internally in the essence, in the

source; the white colour of the branch [1] is from the liberty of the love-lubet, and the brown is the earthly [property] from Saturn's impression, and from the wrath of Mars; and the green, which opens itself above, is Mercury's in the form of Jupiter and Venus.

19. For Jupiter is power, and Venus is love-desire, which hasten towards the sun, as towards their likeness; and the heaven, which is created out of the midst of the water, puts upon them its blue and green-coloured garment according to the stars' might; for the spirit of the stars receives the new child also, and gives him its spirit and body, and rejoices therein: Now the forms are in contest,[2] and Mercury is the faber and separator; Saturn impresses, and Jupiter is the pleasant power in sulphur; Mars is the fire-source, viz. the might in sulphur; Venus is the water, viz. the sweet desire; Mercury is the life, Luna the body, and Sol the heart, viz. the centre to which all forms tend and press.

20. Thus the outward sun presses into the sun in the herb; and the inward sun presses into the outward, and there is a mere pleasing relish and delight of one essence in another; Saturn makes four, Jupiter makes a pleasant taste, Mars makes bitter, by reason of his anxious nature, Venus makes sweet, Mercury distinguishes the taste, Luna takes it into her sack and hatches it; for she is of an earthly and heavenly property, and she gives it the menstruum wherein the tincture lies.

21. Thus there is an instigation in the taste; each form hastens to the sweet water and the sun; Jupiter is pleasant, and ascends up aloft with the love-desire in the sweet source-water, wherein Mars rages, and thinks himself to be master in the house, seeing that he rules the fire-spirit in sulphur, at which Mercury is dismayed, that Mars does so disquiet him, and Saturn makes the flagrat corporeal according to his austere impression, and these are the knots upon the stalk; and the flagrat is salnitral, according to the third form of nature in the first impression to the spirit-life, viz. in the anguish-form, from whence the sulphur takes its original, and in the flagrat Mercury goes up in the salniter on the sides, and takes Venus also into it, viz. the love-desire, from whence grow twigs and branches on the stalk, trunk, or body, be they either herbs, trees, or shrubs; and each branch [or sprig] is then like to the whole plant.[3]

22. But the sun continually by little and little deprives Mars

[1] Shoot, or twig.   [2] Or in their wrestling combat.   [3] Or growth.

of his force, whereupon the salniter extinguishes, and Mars loses his bitter property; then Jupiter and Venus wholly yield themselves to the sun in the moon's cabinet,[1] and the outward sun takes full possession of the inward; understand the inward sun is a Sulphur in Mercury, and is of the divine power's property, from the liberty of God, which imprints itself on all things, and gives life and power to all things. Now when that is done, that Jupiter and Venus have given themselves to the power of the sun, then Jupiter forces no more upwards, but Mars and Mercury do continually more and more wind up the stalk from the earth on high; Jupiter stays still above in the inward and outward sun's power, and there is the pleasant conjunction with time and eternity, there the eternity beholds itself in an image [2] in the time.

23. And paradise springs up [or opens], for the Sulphur and the salt in the Sulphur are here transmuted in the paradise, and the paradisical joy puts itself forth in the smell and taste. This is now the head or knob of the blossoms, wherein the corn grows; the lovely smell is in one part paradisical, viz. from the divine power, from the liberty; and on the other part earthly, according to the outward sun, and the outward world.

24. The heavenly property sets forth its signature with fair colours of the leaves on the blossoms; and the earthly [represents its signature] by the green leaves [or sprigs] about the blossom; but seeing this kingdom of the outward world is only a time (in which the curse is), and Adam could not stand in paradise, the paradisical property soon passes away with its signature, and changes itself into the corn which grows in the blossom; therein the property of the inward and outward sun, viz. of the inward and outward power, is couched, each property in its principle; for God has cursed the earth, and therefore let none think that the outward is divine, only the divine power penetrates and tinctures the outward [being]; for God said, " The seed of the woman shall bruise the serpent's head: " This is now effected after the curse in all things which approach near the Deity, wherein Mercury is a poison; there God bruises its head with the inward and outward sun, and takes away the poisonful might in the anger.

25. O that you would but learn to understand, dear sirs and brethren, wherewith you are to cure; not with the angry Mercury, which in many an herb is an evil poison-source, but with the inward Mercury: If you would be called doctors and

---

[1] Bag, or sack.   [2] Type, or resemblance.

masters, then you ought also to know how you may change the outward Mercury in the Sulphur into love, that he may be delivered from the anguish-source, and brought into a joyfulness, viz. that the earthly [being] be turned into an heavenly, the death into life; this is your doctorship in the right meaning, and not by the officer of reason only.

26. God has placed man above the officer, and ordained him in the understanding to his own dominion: He has ability to change nature, and to turn the evil into good, provided that first he has changed himself, otherwise he cannot; so long as he is dead in the understanding, so long he is the servant and slave of the officer; but when he is made alive in God, then the officer is his servant.

27. Ye haughty caps, let it be told you; pride, and your own honour, and the earthly lust of the flesh, lies in your way, so that you are not masters in the mysteries, but blind children; you will not lay your hands upon the coals, but you take money from the poor and distressed, and give that to many an one which had been far better he had never bought, for which you must give a severe and strict account.

28. Thus it is likewise with the sulphurean seething in the earth with the metals, the power [1] is stronger in metals than in the herbs, the tincture is more heavenly than earthly, if the artist affords it his help, then it changes itself, viz. the earthly into an heavenly, which notwithstanding comes to pass in many places without the artist's ingenuity; as we see, how Mercury in sulphur apprehends the heavenly tincture in its boiling, whereby he changes his made essence (which he makes in the sulphur) into gold and silver by the power and efficacy of the tincture, understand, by that part of the heavenly property; for out of the earth, or out of the mortified property in the salniter, no gold can be made, for there is no fixedness therein.

29. Now we are thus to consider of this process of the boiling in the Sulphur in the earth: Where the earth is in any place sulphureous in the saturnine property, wherein the sun bears chief rule, there is such a boiling; the outward sun hungers after the inward, which dwells in its own principle in the centre in sulphur, and sets its desire upon time; for the time, viz. the creature, longs after eternity, viz. after the liberty, to be freed from vanity; as the Scripture says, that " all creatures do earnestly long with us to be freed from vanity."

30. Even here the liberty gives itself into the solar property

[1] Virtue, or efficacy.

into the time, and when Mercury tastes it, he becomes joyful, and turns his wheel in the joy; then Saturn impresses the meekness; and Mars, which arises in the mercurial wheel in the impression, gives the fire-soul thereinto, so that there is a driving forth and growth; for the liberty puts itself forth in Mercury's property, and Mercury continually separates Saturn and Mars from it; for he will have a fair and pure child to his joy; he suffers Venus to remain on the child, for she is in property akin to the child: copper is nighest to gold by reason of the materia, it wants only the tincture; Mars holds him too hard in possession; if he may be got out, then it is gold, which the artist does well understand.

31. After Venus Mars is akin to gold; for he has swallowed up Venus in his wrath, and uses her for his body, else in his own peculiar property he has no corporeal essence, for he is only wrath, which consumes: He makes him a body out of the water of Venus, which he devours, and Saturn makes it corporeal to him; therefore he does so defile his iron with rust, and that is his property, viz. to be a devourer of his body; but Venus is pleasant, and makes a growing in him, he devours again whatever Venus's property makes in him; for Venus is the food of Mars in the saturnine property; therefore the artist is to consider what lies in Mars; if he has only the solar tincture, he needs nothing else thereto, that he may but deprive Mars of his force, for Mars has his toughness from Venus.

32. Mars in his own peculiar property is only spalt, and causes hardness, as the fire does; but Saturn is the impressure of all things; Venus needs only the tincture, and then she is perfect; but the artist must rightly understand where the possibility lies, viz. in Sulphur, where Saturn has the Sulphur in his belly, and Mercury shews its colour, there he is in the will,[1] but cannot, for Saturn holds him too fast imprisoned; but if the artist gives him his helping hand, that he may but advance his wheel, and give him his mother's food, which she has hid in the centre, then he grows strong, and casts Saturn away, and manifests the child: For so it is also in the earth, where Mercury is quick in his mother, viz. in the Sulphur, that he is not withheld, that he may only reach Venus in his hunger for food, the sun will soon shine forth, for she beams forth in Venus's meekness: He dresses [or seethes] his food with his own fire, he needs no artist thereto; which the artist must well observe, for he has his Mars in himself.

33. Now as the boiling is in the earth, so also it is above the

[1] Or mind.

earth; when the fruit grows out of the earth, it is first sharp [astringent] and bitter, also sour and unpleasant, as the apple upon the tree is so; for Saturn has at first the dominion, he attracts it together, and Mercury forms it, and Mars gives the fire to Mercury, which Saturn receives into his cold property, Venus gives the sap, and Luna takes all into her body, for she is mother, and receives the seed of all the planets into her menstruum, and hatches it; Jupiter gives power thereinto, and Sol is king therein, but at the first Sol is weak; for the materia is too earthly and cold. Now the whole essence in its boiling lies in the body[1] of Sulphur; and in the Sulphur the salnitral flagrat makes a salt in Mars's wheel according to each property; for the Sulphur turns into salt, that is, into taste; and in the same taste there is an oil hid in the centre in the sulphureous property, which [oil] arises from the free love-lubet, viz. out of eternity, and manifests itself with an external essence in the time, which is the manifestation of God.

34. Now in this same oil is the hunger or love-desire after the essence of time, viz. after the manifestation of the Deity; this desire reaches in the essence of time after its property, viz. after the sun, and the sun's property reaches after the oil in the centre of the fruit, and fervently longs after it, and gives itself freely into the fruit, and sucks the virtue into itself, and gives it forth in its joy into the austere property of the fruit, and meekens and sweetens all with the love, which it receives in the centre in the oil of the liberty: Thus a fruit, which at first is sour and sharp, becomes very pleasant and sweet, that a man may eat it; and even thus is the ripening of all fruits.

35. Now by the signature in the external you may see the inward form; for the forms in the salt, viz. in the power, shew themselves externally.

36. There are commonly four colours, as white, yellow, red, and green: Now according to what colour the fruit (as an apple) is most signed, accordingly is the taste also in the salt; as white with a clear thin skin somewhat inclining to dark gives sweetness, which is of Venus property; if the sweet taste be strong and powerful, then Jupiter is potent therein; but if it be weak and fulsom, then the moon is strong therein; but if it be hard, and of a brownish colour, then Mars is strong therein; but if the white colour be of a grayish-brown, then Saturn is strong therein: Venus makes[2] a white colour, Mars red, and bitter in the taste; Mars makes Venus's colour light, Mercury gives a mixt colour,

---

[1] Or womb.   [2] Gives, or yields.

and opens the green in Mars; Jupiter inclines to blue, Saturn to black, almost gray; the sun makes the yellow colour, and gives the right sweetness in the salt, and casts forth the pleasant smell, which takes its rise from Sulphur; Saturn makes astringent [sharp] and sour; and each property represents itself externally, as it is internally in the dominion, so also by the form [or signature] of the leaf, or branches.

37. Every root, as it is in the earth, may be known by the signature for what it is good or profitable, even such a form also has the earth, and it is discerned in the leaves and stalks which planet is lord in the property, much more in the flower; for of what taste the herb and root is, even such an hunger is in it, and such a cure lies therein, for it has such a salt. The physician must know what kind of sickness is risen in the body, and in what salt the loathing is risen in Mercury, that so he may not administer a further loathing [and nausea] to his patient; for if he gives him the herb, in whose property Mercury has before received a loathing, then he ministers poison to him; so that the poison in the loathing of the body does exceedingly inflame itself in Mercury, unless he burns that herb to ashes, and gives it him; then the poison of the loathing loses its might; for these ashes are a death to the poison of the living Mercury.

38. This we find very effectually in the magic; this also the physician must know, that all sicknesses arise from the loathing in the form of nature: As when one form in the life is superior, if then a contrary thing quite opposite to its property be by force introduced into it, let it be either from the stars, or from the elements, or from the seven forms of life, then it deprives this superior [or chiefest] form (which is the leader and ruler of the life) of its strength and power in its salt; then the Mercury of this superior form begins effectually to work, that is, to hunger and loath; and if he gets not his own peculiar property, understand the bodily form, which is chief in the body among the seven properties or forms, then he enkindles himself in his own poison-source according to his vital [1] property, and does so forcibly strive so long, till he becomes fiery, and then he awakes his own Mars, and his own Saturn, which impress him, and consume the flesh of the body in the poison-fire, and wholly consume the oil of light; even then the life's light goes out, and it is past recovery.

39. But if the form of life, wherein [2] Mercury is inflamed in the loathing [3] in the anguish and poison-source, may obtain

[1] Or life's.   [2] Or whereby.   [3] Or nausea.

that property into its hunger, of which the spirit and body is chief, then he obtains his own natural food, of which he lives, and does again rejoice, and puts away the nauseate,[1] and then the nauseate dissipates [or dissolves] and is spewed out; but the physician must have a care, whether or no that thing which he will administer to his patient be in its property strong also in the same essence, from whence the nauseate is risen in the body.

40. As for example; A jovial man receives a nauseate [or loathing] from the lunar property; now if the physician knew that he had so gotten his nauseate, and prepared him a jovial cure according to the hunger of his own spirit or mercury, this now would be right; but if the moon's property be strong in the salt which he would administer for the nauseate, then he gives him a nauseate; but if the jovial cure be free from the moon, then the jovial Mercury receives its own food with great desire, and quits the nauseate: And thus it is likewise with diseases which arise in the salniter, viz. from fear or frightening; thereto belongs also such a flagrat as the first was, and then there is a present cure, or such an herb, wherein the salniter lies in such a property as it lies in that man.

41. I know, and it is shewn me, that the sophister will cavil at me, because I write, that the divine power is in the fruit, that God's power does appropriate [2] itself into the generation of nature: But hear, my dear friend, become seeing, I ask thee, How was paradise in this world? Was it also manifest in nature? Was it also in the fruit? Was it in the world, or without the world? Did paradise stand in God's power, or in the elements? Was the power of God manifest in the world, or hidden? Or what is the curse of the earth, and the putting of Adam and Eve out of paradise? Then tell me, Does not God dwell also in time? Is not God all in all? It is written, " Am not I he who filleth all things? " Also, " Thine is the kingdom, the power, and glory, from eternity to eternity."

42. Here consider thyself, and leave me uncensured: I do not say, that the nature is God, much less the fruit proceeding from the earth; but I say, God gives power to every life, be it good or bad, to each thing according to its desire, for he himself is All; and yet he is not called God according to every being, but according to the light wherewith he dwells in himself and shines with his power through all his beings; He gives in his power to all his beings and works, and each thing receives his power

---

[1] Or loathing.   [2] Unite, or give in.

according to its property; one takes darkness, the other light; each hunger desires its property, and yet the whole essence [or being] is all God's, be it evil or good, for from him and through him are all things, what is not of his love, that is of his anger. Paradise is yet in the world, but man is not therein, unless he be born again of God; then as to that new regeneration he is therein, and not with the Adam of the four elements. O that we would but once learn to know ourselves, and even understand it by the created essence [or being].

43. Lo! in Saturn there lies gold shut up in a very disesteemed and contemptible form and manner, which indeed resembles no metal; and though it be cast into the fire and melted, yet a man shall have nothing, but a contemptible matter void of any form of virtue, till the artist takes it in hand, and uses the right process about it, and then it is manifest what was therein.

44. So likewise God dwells in all things, and the thing knows nothing of God; he likewise is not manifest to the thing, and yet it receives power from him, but it receives the power according to its property from him, either from his love, or from his wrath; and from which it receives, so it has its signature [1] externally; and the good is also in it, but as it were wholly shut up [or hidden] to the iniquity [or evil]; an example of which you have in bushes, and other thorny and pricking briars, out of which notwithstanding a fair well-smelling blossom grows; and there lie two properties therein, viz. a pleasant and unpleasant; which overcomes, that shapes [forms or marks] the fruit.

45. Thus also it is with man; he was created a fair blossom and fruit of paradise, but the devil raised up in him his thorny property by the serpent, understand the centre, the property of the wrathful nature, which in his paradisical source was not manifest in him; but when his hunger entered into the thorny false property of the serpent, viz. into death, then the property of death, and the false serpent in the devil's desire, pressed into his hunger, and filled soul and body, so that the hunger of the false serpent began effectually to work in him, and death awaked in him, and then paradise hid itself in him: For paradise entered into itself, and the poison of the serpent in death's property dwelt also in itself; here was now the enmity; then said God to him, " The seed of the woman shall bruise the serpent's head, and thou shalt sting the heel with death's poison."

46. Understand the paradisical image which is shut up, and

---

[1] Or so it is signed, or marked.

captivated in the wrathful death, in which the word of the Deity, viz. the divine Mercury, ruled and wrought, did disappear; as the gold is disappeared in Saturn, so that nothing is seen but a contemptible matter, till the right artist sets upon it, and again awakens the Mercury in the inclosed gold, and then the dead inclosed body of the gold does again revive in Saturn; for Mercury is its life, who must be introduced into it again, and then the dead body of the gold appears,[1] and overcomes the gross Saturn, wherein it lay shut up, and changes its mean contemptible old body into a fair glorious golden body.

47. Thus likewise it is with man; he lies now shut up after his fall in a gross, deformed, bestial dead image; he is not like an angel, much less like unto paradise; he is as the gross ore in Saturn, wherein the gold is couched and shut up; his paradisical image is in him as if it were not, and it is also not manifest, the outward body is a stinking carcass, while it yet lives in the poison: He is a bad thorny bush, from whence notwithstanding fair rose-buds may bloom forth, and grow out of the thorns, and manifest that which lies hidden, and shut up in the wrathful poisonful Mercury, till the artist who has made him takes him in hand, and brings the living Mercury into his gold or paradisical image disappeared and shut up in death; so that the inclosed image, which was created out of the divine meekness and love-essentiality, may again bud and spring forth in the divine Mercury, viz. in the word of the Deity, which entered into the humanity shut up [and closed in the death and curse].

48. And then the divine mercury changes the wrathful Mercury into its property, and Christ is born, who bruises the head of the serpent, viz. of the poison and death in the anger of God, understand the might of wrathful death; and a new man arises in holiness and righteousness, which lives before God, [and his divine image] appears and puts forth its lustre as the hidden gold out of the earthly property: And hereby it is clearly signified to the artist chosen of God how he shall seek; no otherwise than as he has sought and found himself in the property of the pure gold; and so likewise is this process, and not a whit otherwise; for man and the earth with its secrets lie shut up in the like [or same] curse and death, and need one and the same restitution.

49. But we tell the seeker, and sincerely and faithfully warn him as he loves his temporal and eternal welfare, that he do not first set upon this way to try the earth, and restore that which

---

[1] Or puts itself forth. Text, glances forth.

is shut up [in death], unless he himself be before born again through the divine mercury out of the curse and death, and has the full knowledge of the divine regeneration,[1] else all that he does is to no purpose, no learning [or studying] avails; for that which he seeks lies shut in the curse, in death, in the anger of God: If he will make it alive, and bring it into its first life, then that life must be before manifest in him, and then he may say to the mountain, " Get thee hence, and be cast into the sea; " and to the fig-tree, "No fruit grow on thee henceforth;" and it shall come to pass; for if the divine mercury lives, and is manifest in the spirit, then when the spirit of the soul's will imagines into anything, Mercury also goes along with it in the imagination, and enkindles the Mercury fast apprehended in death, viz. the similitude of God, or the manifestation, with which the living God has made himself manifest.

50. I know and see, that the mocker in the devil's vizard will yet bring my writing into a misapprehension, and make me more dark and doubtful, because I write of the inward and outward Mercury, and understand by the inward the word of God, or the divine voice, viz. the manifestation of the eternity of the abyss; and by the outward [mercury] I understand the officer in nature, viz. the instrument, which the inward, living, powerful word, or divine voice uses, wherewith it forms [2] and works. Now the sophister will falsely interpret it, and say, that I mix them both together, making no difference, and hold [3] nature for God, as Babel has already done to me: But I bid him view my words well, and learn to understand them right; for I speak sometimes from the heavenly Mercury, and see that only, and then presently I name the instrument of the heavenly, therefore let him have regard to the sense: I write not heathenishly, but theosophically, from a higher ground than the outward faber [4] is, and then also from the same.

---

[1] Or has the new-birth in perfect knowledge.
[2] Or makes.   [3] Or take.   [4] Archeus, or separator.

CHAPTER IX

1. THE whole outward visible world with all its being is a signature, or figure of the inward spiritual world; whatever is internally, and however its operation is, so likewise it has its character externally; like as the spirit of each creature sets forth and manifests the internal form of its birth by its body, so does the Eternal Being also.

2. The Being of all beings is a wrestling power; for the kingdom of God consists in power, and also the outward world, and it stands especially in seven properties or forms, where the one causes and makes the other, and none of them is the first or last, but it is the eternal band; therefore God has appointed six days for man to work, and the seventh day is the perfection wherein the six do rest; it is the centre to which the desire of the six days tend; therefore God calls it the Sabbath or resting-day, for therein the six forms of the working power rest: It is the divine sound [1] in the power, or the kingdom of joy, wherein all the other forms are manifest; for it is the formed world, or divine corporality, by which all things are generated and come forth to a being.[2]

3. This formed world has manifested itself with the motion of all forms with this visible world, as with a visible likeness, so that the spiritual being might be manifest in a corporeal comprehensive essence; as the desire of the inward forms has made itself external, and the internal being is in the external; the internal holds the external before it as a glass, wherein it beholds itself in the property of the generation of all forms; the external is its signature.

4. Thus everything which is generated out of the internal has its signature; the superior form, which is chief in the spirit of the working in the power, does most especially sign the body, and the other forms hang to it; as it is to be seen in all living creatures, in the shape and form of the body, and in the behaviour and deportment, also in the sound, voice, and speech;

[1] Voice, or harmony.   [2] Or essence.

and likewise in trees and herbs, in stones and metals; all according as the wrestling is in the power of the spirit, so is the figure of the body represented, and so likewise is its will, so long as it so boils in the life-spirit.

5. But if the artist takes it in hand with the true Mercury, then he may turn the weakest form to be uppermost, and the strongest undermost, and then the spirit obtains another will, according to the most superior form; that which before must be servant becomes now lord and master in the seven forms; as Christ said to the sick, " Arise, thy faith hath made thee whole," and they arose: And thus likewise it is here, each form hungers after the centre, and the centre is the voice of life, viz. the Mercury, the same is the faber or former of the power; if this voice gives itself into the hunger of the meanest form in the strong combat [1] then it lifts up its property (understand the property of that form), and thus its desire or faith has saved it; for in the desire Mercury lifts up [or sublimes] itself; and thus it was in Christ's patients.

6. Sickness had taken possession of them, and the poison of death had gotten the upper hand in Mercury; but now the form of life in the centre did set its hunger as a famished and mean property after the liberty to be freed from the abomination; but seeing the Mercury was revived in Christ the divine property, therefore the weak hunger entered into Christ's strong hunger after the salvation of man, and so the weak hunger received the strong in the power; and then the divine voice in Christ said, " Arise, lift up thyself, thy faith " (that is, thy desire which thou hast introduced into me) " hath saved thee."

7. Thus the life prevails over the death, the good over evil; and on the contrary, the evil over the good, as came to pass in Lucifer and Adam, and still daily comes to pass: And thus everything is signed; that form which is chief receives the taste, and also the sound in Mercury, and figures [2] the body after its property; the other forms hang to it as co-helpers, and also give their signature thereto, but very weakly.

8. There are especially seven forms in nature, both in the eternal and external nature; for the external proceed from the eternal: The ancient philosophers have given names to the seven planets according to the seven forms of nature; but they have understood thereby another thing, not only the seven stars, but the sevenfold properties in the generation of all essences: There is not anything in the Being of all beings, but it has the

---

[1] Text, wrestling power.   [2] Or shapes.

seven properties in it; for they are the wheel of the centre, the cause of Sulphur, in which Mercury makes the boiling in the anguish-source.

9. The seven forms are these; viz. the desire of the impression is called Saturn, into which the free lubet of eternity gives itself; this in the impression is called Jupiter, by reason of its pleasant commendable virtue; for the saturnine power encloses and makes hard, cold, and dark, and causes the Sulphur, viz. the vital spirit, understand the moving vital spirit, viz. the natural; and the free lubet makes the impression to long to be freed from the dark astringent hardness, and it is very rightly called Jupiter, being a desire of the understanding [1] which opens the darkness, and manifests another will therein.

10. In these two properties is pourtrayed and exactly deciphered God's kingdom, viz. the original, and also the kingdom of God's anger, viz. the dark abyss, which is a cause of the motion in Saturn, viz. in the impression; the impression, viz. Saturn, makes the nothing, viz. the free lubet movable and sensible, and also opposite, for it causes it to be essence; and Jupiter is the sensible power proceeding from the free lubet to manifestation out of the nothing into something, in the impression of Saturn; and they are two properties in the manifestation of God according to love and anger, viz. a model of the eternal form, and are as a wrestling combat, viz. an opposite desire against each other; one makes good, the other evil, and yet it is all good; only if we will speak of the anguish-source, and then also of the joyful source, then we must distinguish, that the cause of each source may be understood.

11. The third form is called Mars, which is the fiery property in the impression of Saturn, where the impression introduces itself into great anguish, viz. into a great hunger; it is the painfulness, or the cause of feeling, also the cause of the fire and consuming, also of enmity and malignity; but in Jupiter, viz. in the free lubet, in the nothing, it causes the fiery love-desire, that the liberty, viz. the nothing, is desirous, and introduces itself into sensibility, viz. into the kingdom of joy: In the darkness it is a devil, viz. God's wrath, and in the light it is an angel of joy, understand such a property; for when this source became dark in Lucifer, he was called a devil, but while he was in the light he was an angel; and thus also it is to be understood in man.

12. The fourth property or form is called Sol, viz. the light of

[1] Or original.

nature, which has its original in the liberty, viz. in the nothing, but without splendour, and gives itself in with the lubet into the desire of the impression of Saturn, even to the wrathful or fiery property of Mars; and there the free lubet, which has sharpened itself in the impression, in the property of Mars, in the consuming anguish, and in the hardness of Saturn, displays, or powerfully puts itself forth in Jupiter, as a sharpness of the liberty, and an original of the nothing, and also of the sense; [1] and the effluence [2] from the heat and anguish of Mars, and from Saturn's hardness is the shining of the light in nature, which gives the understanding in Saturn, Jupiter, and Mars, viz. a spirit, which knows what itself is in its properties, which hinders or prevails against the wrath, and brings it out of the anguish, out of the property of Mars, into Jupiter's, viz. out of the anguish into a love-desire.

13. In these four forms the spirit's birth consists, viz. the true spirit both in the inward and outward being, viz. the spirit of power in the essence; and the essence or corporality of this spirit is Sulphur.

14. Ye rabbies and masters! that you could but understand, how faithfully that is given and revealed to you, which your predecessors have intended and aimed at, wherein you have been a long time blind, the cause of which is your pride: This God, the most high understanding, sets before you by mean, and heretofore ungrounded instruments, which he himself has grounded, if you would yet once see, and escape the tormenting source.

15. The fifth form is Venus, the beginning of all corporality, viz. of the water, which arises in the desire of Jupiter and Mars, viz. in the love-desire, out of the liberty, and out of nature, viz. out of the impression's desire in Saturn, in Mars, in the great anguish, to be freed from the anguish: And it carries two forms in the desire of its property, viz. a fiery from Mars, and a watery [property] from Jupiter, understand an heavenly and earthly desire; the heavenly arises from the heavenly impression of the union [or free effluence] of the Deity in nature to its own manifestation; and the earthly arises from the impression of the darkness in Mars, viz. in the wrathful fire's property; therefore the essence of this desire consists in two things, viz. in the water, from the original of the liberty, and in Sulphur from the original of nature according to the impression.

16. The outward similitude of the heavenly [Being] is water

---

[1] Perception, or sensation.   [2] Or breathing forth.

and oil; understand, according to the sun it is water, and according to Jupiter it is oil, and according to the hard impression of Saturn after the heavenly Being according to Mars, it is copper, and according to Sol gold, and according to the earthly impression, according to the property of the darkness, it is in Sulphur grit, gravel and sand; according to the property of Mars a cause of all stones; for all stones are Sulphur from the powerful predominance of Saturn and Mars in the property of Venus according to the dark impression, understand according to the earthly part.

17. O ye dear wise men! if you did but know what lies in Venus, you would not so sumptuously adorn your roofs: The potentate often loses his life for the servant's sake, and he puts the master upon his roof, therefore he is blind; this his false Venus-desire causes in him, that he forms it in Saturn and Mars, and brings it forth in Sol; if he formed his Venus-desire in Jupiter, then he might rule over the fiery Mars which lies in Venus, and has put his coat upon Venus in Sulphur.

18. Thus Mars clothes all his servants which love him and Saturn with his garment, that they only find the copper of Venus, and not its gold in the copper; the spirit of the seeker enters into Sol, viz. into pride, and supposes that he has Venus, but he has Saturn, viz. covetousness; if he went forth in the water, viz. in the resigned humility of Venus, the stone of the wise men would be revealed to him.

19. The sixth form is Mercury, viz. the life and separation, or the form in the love, and in the anguish: In Saturn and Mars, on the one part he is earthly according to the hard impression, where his motion and hunger is a pricking, adverse, and (according to the fire) a bitter pain and woe; and according to the water in the earthly Sulphur, viz. in the mortification, a poison-source.

20. And according to the other part, according to the lubet of the liberty, he is the pleasant property of joy in Jupiter and Venus, also of springing and growing; and according to the impression of the heavenly Saturn, and according to Mars in the love-desire, he is the sound in the spirit, understand, the separator of the sound, viz. of the tone; also of all pronunciations of speeches, and all the several cries and notes; all whatever sounds is distinguished by his might; Venus and Saturn carry his lute, and he is the lutanist, he strikes [1] upon Venus and Saturn, and Mars gives him the sound from the fire; and thus Jupiter rejoices in Sol.

[1] Or plays.

21. Here lies the pearl, dear brethren: Mercury makes the understanding in Jupiter, for he separates the thoughts,[1] and makes them act and move; he takes the infinity of the thoughts into his desire, and makes them essential; this he does in Sulphur, and his essence is the manifold power of the smell and taste, and Saturn gives his sharpness thereinto, so that it is salt.

22. But I understand here the virtual salt in the vegetable life: Saturn makes the common salt in the water: He[2] is an heavenly and an earthly labourer, and labours in each form according to the property of the form; as it is written, " With the holy thou art holy, and with the perverse thou art perverse." In the holy angels the heavenly Mercury is holy and divine, and in the devils he is the poison and wrath of the eternal nature according to the dark impression's property, and so on through all things, as the property of each thing is, so is its Mercury, viz. its life; in the angels he is the hymn of God's praise, and in the devils he is the cursing and awakening of the opposite will of the bitter poisonful enmity.

23. Thus likewise it is to be understood in men and all creatures, in all whatever lives and moves; for the outward Mercury is the outward word in the outward world: He[3] is the outward verbum, and Saturn with the impression is his fiat, which makes his word corporeal; and in the inward kingdom of the divine power he is the eternal word of the Father, whereby he has made all things in the outward [principle], understand, with the instrument of the outward Mercury.

24. The outward Mercury is the temporal word, the expressed word; and the inward [Mercury] is the eternal word, the speaking word; the inward word dwells in the outward, and makes through the outward all outward things; and with the inward, inward things: The inward Mercury is the life of the Deity, and all divine creatures; and the outward Mercury is the life of the outward world, and all external corporality in men and beasts, in vegetables and animals, and makes a peculiar principle, viz. a likeness of the divine world; and this is the manifestation of the divine wisdom.

25. The seventh form is called Luna, the amassed essence: What Mercury has comprised in Sulphur, that is a corporeal or substantial hunger of all forms; the property of all the six forms lies therein, and it is as a corporeal being of all the rest; this property is as a wife of all the other forms; for the other forms do all cast their desire through Sol into Luna; for in Sol they

---

[1] Or distinguishes the senses.　　[2] Viz. the Mercury.　　[3] Viz. Mercury.

are spiritual, and in Luna corporeal: Therefore the moon assumes to it the sunshine, and shines from the sun; whatever the sun is, and makes in the spirit-life in itself, the same Luna is, and makes corporeal in itself.

26. It is heavenly and earthly, and rules the vegetative life; it has the menstruum, viz. the matrix of Venus in it; all whatever is corporeal does congeal[1] in its property; Saturn is its fiat, and Mercury is its husband, which impregnates it, and Mars is its vegetable soul, and the sun is its centre in the hunger, and yet not wholly in the property; for it receives only the white colour from the sun, not the yellow, or the red, viz. the majestic; therefore in its property lies silver in metals, and in the property of Sol gold; but seeing Sol is a spirit without essence, thereupon Saturn holds the sun's corporeal essence in himself to lodge in; for he is the fiat of the sun; he keeps it shut up in his dark cabinet, and does only preserve and keep it; for it is not his own essence, till the sun sends him his faber Mercury, to whom he gives it, and to none else.

27. Observe this, ye wise men! It is no fiction or fallacy; let the artist but understand us right; he must bring the jewel shut up in Saturn into the mother of generation, viz. into Sulphur, and take the faber, and divide all forms, and separate the variety of hungers, which the faber himself does, when the artist brings the work into the first mother, viz. into Sulphur: But he must first baptize the froward child with the philosophical baptism, lest he makes a bastard of Sol; and then let him lead him into the desert, and try whether Mercury will eat manna in the desert after the baptism; or whether he will make bread of stones; or whether he will aspire aloft as an haughty spirit, and precipitate himself from the Temple; or whether he will worship Saturn, in whom the devil sits hidden: This the artist must observe; whether Mercury, the wicked poisonful child, receives the baptism; whether he can feed of God's bread or no.

28. If he now does eat, and stands out in the temptation, then will the angels appear to him after forty days, and then let him go out of the desert, and eat his own food; and so the artist is ready and fit for his work; if not, then let him by all means leave it, and as yet account himself unworthy of it.

29. He must have the understanding of the generation of nature; else all his labour and pains are to no purpose, except the grace of the Most High has bestowed upon him some particular, that so he is able to tincture Venus and Mars, which is

---

[1] Thicken, or curdle.

the shortest [and most ready way], if God shews him such an herb wherein the tincture lies.

30. The lunar body of metals lies in the seething of the earth, in Sulphur and Mercury, covered internally with the coat of Venus, and clothed externally with the cloak of Saturn, as we see plainly, and is a degree more external than the solar body: Next after Luna, Jupiter's body is also a degree more external; but Venus is a sly bird, she has also the inward solar body; she takes the coat of Mars upon her, and hides herself in Saturn's cabinet; but she is manifest, and not hidden.

31. Next Venus Mars is likewise a degree more external, and nearer to earthliness; and next Mars Mercury's body is a *particula* of all the rest; on one part most nigh to the earthly corporality, and on the other part nearest the heavenly; and next Mercury Luna is on the earthly part wholly earthly, and on the heavenly part wholly heavenly; it carries an earthly and heavenly face towards all things;[1] to the evil it is evil, and to the good it is good; to a pleasant creature it gives its best in the taste, and to a bad creature it gives the curse of the corrupted earth.

32. Now in all this, as the property of each thing is internally, so it has externally its signature, both in animals and vegetables; and this you shall see in an herb, so likewise in trees and beasts, and in men also.

33. If the saturnine property be predominant, and chief in a thing, then it is of a black, greyish colour, hard and spare, sharp, sour, or salt in taste; it gets a long lean body,[2] grey in the eyes,[3] of a dark blue, of a very slender body, but of a hard touch, though the property of Saturn is very seldom alone master in a thing; for he soon awakens Mars with his hard impression, who makes his property bending and crooked, full of knots, and hinders the body from growing high, but is full of branches and rugged, as is to be seen in oak-shrubs, and the like trees.

34. But if Venus be next to Saturn[4] in any place in the sude or seething of the earth, then the sude in the Sulphur of Saturn causes a tall strong body; for it gives its sweetness into Saturn's impression, whereby Saturn becomes strong and lusty, and if Venus be not hindered by Mars, it grows a great, tall, slender tree, herb, beast, or man, or whatever it be.

35. But if Jupiter be next to him in the property of Venus,

---

[1] It gives a cursing or a blessing aspect.
[2] Stalk, or blossom.　　　　　[3] Or of whitish buds in vegetables.
[4] In conjunction with Saturn.

so that Jupiter is stronger in Saturn than Venus, and Mars under Venus, then it falls out to be a very excellent fair body, full of virtue and power, also of a good taste; its eyes are blue, and somewhat whitish, of a meek property, but very potent: If it falls out that Mercury is between Venus and Jupiter, and Mars undermost, then is this property in Saturn graduated in the highest degree with all power and virtue, in words and works, with great understanding.

36. If it be in herbs, then they are long, of a middle-sized stature or stalk, of a very curious form, fair blossoms, white, or blue; but if the sun also casts the influence of his property into it, then does its colour by reason of the sun incline to yellow; and if Mars hinders not, then is the universal very sovereign in the thing, be it either a man, or other creature, or an herb of the earth: This let the magus well observe, it withstands all malignity, and false influences and assaults from the spirits, whatever they be, so far as a man himself is not false and wicked, and inclines not his desire to the devil, as Adam did, in whom also the universal was wholly complete.

37. With these herbs a man may cure, and heal without any art of the artist; but they are rarely and seldom found, yea not one among many sees them, for they are nigh to paradise: The curse of God hides the eyesight of the wicked, that it does not see, although they should stand before his eyes: Yet in such a conjunction of the planets they are manifest, and may not be hidden; therefore there lies a great secret in many an herb and beast, if the artist knew it, and had the true skill to use it; the whole magia lies therein: But I am bidden to be silent by reason of the wicked, who is not worthy of it, and is justly plagued with the plague with which he plagues other honest people, and tumbles himself in the mire.

38. But if Mars in his property be next Saturn, and Mercury casts an opposite aspect, and the power of Venus be under Mars, and Jupiter under the property of Venus, then out of this property all is corrupted and poisoned; a poisonful herb, tree, beast, or whatever it be; if it falls into the corrupt human property, then it is fitted and prone to evil, but if the moon brings its powerful influence thereinto, then is the false magia ready in the lunar menstruum, and witchcraft is manifest, of which I must here also be silent, and will only shew the signature.

39. In an herb, if the blossom be somewhat reddish, and wreathed, or streaked, and inclined to white by the red, then is the power of Venus there, which makes resistance therein; but

if it be only reddish, and of dark wriths or streaks, with a rough peel or skin on the stalk, branch, and leaf, then does the basilisk lodge there.

40. For Mars makes it rugged, and Mercury is poisonful therein, which gives a streaked colour, and Mars the red, and Saturn the dark, which is a pestilence in the lunar menstruum; but to the artist it is an herb against the pestilence, if he takes the poison from Mercury, and gives him Venus and Jupiter for food, then Mars brings forth the vegetable soul in Sol, and turns his wrathful fire into a love-fire, which the artist must know, if he will be called a doctor.

41. This property likewise signs the living creatures both in their voice and visage; it gives a gross, dull sound, somewhat inclining to a shrill voice by reason of Mars, soothing, flattering, and very false, lying, commonly red pimples [or streams] in the eyes, or blinking, and rolling unsteady eyes: In herbs this property likewise yields a taste very loathsome, from whence in man's life, viz. in Mercury, if it takes it down, a stirring boiling poison arises, which darkens and obscures the life.

42. The physician must have a care of the herbs of this property; they are not to be taken into the body, but they are poisonful, of what name soever they be; for there often happens such a conjunction of the planets, which sometimes so prepares an herb, which is good if it be subject to Saturn and Mars: So likewise it falls out sometimes, that an evil herb, by reason of a good conjunction, if in its beginning it stands in the menstruum, may be freed from the malignity, which is to be known by the signature; therefore the physician, who understands the signature, may best of all gather the herbs himself.

43. But if Mars be next Saturn, and Mercury very weak, and Jupiter also under Mars in the property, and Venus casts an opposite aspect or dissent with its desire, then it is good; for Jupiter and Venus change the wrath of Mars into joy, which produces hot wholesome sovereign herbs, which are to be used in all hot diseases and hurts; the herb is rough, and somewhat prickly the leaves on the branches; so likewise the stalk is fine and thin, according to the nature of Venus, but the virtue and power is of Mars and Jupiter, well mixed and tempered, commonly with brownish blossoms forcing forth in the property, and that because Mars is strong therein with his wrath; but seeing his wrath is changed by Jupiter and Venus into a pleasant property, the wrath becomes a desire of joy.

44. The physician must not give Saturn without Mars in hot

diseases, not cold without heat, else he enkindles Mars in the wrath, and stirs [1] up Mercury in the hard impression in the property of death; Mars belongs to the cure of every Mars-like sickness, which is of heat, and pricking pangs: But let the physician know, that he must first correct and qualify Mars, which he intends to administer, with Jupiter and Venus, that the wrath of Mars may be changed into joy, and then he will also change the sickness in the body into joy; cold is quite contrary to it.

45. If the physician administers Saturn only and by itself to a martial disease or hurt, then Mars is dismayed with death, and falls down with his force and strength into death's property; and now seeing he is the fire in the body, the life's fire becomes thereupon deadly in the elemental property; for he soon awakens Mercury in the property of cold: But yet the physician must have a care that he administers not in an hot disease the raw undigested hot Mars, in which Mercury is wholly inflamed and burning; for he enkindles the fire more vehemently in the body; he must first mollify Mars and Mercury, and put them into joy,[2] and then it is right and good.

46. The hotter an herb is, the better it is hereunto; yet its wrathful fire must be changed into love, and then he can also change the wrath in the body into joy; all according as the property of the disease is, that the disease be able to bear it; for to a weak fire in the body, which is tired and languished by reason of the heat, and rather inclines to cold, viz. to the poison of Mercury, where the life is in danger, there belongs a cure with a fine subtle heat, wherein Venus is strong, and Mars very tender and mild by reason of the power of Venus; Jupiter need not be strong there, lest he make Mars and Mercury too strong, so that the weak life, before it is quickened and refreshed, is overwhelmed, and brought into the mercurial poison.

47. An herb in this aforesaid property grows not high, it is somewhat rough in the touch; the rougher it is, the stronger is Mars therein; it is better to be used outwardly to wounds and sores, than inwardly: The fine and subtle part is to be taken into the body, and is expulsive; the more subtle it is, the nigher it is to the life in the body, which the physician may very well know by its salt; for no rough wild property is to be taken into the body, unless the body be inflamed with a sudden poison, where the life also is fresh and strong, then a vehement resistance must be used; yet Mercury and Mars must not be administered

---

[1] Text, that he stirs.   [2] Sublime them.

in the wrath, but in their strongest power, Mars in the greatest heat, but before changed into joy; and then he also changes Mercury according to himself: Jupiter belongs to the transmutation of wrathful Mars, but he must be first introduced into Sol's property, and then he is rightly fit for it.

48. Every living creature, according to its kind in the foregoing property, is friendly and pleasant, if you deal friendly and gently with it; but if it be dealt roughly with, then Mercury is stirred up in the poison-property, for Mars soon boils up, and gets aloft in the bitter property, and then the anger springs forth; for the ground of all malignity lies therein; but if it be not stirred up, then it is not manifest; as a great sickness which lies in the body, but while the same is hid, and not enkindled, it is not manifest and apparent.

49. But if Mercury be next Saturn in the property, and next him the moon, and Venus and Jupiter beneath, and also weak, then let Mars stand where he will, yet all is earthly; for Mercury is held in the austere impression in the cold property, viz. in death's form, and his Sulphur is earthly; if Mars comes near to it, then it is poisonful also, but if Venus makes an opposition therein, then the poison is resisted, yet it is but earthly; it gives a greenish colour from the power of Venus.

50. But if Venus be next Saturn in the property, and the moon not opposed by Mars, and Jupiter likewise goes in his own power, then all is pleasant [and lovely under that property or constellation]; the herbs are slender, single, and soft in touch, of white blossoms, unless Mercury brings in a mixt colour from the power of the sun, viz. from Mars half red, and from Jupiter bluish, and it is weak in the property, and of little use in physic, yet not hurtful: In the creature it gives a pleasant, courteous, humble life, with no deep reason [reach or capacity], but if Mars comes thereunto, the creature is small, or thin, of a white, weak, and effeminate nature.

51. There are three special salts which may be used to cure, which belong to the vegetable life, viz. Jupiter, Mars, and Mercury; these are the working life, in which the sun is the right spirit which makes these salts operative.[1]

52. The salt or power of Jupiter is of a pleasant good smell and taste from the inward original [of the property] of the liberty of the divine essence, and from the external [principle or original] of the property of the sun and Venus, but yet it is not alone of itself of sufficient power in nature; for the outward

[1] Working, powerful, or virtual.

nature consists in fire and anguish, viz. in poison, and Jupiter's power[1] is opposed to the fiery poison life, which makes a temperature in the poisonful nature, viz. a desire of meekness out of the enmity.

53. The salt of Mars is fiery, bitter, and austere, and the mercurial salt is anxious and raging, like a poison, inclined both to heat and cold; for it is the life in Sulphur, and unites [or assimilates] itself, according to each thing's property; for if it comes into Jupiter's salt, it causes joy and great power; but if it comes into Mars's salt, it makes bitter pangs, stitches, achings, and woe; but if it comes into Saturn's earthly salt, it makes swellings, anguish, and death, if it be not hindered by Jupiter and Venus: Venus and Jupiter are opposite to Mars and Mercury, that so they might temper them both; and without the power of Mars and Mercury there would be no life in Jupiter, Venus, and Sol, but only a stillness; " therefore the worst is as profitable as the best," and the one is the cause of the other.

54. But the physician is to heed and mind what he takes in hand, lest he inflame the mercurial poison more and more in his patient, or introduce it into another adverse source: He ought indeed to use the martial and mercurial salt for his cure, but he must first reconcile Mars and Mercury with Venus and Jupiter, that so both these angry adversaries may resign their will into Jupiter's will, so that Jupiter, Mars, and Mercury may all three obtain one will in the power, and then the cure is right, and the sun of life will again enkindle itself in this union and agreement, and also temper the nauseate of the disease in the contrariety in the salt of the disease, and turn Mercury's poison, and the bitter fire of Mars into a pleasant Jupiter.

55. This is now to be understood only concerning the vegetable soul, viz. concerning the outward man, which lives in the four elements, and concerning the sensible and feeling property.

56. Reason likewise is to be cured with its likeness; for as reason may be brought by words into a sensible sickness and disease, so that reason may vex, fret, and torment itself, and at last fall into an heavy sad sickness and death; so also it may be cured with the application of the same thing [with its own assimilate].

57. As for example: An honest man falls into great debts, care, trouble and distress, which does even afflict him nigh to death; but if a good friend comes and pays his debt for him, then is the cure soon effected with its likeness: Even thus it is

[1] The jovial virtue.

in all things; from whence the disease is risen, even such a like cure is requisite for the restoring its health; and thus it is likewise in the mental soul.

58. The soul of the poor sinner is poisoned in the anger of God, and the Mercury (understand the eternal Mercury in the eternal nature) is inflamed in the soul's property in the fiery Mars of God's anger, which does now burn in the eternal Saturn, viz. in the horrible impression of darkness, and feels the sting of the poisonful angry Mars; his Venus is imprisoned in the house of misery, his water is dried up, his Jupiter of understanding is brought into the greatest folly, his sun is quenched, and his moon turned to dark night.

59. Now he cannot be cured and remedied any other way, but with the likeness; he must again appease the mental Mercury; he must take Venus, understand the love of God, and introduce it into his poisonful Mercury and Mars, and tincture the Mercury in the soul again with love, and then his sun will again shine in the soul, and his Jupiter will rejoice.

60. Now if thou sayest that thou canst not, and that thou art too strongly captivated; I say also, that I cannot; for it lies not in my willing, running, and toiling, but it lies in the compassion of God; for I cannot by my own strength and ability overcome the wrathful anger of God which is enkindled in me; but seeing his dear heart has freely given itself again out of love, and in love, into the humanity, viz. into the poisonful enkindled Mercury in the soul, and tinctured the soul, viz. the poison-source of the eternal nature in the eternal Father's nature's property; therefore I will cast my will into his tincture, and I will go with my will out of the enkindled poison-source, out of the evil Mercury in God's anger into his death, and with my corrupted will I will die with him in his death, and become a nothing in him, and then he must be my life.

61. For if my will is a nothing, then he is in me what he pleases, and then I know not myself any more, but him; and if he will that I shall be something, then let him effect it; but if he wills it not, then I am dead in him, and he lives in me as he pleases, and so then if I be a nothing, then I am at the end, in the essence out of which my father Adam was created; for out of nothing God has created all things.

62. The nothing is the highest good, for there is no *turba* therein, and so nothing can touch [or annoy] my soul; for I am a nothing to myself, but I am God's, who knows what I am; I know it not, neither shall [or ought] I to know it.

63. And thus is the cure of my soul's sickness; he that will adventure it with me shall find by experience what God will make of him: As for example; I here write, and I also do not do it; for I, as I, know nothing, and have also not learned or studied it; so then I do it not, but God does it in me as he pleases.

64. I am not known to myself, but I know to him what and how he pleases: Thus I live not to myself, but to him; and thus we are in Christ only one, as a tree in many boughs and branches, and he begets and brings forth the fruit in every branch as he pleases, and thus I have brought his life into mine, so that I am atoned with him in his love; for his will in Christ is entered into the humanity in me, and now my will in me enters into his humanity; and thus his living Mercury, that is, his word, viz. the speaking Mercury, tinctures my wrathful evil Mercury, and transforms it into his. And thus my Mars is become a love-fire of God, and his Mercury speaks through mine, as through his instrument, what he pleases; and thus my Jupiter lives in the divine joy, and I know it not; the true sun shines to me, and I see it not; for I live not to myself, I see not to myself, and I know not to myself: I am a thing, and I know not what; for God knows what I am; and so now I tend and run to and fro as a thing, in which the spirit drives [or actuates] me as he pleases; and thus I live according to my inward will, which yet is not mine.

65. But yet I find in me another life, which I am, not according to the resignation [or self-denial], but according to the creature of this world, viz. according to the similitude of eternity; this life does yet stand in poison and strife, and shall yet be turned to nothing, and then I am wholly perfect: Now in this same life, wherein yet I find my selfhood, is sin and death, and these likewise shall be brought to nothing: In that life, which God is in me, I hate [1] sin and death; and according to that life which yet is in my selfhood, I hate the nothing, viz. the Deity: Thus one life fights against the other, and there is a continual contest in me; but seeing Christ is born again in me, and lives in my nothingness, therefore Christ will, according to his promise made in paradise, bruise the head of the serpent, viz. of my selfhood, and mortify the evil man in myself, so that he himself may truly live [in me].

66. But what shall Christ do with the evil man? Shall he cast him away? No. For he is in heaven, and does thereby

[1] Or I am an enemy to.

accomplish and effect his wonders in this world, which stands in the curse: Now each labours in its own [vineyard]; the outward man labours in the cursed world, which is evil and good in the wonders of God, viz. in the mirror of glory, which yet shall be revealed in him; and the inward man is not its own, but God's instrument, with whom God makes what he pleases, till the outward with its wonders in the mirror shall also be manifest in God; and even then is God all in all, and he alone in his wisdom and deeds of wonder and nothing else besides; and this is the beginning and the end, eternity and time.

67. Now understand it right; to the outward man there belongs a cure from the outward, viz. from the outward will of God, who has made himself external with this visible world; and for the inward man there is a cure from the inward world, in which God is all in all; only one, not many, one in all, and all in one: But if the inward penetrates the outward, and illustrates it with its sunshine, and the outward receives the sunshine of the inward, then it is tinctured, cured, and healed by the inward, and the inward illustrates it, as the sun shines through the water, or as the fire sets the iron quite through of a light glee; here now needs no other cure.

68. But seeing the devil in the wrath of the eternal nature opposes the soul, as an enemy of the soul, and continually casts his poisonful imagination at the soul to tempt and try it, and the anger or wrath of the eternal nature is manifest in the outward man, which Adam awakened and stirred up; thereupon this wrath is oftentimes stirred up by the devil and his servants, that it effectually works and burns in the outward body, and even then the inward love-fire goes out in the outward man, as a red-hot iron is quenched in the water; yet not so soon in the internal, but in the external [man], unless the outward man continues lying in the mire [1] of sin; so that the soul, which had given itself into the nothing, viz. into the liberty, into the life of God, does enter again with its desire into the outward sinful man, then it loses the inward sun; for it goes again out of the nothing into the something, viz. into the source.

69. Thus the outward body must then have an outward cure; and though the inward man yet lives in God, yet whereas the soul has imagined into the outward wrath, so that the divine tincturation is no longer in the outward man, the outward Mercury, viz. the expressed [2] word, must have a tincturation

---

[1] Or water.   [2] Outspoken.

from the outward expressed love and light, unless the will-spirit of the soul does wholly re-enter into the inward hidden man, and be again transmuted;[1] and then the cure may be again introduced into the outward man, being the thorough-shining love of God in the light,[2] which is exceeding precious.

70. But now this herb is rarely to be found upon the earth; for men eat only of the forbidden tree; therefore the poison of the serpent does so spring up in them in the wrath of the eternal and external nature, so that they must also have an external cure for their serpent's poison in the outward Mercury.

71. It is indeed possible for a man to live without sickness, but he must bring the divine tincturation from the inward man through the outward, which is very difficult [to do] in the world; for the outward man lives among the thorns of God's wrath, which gall and sting him on every side, and blow up the wrath of God, so that it burns in the outward man, and then the tincturation of God's love may not continue there: It is indeed there, but not in the outward enkindled abominations, but it dwells in itself, like as the light dwells in the darkness, and the darkness comprehends it not, also knows nothing of it; but when the light is manifest in the darkness, then is the night changed into day.

72. Thus it is likewise with man; of what light man lives, of that also comes his cure; if he lives in the outward world, then the outward goodness and love, viz. the outward Jupiter and Venus with the sun must be his cure, or he remains in the angry Mars, and in the poisonful Mercury, in the earthly moon captivated in the impression of Saturn, viz. in the earthly Sulphur; which however is made manifest, and awakened in the outward man by Adam, for whose sake the outward man must die, putrify, and so enter again into the nothing, viz. into the end, or as I might better say and signify it, into the beginning of the creation, into the essence, out of which it went and departed with Adam.

[1] Transformed.
[2] The transforming light of God in the dark soul, such as shined in Enoch, Elijah, Paul, etc.

CHAPTER X

1. LET the lover of God understand us right; we do not go upon an historical heathenish conjecture, nor only upon the light of the outward nature; both suns shine to us. Understand us right, and see how God has cured man when the poison of the serpent and devil held him imprisoned in death, and how he yet still cures the poor soul captivated in God's anger; the like process also must the physician keep in curing the outward body.

2. The divine light and love were extinguished in Adam, because he imagined into the serpent's property, viz. into evil and good, so that the poison of death began effectually to work in Mercury, and the source of anger was inflamed in the eternal Mars, and the dark impression of the eternal nature's property took possession of him: His body became earth in the dark impression in the poison of the enkindled Mercury, and was an enmity against God: he was utterly undone, and there was no remedy for him by any creature, neither in heaven, nor in this world; the wrathful death captivated him in soul and body.

3. Now how did God do to cure him and tincture him again? Did he take a strange thing thereunto? No, he took the likeness, and cured him with that which was corrupted in him, viz. with the divine Mercury, and with the divine Venus, and with the divine Jupiter; understand; in man was the expressed word, which I call the eternal Mercury in man; for it is the true ruling acting life; it was inspired or in-spoken into man's image (which God created out of his essence into an image according to God) as into a creaturely image, which was the soul with the property of all the three worlds, viz. with the world of light and understanding, which is God; and with the fire-world, which is the eternal nature of the Father of all beings; and with the light, love-world, which is heavenly corporality; for in the love-desire is the essence, viz. the corporality.

4. The desire of love is spirit, and is the heart of God, viz. the right divine understanding: In the love-essence Mercury is God's word, and in the fiery nature he is the wrath of God, the

original of all mobility and enmity, also of strength and omnipotence; the fiery property makes the light, viz. the liberty, desirous; so that the nothing is a desire, and this desire is the love of God, which Adam extinguished in him: For he imagined after evil and good, that is, after earthliness; the earthliness came forth into a being both out of the wrath, and out of the love-being, and that through God's motion, that the wonders of the abyss and byss might be made manifest, that good and evil might be made known and manifest: And this Adam, being the image of God, should not do, for God had created him to his image: He should have tinctured the fire-world and outward world with the word of love, that so none of them should be manifest in him, like as the day holds the night swallowed up in itself.

5. But by false imagination he has awakened and manifested the dark and poisonful mercurial fire-world in him, so that his bodily essence of the dark impression is fallen to the evil part in the poisonful mercurial property, and the soul is become manifest in the eternal nature in the Father's fire-property, viz. in the poisonful hateful Mercury; according to which God calls him an " angry and zealous God," and " a consuming fire."

6. Now to help and restore this again, viz. the image of God, God must take the right cure, and even the same which man was in his innocence: But how did he effect it? Behold, O man, behold and see, open thy understanding; thou art called.

7. He introduced the holy Mercury in the flame, viz. in the fiery love with the desire of the divine essentiality, or after the divine essentiality again (which desire makes divine corporality in itself) into the expressed word, viz. into the mercurial fire-soul (understand, into the soul's essence in the womb of Mary), and became again that same image of God: He tinctured the poison, viz. the wrath of the Father of all essences, with the love-fire: He took only that same Mercury which he had breathed into Adam for an image, and formed into a creature: He took only that same property, yet not in the fire's property, but in the burning love: He did with the love introduce again the light of the eternal sun into the human property, that he might tincture the wrath of the enkindled Mercury in the human property, and inflame it with love, that the human Jupiter, viz. the divine understanding, might again appear and be manifest.

8. Ye physicians, if you here understand nothing, then you are captivated in the poison of the devil: Behold, I pray, the right cure, with which the enkindled Mercury in man's life is to

be remedied; it must be a Mercury again, but first enkindled
in Venus and Jupiter; it must have the sun's property, which
it attains to by Jupiter and Venus: As God deals with us poor
men, so must the outward poisonful sick Mercury be tinctured
with such an external cure; not with the dark impression of
Saturn, with cold (unless it be first sweetly appeased and
qualified with Jupiter and Venus, that the sun does again shine
in Saturn), but with meek love; this is his right physic, whereby
the death is changed into life; yet this is only a common manual
cure, which the vulgar may learn.

9. But it behoves the doctor, if he will be called a doctor,
to study the whole process, how God has restored the *universal*
in man; which is fully clear and manifest in the person of Christ,
from his entrance into the humanity, even to his ascension,
and sending of the Holy Ghost.

10. Let him follow this entire process, and then he may find
the universal, provided he be born again of God; but the selfish
pleasure, worldly glory, covetousness and pride lie in the way.
Dear doctors, I must tell you, the coals are too black, you defile
your white hands therewith; the true unfeigned self-denying
humility before God and man does not relish with you; therefore
you are blind: I do not tell you this, but the spirit of wonders
in its manifestation.

11. But we will give direction to the desirous seeker, who
would fain see if he knew the way fitly to attain his intent; for
the time is at hand, where Moses is called from the sheep to be a
shepherd of the Lord, which shall shortly be manifest, notwithstanding all the raging and raving of the devil: Let not the
dear and worthy Christendom think, seeing now it seems as if
she should go to wrack and ruin, that it is utterly undone; No:
the Spirit of the Lord of Hosts has out of his love planted a new
branch in the human property, which shall root out the thorns
of the devil, and make known his child Jesus to all nations,
tongues and speeches, and that in the morning of the eternal day.

12. Dear brethren, behold, I pray, the right cure: What did
God with us when we lay sick in death? Did he quite cast
away the created image, understand the outward part, viz. the
outward corrupt man, and make wholly another new man? No.
He did it not: For though he introduced divine property into
our humanity, yet he did not therefore cast away our humanity,
but brought it into the way or process to the new-birth.

13. What did he? He suffered the outward humanity, viz.
the outward water, understand the essentiality of Venus, which

was shut up in the wrath of death, to be baptized with the water
of the eternal essence, and with the Holy Ghost, that the incentive of the outward essentiality shut up in death might again
glow, as a fire that falls into tinder: Afterwards he withdrew
his outward food from the outward body, and brought it into
the desert, and let it hunger, and then the spark enkindled from
the fire of God must imagine into God,[1] and eat manna of divine
essentiality forty days, of which Israel was a type in the wilderness of Sinai with their manna: The essence of eternity must
overcome the essence of time, therefore it is called a temptation
of the devil; for the devil as a prince in the wrath of God did
there tempt the outward humanity, and represented all that to
it wherein Adam fell, and became disobedient to God.

14. There now it was tried whether the image of God would
stand, seeing internally there was God's love-fire, and externally
the baptism of the water of eternal life: Here the soul was
tempted, whether it would be a king, and an angelical throne
instead of the fallen angel, and possess the elected throne of
God in the royal office, from which Lucifer was taken, and thrust
into the darkness, viz. into the throne of poison and death; but
seeing he stood (in that the soul did resign and submit its will
alone into God's love-fire, and desired no earthly food, nor the
earthly kingdom good and evil for outward dominion) the
process to the universal, viz. to the restoration of all that which
Adam had lost, did further proceed and go on: *He turned water
into wine.*

15. Ye physicians, observe this, it concerns you in your
process, you must also go the same way to work: *He healed the
sick ;* so you must likewise make the form in your poisonful
Mercury whole and sound by the power of the philosophical
baptism: He made the dead alive again, the dumb to speak,
the deaf to hear, the blind to see, and cleansed the lepers; all
this must go before, that all the forms in Mercury may be pure,
sound, and living, which Mercury himself does make after the
baptism and temptation; as the living speaking Mercury did
this in the person of Christ; the artist cannot do it, only there
must be faith; for Christ also testifies, that he could not do
many wonders at Capernaum, only heal a few diseased; for the
faith of those at Capernaum would not enter into the divine
Mercury of Christ.

16. So that we see there, that the person of Christ, viz. the

---

[1] Put its desire, hunger, and imagination into the nothing, the highest
good or omnipotence, and eat of God's bread.

creature, could not work the wonders in its own power, but the Mercury, viz. the living, speaking word in him; for the person did cry and call into God, viz. into the speaking word, and set its desire thereinto; as we may see in the Mount of Olives where he prayed, that he sweat drops of blood; and by Lazarus, when he would raise him up, he said, " Father, hear me; but I know that thou always hearest me; yet because of those that stand by, I say it, that they may believe that thou workest by me."

17. Thus the artist must not arrogate anything to himself, the Mercury does itself, after the philosophical baptism, work these wonders before it manifests the universal; for all the seven forms of nature must be crystallised and purified, if the universal shall be revealed; and each form carries a peculiar process when it is to be brought out of the property of the wrath, and entered into the pure and clear life; and it must transmute itself into the crystalline sea which stands before the throne of the ancient in the Revelation, and change itself into paradise; for the universal is paradisical; and Christ also came for that reason into our humanity, that he might again open or make manifest the universal, viz. the paradise, again in man: The speaking word in Christ wrought wonders through all the seven properties or forms, through the expressed word in the humanity, before the whole universal was manifest in the body of the human property, and the body glorified.

18. Even thus it is in the philosophical work, when the Mercury shut up in death receives into it the baptism of its refreshment in love, then all the seven forms manifest themselves in this property, as it came to pass in the process of Christ in his miracles, but as yet they are not perfect in the operation of the manifestation of their properties.

19. The universal is not yet there, till all seven give their will into one, and forsake their property in the wrath, and depart from it with their will, and take into them the love's property: They must take in the will of the nothing, that their will be a nothing, and then it can subsist in the wrath of the fire, and there is no further turba therein; for so long as the desire of the wrath is in the form, it is adverse and opposite to the second form,[1] and inflames the second form with its wrathful property, that is, it strikes the signature of the second, and awakens it in the wrath, and then the voice or sound of the second enkindles the first form's property in Mercury, and so no form can attain to any perfection, that it might enter into love.

[1] Or other forms.

20. Therefore the artist can effect nothing, unless he gives a meat to the forms, which they all desire, and love to eat, wherein there is no turba: Now the properties cannot eat, seeing their mouth is frozen up in the impression of Saturn; the artist must first open their mouth, and make them alive in their zeal, that all the forms may be hungry, and then if there be manna, they all eat together of it, and so the precious grain of mustard-seed is sown.

21. Now when Mercury does thus awake from the death of the impression of Saturn, and gets manna into the mouth of his property of the poisonful death's source, then arises the flagrat of the kingdom of joy, for it is as a light which is enkindled in the darkness, for the joy or love springs up in the midst of the anger: Now if Mercury apprehends the glimpse or aspect of the love in Mars, then the love dismays the wrath, and it is as a transmutation, but it is not fixed and steadfast; and as soon as this comes to pass, the angelical properties appear in view.

The Process in the Temptation

22. Jesus was led by the Spirit into the wilderness, and the devil came to him, and tempted him. When the soul of Christ did hunger, the devil said to Jesus, Open the centre in the stones, that is, the impressed Mercury, and make thee bread, eat the substance of the soul's property: What, wilt thou eat of nothing, viz. of the speaking word? Eat of the expressed word, viz. of the property of good and evil, and then thou art lord in both; this also was Adam's bit, wherein he did eat death: Then said Christ Jesus, " Man liveth not by bread alone, but by every word which proceedeth from the mouth of God."

23. Mark! Whence had the person of Christ the will, that he would not eat with the soul's hunger of the bread which could have been made of stones, which he could well have performed? Or how had it been, if the hunger of the human property had after the unction of baptism eaten in the temptation of the Mercury in the impression of death, viz. of the Sulphur of the expressed word, in which was the anger, and from whence the love was fled, as it is so in the earthly property?

24. Observe! The will and desire to eat of the speaking word came into the soul's property from the motion of the Deity: When the same had moved itself in the soulish essence, shut up in death in Mary his mother in her essence or seed, and introduced the aspect of the eye of God in the love into the dead

soul's essence, and had manifested the love in death, then one divine property desired the other; and the desire of the bodily hunger to eat of God's bread or essence came from the baptism: When the water of the body, which in the impression of the substance was enclosed in death, did taste the water of eternal life in the Holy Spirit, viz. the Holy Spirit's corporality or essentiality in the baptism, then the incentive of the divine hunger of the ardent desire after God's essence did arise in the flesh, as a divine hunger, a glimmering or shining incentive of divine property.

25. Now the man Christ must hereupon be tempted in body and soul, of which he would eat; on one part the expressed word of love and anger was represented before body and soul, in which the devil would be lord and master, and rule therein omnipotently; and on the other part the speaking word in the love-property was only represented to the soul and body.

26. Here now began the combat which Adam should have undergone in paradise; for on one side God's love-desire, which had manifested itself in the soul, did eagerly attempt the soulish and bodily property, and introduced its desire into the soul's property, that the soul should eat of it, and give the body manna thereof; and on the other side the devil in God's wrathful property did assault in the soul's property, and brought his imagination into the property of the first principle, viz. into the centre of the dark world, which is the soul's fire-life.

27. Here was the contest about the image of God, whether it would live in God's love or anger, in the fire or light; for the property of the soul, as to its fire-life, was the Father's according to the fire-world; and seeing the soul in Adam had quenched the light-world, the light-world was again incorporated with the name Jesus, which came to pass in the conception of Mary.

28. Now it was here tried in the temptation of which property man would live; whether of the Father's in the fire, or of the Son's in the light of love: Here the whole property of Christ's person was tempted: The devil said, as he had also said to Adam, Eat of the evil and good: Hast thou not bread? Then make bread of stones: Why dost thou hunger so long in thy own property? Then said the divine desire, "Man liveth not of bread alone, but of every word of God."

29. Thus the property of the fiery soul resigned itself with its desire into the love, viz. into the speaking word's property, and the fiery desire did eat manna in the love-desire. O ye philosophers! observe it well; when this was done, the love trans-

muted the fiery property into its love-property; here the Fathe r
gave the fire-soul to the Son, understand the fiery property of
the expressed Mercury to the speaking Mercury in the light;
for Christ also said so afterwards, "Father, the men were thine,
and thou hast given them me, and I give unto them eternal life."

30. Here God's love gave the eternal love-life to the corrupted
humanity; the love did wholly give itself in unto the fire-wrath,
and transmuted the wrath of the soul into a triumphant joyful
love; but if the soul's and body's property had obeyed the
devil in God's wrath, and made bread of the enclosed Mercury,
and eaten thereof, then had the will entered again into its self-
hood, and could not have been transmuted.

31. But seeing it entered into resignation, into the speaking
word of God, and was willing to be and do whatever that pleased,
then the will went from its selfhood, through the wrathful death
of God's anger, viz. from the expressed word, which the devil
had poisoned with his imagination, quite through the property
of the wrath, and sprang forth afresh with a new love-desire in
God; here the will was paradise, viz. a divine love budding in
death.

32. Thus now the love-will being set in opposition to the
poisonful Mercury of the soul's property in the anger of God,
then came the devil, and said, Thou art the king, who hast
overcome, come and shew thyself in thy miracles and deeds of
wonder; and he brought him upon the pinnacle of the Temple,
and said, "Fall down, that men may see it; for it is written,
He hath given his angels charge over thee, that they should
bear thee up in their hands, lest thou dash thy foot against a
stone." Here the devil would fain that he should use again the
fire's might, viz. the soul's selfhood in its own fiery property,
and depart out of the resignation into an arrogation of self in
its own fire-will, as he had done, and also Adam, when he went
with the desire in his own might into evil and good, and would
have his eyes open in evil and good, as Moses writes thereof,
that the serpent did persuade them to it.

33. Here came the fine adorned beast again, and tempted the
second Adam also; for God gave him leave, seeing he said the
fire's matrix had drawn him, he could not stand: Here now that
should be tried; for he was an angel also, as well as the human
soul, which he had seduced: But the human property in body
and soul in the person of Christ had once cast itself into the
resignation out of its selfhood into God's mercy, and stood still
in the resignation, viz. in the divine will, and would not cast

himself down, or do anything but what God alone did by it, and said to the devil, " It is written, Thou shalt not tempt the Lord thy God;" which is as much as if he had said, A creature of God shall will nor do nothing but what God wills and does by it: There must be no other god besides the only one to rule and will, the creature must go and do as the will-spirit of God leads it; it must be God's instrument, with which he works, and does only what he pleases.

34. In this proof Adam did not stand; for he went from the resignation into an arrogation of self, into an own self-will, and would try evil and good, love and anger, and prove how evil and good tasted. Here, dear man, was the trying state before the tree of temptation in paradise, and that was fulfilled which the first Adam could not, and would not do in divine obedience in resignation.

35. When the devil saw that in this also he had no success, that the humanity would not give way to depart out of the resignation, out of God's will, he carried the humanity upon a high mountain, and shewed it all the riches of the world, all whatever does live and move in the expressed word, all the dominions and might in the outward nature, over which he calls himself a prince, but has only the one part in the wrath of death in possession, and said to it (understand to the human property), " If thou fallest down and worshippest me, I will give thee all this."

36. The humanity should again depart out of resignation into a desire of propriety, and desire to possess something of its own in arrogation of self in the cursed property, evil and good; this had been a dainty dish and delight to the devil; then had he remained king, and his lies had been truth: In this Adam also was corrupted, and entered into selfish propriety, and desired worldly dominion and covetousness (which may be seen in Cain), which is the heart of the poisonful Mercury, viz. its hunger's desire, which makes itself essence according to the property of its hunger, not manna, but earth; as we may see in the wild earth, what he has made in the enkindling, or motion of the Father in his fire's property, in which inflammation (viz. in the poisonful wrath of the expressed Mercury) the devil thought to be a prince, and is so in the same property in the wicked, and also in the government of the world in the wrath; but God holds him captive with the water and light of the third principle, so that he is not prince in the dominion of the expressed word, but the judge's executioner; he must look where *turba magna* is

enkindled in the wrath, and there he is busy as far as *turba magna* goes in the wrath, further his courage is cooled.

37. He would give the humanity of Christ this whole dominion to rule in, and above all in the essence of all things, as a mighty god, which notwithstanding he only possesses in the part of the turba in the wrath of God, and has it not in his full dominion: He should but set his desire thereinto, and introduce his will into him, and he would bring his Mercury of the creature into the greatest omnipotence, that he should be a lord over good and evil, and have all things at command, to do therewith as he pleased, for so Adam had fooled it.

38. His Mercury went with the desire into the impression, whence cold and heat arise, and imagined thereinto, and so the property of the cold and hot fire did presently boil up in the Mercury of the creature; and so also the outward heat and cold did soon pierce into the enkindled Mercury of the human property, so that the body now suffers pain from the heat and cold, which property before (when it stood in the free-will of God in the resignation) was not manifest; and thus evil and good did rule and domineer in Adam.

39. For the centre of wrath, viz. the dark world's property, was manifest in him, in a poisonful death's property, as the Mercury in man is yet to this day so poisonful, and of a venomous source; whereas indeed he is changed in the vital [1] light into a solar property, but yet the poison and property of death hangs to it, and it is his root; as we plainly see, that as soon as the ready instrument of his martial fiery property's signature or form is a little struck or played upon, that his evil poisonful fiery property comes forth, and shews itself, and inflames the body, that it even trembles and shakes for the very poison of wrath, and will ever enter into the enkindled poison-source in him who has awakened and enkindled the same, and assimilate in his malice with the malignant fomenter's malice, and wrestle in the poisonful property's right; and then must the body set to its strength as a servant, and accomplish the poison's will, and wrangle and contest with his adversary, and beat him, or be beaten by him; let it be either by hand-blows, or words; it is all in this property and desire of this poisonful Mercury.

40. From hence arises all war and contention, namely, from the dominion of God's anger in the corrupt and enkindled Mercury of the expressed word, which does so act its delight and sport in the poisonful wrath's and dark world's property in man.

[1] Or life's light.

41. Therefore the warrior is a servant of God's anger: He is the axe wherewith the angry husbandman cuts up his thorns and briars from off his ground: He is the chief worker and accomplisher of the wrathful anger of God: God's anger according to his fire's property will have it so, and not his love; and he that suffers himself to be made use of thereunto, he serves the anger of God according to the dark and fire-world's desire and property, which in the heavy fall of Adam has manifested itself in the human property, and brought man, viz. the angelical image, into an half-devilish vizard and likeness; in which property and image of his will in the expressed creaturely Mercury or vital word he cannot inherit God's kingdom, but must be born anew in his Mercury and will, with and in Christ, in God's love, viz. in the holy speaking Mercury and word of life, that a new obedient will wholly resigned into God's love may proceed from his creaturely Mercury, which neither wills or acts anything but what the will of the speaking divine Mercury wills, who in his selfhood, and selfish arrogation in his own will, is as dead, that he may be the instrument of the great God, whereby he should act, work, and do how and what he pleases: And then is God all in all in him, his will and deed, and he is a branch in the great tree which draws sap, power, and life from the tree of God, and grows and lives in him, and brings forth his fruit; then is the Mercury of the human life a pro-created or expressed fruit, which grows upon the paradise-tree of God, and gives forth its note and sound, and strikes the signature in the speaking word of God, viz. God's harp and lute, in his praise, for which end man is created, not that he should necessarily play upon the instrument of anger and death according to the devil's will.

42. The devil has given himself to be such a lutanist who contrives and helps to act and drive on the play in the wrath, viz. in the darkness: He is the instrument and actor in the wrath of the eternal nature, which has its effects and achievements with him and in him,[1] as its instrument: The like also must the wicked man do, as Saint Paul speaks thereof; " The holy man is unto God a sweet savour unto life, and the wicked a sweet savour unto death." All whatever does live and move must enter [2] into the glory of God; one works in his love, the other in his anger: All is generated and created in the infinite being to the manifestation of the infinite great God; out of all the properties of evil and good, creatures were brought forth

---

[1] And all his legions of evil spirits.   [2] Agree, or make for.

by the will of the speaking word; for the property of the darkness and the fire was as well in the speaking as the property of the light; and therefore there are evil and good creatures.

43. But the angels and men were spoken forth in the image of God's love; they ought not to speak and incline their will into the fire and dark world, and introduce their desire thereinto; also not at all will to be their own, but continue steadfast in the resignation in the speaking will of God, as a form of the speaking will, and bear no inclination to anything, but only to the *speaking;* in which figure they stand as an image or platform of the expressing, as a spoken word, wherewith the speaking word beholds itself in its own likeness, whereby it there manifests the eternal knowledge of the eternal mind, and sets the Spirit's will into a form,[1] and plays therewith.

44. As a limner that pourtrays his own image, and does thereby behold what he is, and how his form and features are; or as a musician composes a curious lesson or song, and so plays and melodises with his life, and will of life, viz. with the sound of his own life's Mercury, in the tune of the song, or upon some musical instrument, as it is agreeable to his life's Mercury, wherewith his vital Mercury does rejoice and delight itself.

45. Thus likewise God created us to his love-consort[2] to his joy and glory, whereby he exalts his speaking eternal word, or plays in the same with us as with his instrument.

46. Therefore, when this melodious instrument was broken in its sound by the wrathful might of his anger, that is, when man's image would play in its own might both in evil and good, in love and anger, viz. in its own self-will, and would not yield itself to be used to what the speaking word had created it, and departed out of resignation into an arrogation of self, and would play as itself pleased, now good, then bad, then this instrument was against the love of God, in which no voice, breath, or smallest degree of anger is manifest or can be, as in the light of the fire no pain of the fire is manifest.

47. For the will of the human Mercury went out from the will of the divine speaking word into its own self-will: Thus it fell into the centre of the pregnatress of all essences, viz. into the anguish, poison, and death, where God's anger, viz. the speaking in the wrath, took possession of it.

> Here now was our distress, we were forlorn,
> Opprest in wrathful death, and woeful scorn;
> If God had not restored us again,
> We should have still been rowling in death's plain.

---

[1] Image, or likeness.   [2] Melody, harmony, delight, or play.

48. Thus, dear reader, it is clearly set before you wherein Christ was tempted; namely, whether the soul, and the whole man, viz. the image of the speaking word (after that God had introduced the spark of his love again into the human property, and freely given itself again with the love into it), would now again enter into its first place, and be God's melodious instrument in his love, or not; or whether it would be a selfish arrogator in its own will, and do what its own speaking would bring forth in the enkindled Mercury of its life; whether it would suffer God's will to strike the signature upon its instrument, or the anger of God to strike it, as before came to pass [viz. in the first Adam].

49. Here it was tried: Therefore said the devil, viz. the organist in God's anger, to Christ, that he should fall down and worship him, and then he would give him all dominion, power, and glory; he should and might do what he pleased, he should live and delight in his own self-will; he should only give the devil his will, and forego resignation, and depart out of God's mercy and love-will: And if this had come to pass, then had the fair instrument been once again broken, and the human melody in God's love and deeds of wonder had ended; but Christ said, "Get thee hence, Satan: It is written, Thou shalt worship the Lord thy God, and serve him only. Then the devil left him, and the angels came and ministered unto him."

THE MAGICAL PROCESS

50. Herein (as it is already mentioned at large) the magus must well consider his purpose and intent; not desiring with the covetousness of the devil to possess the earthly kingdom, also not to fly [or cast himself down] from the Temple, much less to work out his intent from the stones; he must think that he is God's minister and servant, not a selfish lord, of whom becomes a fool: If he will help the poor captive shut up in the anger of God out of the bands of darkness, wherein he is swallowed up in the curse of the earth, and deliver him from the anger of God, then he must think and well observe how God with his entrance [viz. into the humanity] hath redeemed him; he must very exactly and intimately consider the temptation of Christ, not blindly grope after it with outward manual art, and think with himself, I have a dead stone before me; it neither knows or feels anything, I must by force set upon it, that I may compel it, and take its jewel, which it has hidden in it.

51. He that does so is a fool, and goes on in his own self-will, and is altogether unfit for the work; let him not meddle with it; we desire faithfully to admonish him, that if he will seek aright, then let him consider the process of Christ, how God has again regenerated the universal shut up in death in the human property.

52. For God did not take man as he lay closed up in death, and cast him into a furnace, and melted him in the wrath, as the false magus does; but he gave his love first into his human essence, and baptized the humanity; afterwards he brought him into the wilderness, and set the devil opposite to him, not into him; he let him first fast and hunger forty days, and gave no outward food to the humanity: He must eat of his life's Mercury, that God might see whether the humanity would bring its desire into God; and when the humanity introduced its desire into the Deity, and received the manna, then he let the devil set upon the humanity, who introduced all his subtlety and desires into the humanity, and tempted him: Dost thou not understand anything here? What shall I say more to thee? If thou art a beast, then I give thee not my pearl; it belongs to God's children.

53. God must become man, man must become God; heaven must become one thing with the earth, the earth must be turned to heaven: If you will make heaven out of the earth, then give the earth the heaven's food, that the earth may obtain the will of heaven, that the will of the wrathful Mercury may give itself in unto the will of the heavenly Mercury.

54. But what wilt thou do? Wilt thou introduce the poison-ful Mercury (which has only a death's will in itself) into the temptation, as the false magus does? Will you send one devil to another, and make an angel of him? In deed and in truth I must needs laugh at such folly: If thou wilt keep a corrupt black devil, how dost thou think to turn the earth by the devil to heaven? Is not God the creator of all beings? Thou must eat of God's bread, if thou wilt transmute [1] thy body out of the earthly property into the heavenly.

55. Christ said, " He that eateth not the flesh of the Son of Man hath no part in him: " And he says further, " He that shall drink of the water that I shall give, it shall spring up in him to a fountain of eternal life." Here lies the pearl of the new-birth: It is not enough to play the sophister; the grain of wheat brings forth no fruit, unless it falls into the earth; all

[1] Or change.

whatever will bring forth fruit must enter into its mother from whence it came first to be.

56. The mother of all beings is Sulphur, Mercury is her life, Mars her sense, Venus her love, Jupiter her understanding, Luna her corporeal essence, Saturn her husband: You must reconcile or lovingly betroth the man with the woman; for the man is angry, yet give him his dear spouse into his arms; but see that the spouse be a virgin, wholly chaste and pure; for "the woman's seed shall break the serpent's head," viz. the man's anger: The virgin must be in real love, without any falsehood or unfaithfulness, a virgin which never touched any man in anger according to his manhood; for the pure Deity does so espouse itself in clear love with the humanity, even as Mary said, "Be it unto me as thou hast spoken, for I am the Lord's handmaid;" and so the humanity assumed the Deity, and also the Deity the humanity.

57. The chaste virgin signifies in the philosophic work the clear Deity, the humanity is Mercury, Sulphur, and Salt, both heavenly and earthly; the heavenly property is disappeared, and as a nothing; the deadly property in the wrath is stirred up, and lives to the anger, and in the properties of the anger; the humanity, both in Adam and in Christ, was tempted. Dost thou ask, wherewith? With the like opposite in the wrath, even with such a devil as had all these properties in him, as a potent prince [in all the properties of the anger].

58. The properties in Sulphur were tempted with the likeness of the Sulphur; in the Sulphur, or from the sulphureous property, the temptation did come and arise, and its forms are[1] three, as one in the impression, which the philosophers call Saturn, which the human spirit or will should open in the property of Venus, and therewith satiate or feed its hunger, viz. the fire; the other property was, that he should live in his own awakened and opened Venus out of Saturn's property, and aspire in self-will.

59. The third property was, he should introduce his will through the awakened love-desire again into the centre, viz. into the sulphurean mother, which arises in the impression in the anguish: And this he would not do, but the first Adam did it; and therefore God when he would help him tempted him in the Sulphur, viz. in the first mother to the humanity, and suffered a wrathful devil, which was enkindled in the Sulphur, to tempt him with his enkindled malignity and malice in the Sulphur:

[1] Or were.

Dost thou not understand this? What then shall I say more to thee?

60. Sulphur is the womb whereinto we must enter, if we would be new born. Nicodemus said well; " How can one being old enter into his mother's womb, and be born again? " But Christ said, " Except you be converted, and become as children, you cannot see the kingdom of heaven." The self-will must enter again into the first mother which brought it forth, viz. into the Sulphur, by the will understand Mercury.

61. But now who will persuade it to do so? For it is become a selfish thing, and must enter again into the mother, and become nothing; this seemed a strange and wonderful thing to Nicodemus, but the Lord said to him, " The wind bloweth where it listeth, and thou hearest the sound thereof, but thou knowest not from whence it cometh, or whither it goeth; even so is every one that is born of God." Behold, who persuaded the will of Christ in his humanity, to enter again with the will into the filiation or adoption, as it were in the mother's womb, and eat nothing forty days, and would also [eat] nothing, but remained in full steadfast resignation in the mother? Did not the Deity do it, which was entered into the humanity?

62. Thus likewise it goes in the philosophic work, therefore let the artist well observe, and rightly understand us: He must seek the evil stubborn child (which is fled from the mother, and entered into the centre, and would be a selfish thing) in Saturn; for the wrath of God has shut him up with its impression in the chamber of death.

63. Not that he has made him to Saturn, but he holds him shut up in the saturnine death; the same he must again take and bring into the mother's womb, and then send the angel with a message to Mary, and tell her, " She shall bring forth a son, whose name shall be called Jesus: " And if the mother shall yield her consent thereunto, and receive the name Jesus, then the new humanity shall begin in the mother, with the new child in the old apostate captivated in the anger of God, and the name Jesus will first give in itself to the dead child which lay captivated in Saturn, and eagerly draw the will of the evil dead child to itself: This is the fair bride, which shews her crown of pearl to her apostate bridegroom; he should but again receive her, and she would again give him her love. Now if the apostate youth shut up in death does again receive her, then is the artist well prepared, and counted worthy by God to finish his purpose: Now will the bride love the bridegroom, and a virgin bring forth

a son, at which all the world will wonder; the virgin shall embrace the man; but he is a man, and not a woman, and has the virgin's heart.

64. Now he must be tempted, whether or no he will live in virgin-like chastity, and in full resignation of his will to God, for he must be a valiant champion, and destroy the devil's fortress [1] of prey (which he has in his mother) in seven kingdoms; then let the devil set his mother's house on fire with his wrath, and tempt him, he will now well enough defend himself with Christ against the devil.

65. This being done, the young man with his virgin-like heart will wholly give himself up to the mother, when the tempter comes and assaults him, and the mother will wholly swallow him up into herself through the devil's wrath: He gives himself forth wholly out of his own will into the nothing. Now, thinks the artist with himself, I have lost all; for he thinks that he has lost heaven; for he seeks nothing, and does not consider that a virgin has now brought forth: But let him have patience; that which is impossible to the artist, that is possible to nature; after the night it is day; when the tempter has finished all his temptations, then comes the sign [or appearance] of the angels; then the devil which has tempted him must depart.

66. Let the artist well observe this, and pack away the devil, and suffer the young man with his virgin-like heart to lie in his bed, and eat his former food, for he is now become a physician of his sisters [2] in his mother's house; he will do great wonders in all the seven kingdoms of his mother (which are the seven forms of life) as Christ has done.

67. In Saturn he will raise the dead, understand, he will awaken the dead essence which held him captive in his former prison; for he shall turn [or make] the earth to heaven: Even as the virgin has raised up his will out of the anger in the love, and made him a wonder-worker; so must he also awaken with his will, which is united to the virgin's heart, the form or signature in his mother's womb, whence she has brought forth him and all her children, and enkindle it with the virgin's and his love-desire: This is effected and done in the Sulphur of Saturn in the young man's own personal [3] property, and in his mother; for before the espousing of the virgin the heavenly essence of the young man lies shut up in death: For when God cursed the earth, then the heavenly paradisical body disappeared, and the impression of Saturn took it in possession, till the restitution,

---

[1] Royal fort, fort rampant.　　[2] Or kindred.　　[3] Text, bodily.

where God shall restore that which is hidden, that paradise does again spring forth afresh in the expressed word, or that the artist does open the same in a part [1] by God's permission.

68. In the second kingdom of the mother, viz. in Luna, he shall also do wonders; for Jesus fed with five barley loaves five thousand people; this is the working in the essentiality or corporality. He turned water to wine: These and the like do all belong to the lunar property, where the champion with his virgin opens paradise, and feeds the body, where nothing is, where the outward Mercury has not laboured and wrought: Thus the forms [2] in the lunar property open themselves as if they are paradisical, even then the artist thinks I am nigh unto it; but he is yet far off from the end.

69. In the third kingdom of the mother, viz. in Jupiter, Christ did make the babes and ignorant, of a very weak and mean capacity, knowing and understanding, viz. of poor fishermen, carpenters, and the like mechanics, he made apostles, and the most understanding men of all; and also of poor, disrespected, vilified people, as of women, and simple ones, he made faithful, devout, dear, godly children, who apprehended in themselves the universal without any art.

70. Thus likewise it goes in the philosophic work; the essentiality which lies disappeared in death, where the Mercury is wholly earthly, cold, and impotent, does now arise in power, as if the whole being and essence were become a new life, at which the artist wonders, and marvels what it is, or how it happens, and yet does also exceedingly rejoice that he sees the divine power to spring forth before his eyes in a half dead essence, and that in the curse of God: He sees all the four elements, each apart, and sees how the wisdom of God represents [3] itself therein, as an harmony of joy, and sees all colours, and the rainbow upon which Christ sits in judgment in the expressed Mercury.

71. The nature of this splendour arises out of the impression of Saturn; the good Jupiter gives himself forth to be seen in such a manner, as God will change the world, and transform it again into paradise; for this is the understanding in the expressed word, even as Christ has made the foolish, rude, ignorant people truly wise and knowing in divine, real, heavenly jovial understanding and knowledge.

72. In the fourth kingdom of the mother of all beings, which

---

[1] By degrees.   [2] Or signatures.
[3] Speculates, or beholds.

is the mercurial in the wheel[1] of the nature of life, Christ made " the deaf to hear, the dumb to speak, and cleansed the lepers " from the poison of Mercury: All apoplexies, the French or poisonful pox and sores arise from the saturnine water in Mercury, which [water] is called *phlegma*, all which Christ healed in the form or signature of the young man and virgin; for the eternal virginity had espoused itself with the young man, viz. with the humanity.

73. This comes to pass also in the philosophic work: The artist will see how the heaven separates itself from the earth, and how the heaven does again sink into the earth, and changes the earth into a heavenly colour; he will see how Mercury purifies the matter, and how the purified colours will appear in antimony in their property, and how the wonder proceeds.

74. In the fifth kingdom of the mother of all beings, Christ expelled the devils out of the possessed, and healed the deaf in this form and property.

75. This likewise the artist will see in the philosophic work, how Jupiter in Mercury will drive up a black twinkling fiery vapour out of the matter, which sticks on like soot; for it is a hunger of the poison in Mercury, and is very rightly compared to the devil, for it is of his property.

76. In the sixth kingdom of the mother of all beings, viz. in the wheel of life, called Venus, Christ loved his brethren and sisters according to the humanity, and washed his disciples' feet, and loved them even to the deepest exinanition, and gave his life into the wrath's property even to death for them, and manifested himself among them that he was Christ: And when they perceived that the king was come that should deprive self-will of its might and dominion, and destroy the devil's kingdom; then they cried out, and said, " We have no king but Cæsar; " they took him in the dark night into their power, bound him, and brought him before their council,[2] mocked him, whipped him, and beat him, stripped him of clothes, and hung him on the cross.

77. This also the artist will see very powerfully in the philosophic work; for as soon as the dark fiery stream, viz. the material devil goes from the matter, then virgin Venus appears in her virginity very glorious and beautiful; for it betokens Christ's love, who did so humble himself, and manifested his love in our humanity; then the artist thinks that he has the philosophic child, then he has now the fine morsel: But he

---

[1] Orb, rotation, or course.   [2] Or judgment-seat.

dances with the Jews, who thought, when they had taken
Christ, Now we have him, we will keep him well enough.   Thus
he also thinks, it is finished, and receives the child; and when
he beholds it in the trial, then he has Venus, a woman, and not
the virgin with the tincture of the fire and light, and is deceived
by the woman.[1]

78. Now observe right, What do the properties, viz. Saturn,
Mars, and Mercury, when they see the child, viz. the champion
in royal colour, and find that he manages no external dominion
and royalty with power and authority as they do, but will only
rule with love in their poisonful fire-might?   They will not
suffer him.

79. For Saturn signifies the worldly dominion, and Mercury
the spiritual dominion, viz. the Pharisees,[2] and Mars signifies
the devil; these three would not endure Christ among them;
for he said that he was a king of love, and the Son of God, and
was come to deliver his people from sin: Then thought the
devil, sure this rhimes not well, thou wilt lose thy kingdom: And
the worldly magistrate thought, Is this a king, and God's Son?
Then he will take away our might; this does not at all like us:
And the mercurial priests thought; This man is too mean for us,
we will have a Messiah who may bring us to worldly dominion,
and make us to be high and rich in the world, that we may
alone possess the honour of the world; we will not receive him,
he is too poor for us; we might so lose the favour and respect of
the worldly magistrate, and should be much damaged; we will
rather abide in our power, respect, and authority, and abandon
this beggarly king with his love-kingdom: In like manner as
yet to this day they are so minded, and serve his messengers so
whom he sends.

80. Thus likewise it goes in the philosophic work, when Venus
manifests herself with love, viz. in her own property in the three
wrathful forms, viz. in Saturn, Mars, and Mercury; they can
by no means endure it, for it is wholly against their austere,
dark, fiery might, but especially against the poison of Mercury,
they flash and lighten against Venus, and shoot their rays, viz.
the mercurial poisonful rays upon her, as the Pharisees did upon
Christ.   In the meanwhile, Jupiter and Luna hold with Venus,
and give their power to Venus; for Venus does here stand forth
in the power of Jupiter; at this the Pharisees laugh, and think
with themselves, We are wise enough already, what need we

[1] Or lets the woman deceive him.
[2] Or priests who call themselves the ministers of Christ, but are not.

knowledge and understanding? We will have might and honour; and Luna signifies the multitude of laymen who stuck to Christ, while it went well with him; so does Luna in the philosophic work to Venus in her lustre, so long as Saturn, Mercury, and Mars do not meddle with and assault her; but when the power of wrath comes, then Luna changes her will, viz. the colour, and looks, arises, and cries also with the rest the *crucifige* : This the artist will see, if he be chosen and accounted worthy of God for the work.

CHAPTER XI

1. THIS now is thus to be considered; We are to know, that
the essence of this world, together with man, consists in two
properties, viz. in fire and light, that is, in love and anger: Now
the fire is twofold, and the light is also twofold, viz. a cold fire
from the impression, and an hot fire from the power of Mercury in
Sulphur; and so likewise there is a cold light from the cold fire,
and a warming light from the hot fire; the cold light is false,
and the hot light is good; not that it is false in its property,
only in the impression, in the cold Sulphur; in the sharpness of
the wrath it turns to a false desire, viz. to a false love, which is
contrary to the meekness; for its desire is Saturn and Mars.

2. It puts forth its sun (understand its lustre of life) in Mars,
and the warming light (which also receives its fiery sharpness in
the impression in Sulphur from Mars) brings its desire again into
the liberty, viz. through the dying in the fire, through the
anguish: It wholly and freely gives itself forth in the dying of
the fire,[1] and forsakes the property of the wrath.

3. And so it becomes a general joy, and not its own only, even
like the sun that gives forth its shining lustre universally: The
sunshine is neither hot nor cold; only Mercury in the spirit of
the great world makes in Mars and Saturn's property a heat
therein; for the sun enkindles their desire, upon which they grow
so very hungry, eager, desirous, and operative, that even a fire
is found to be in the light, which heat is not of the light's own
property, but of the soul of the great world, which does so
sharpen the pleasant light in its splendor, that it is unsufferable
to the eye.

4. And we are highly to consider and know, that if another
fire-desire, which is not like to the outward life in Mercury, would
rule in the austere wrath of the outward nature, that then it

[1] It freely loses itself in the nothing.

would be an enmity contrary to the austere, cold, bitter, and fiery dominion and life, and that they would exalt [or exasperate] their wrath, eagerly desiring to be rid of it: Even as it so came to pass when the divine love-desire did manifest itself with its great meekness to the false, cold, proud, and austere fire-desire of the Saturnalians, Martialists, and especially of the false Mercurialites: It was a great opposition and enmity to them, that love should rule in the death of poison, and dwell therein, this they could not, nor would not endure; for heaven was come into hell, and would overcome the hell with love, and take away its might; as it is to be seen in the person of Christ; he loved them, and did them all manner of good, and healed their plagues [or diseases], but in that he was not arisen from their wrathful might, and that he said he was descended from above, and was God's Son; this was unsavoury to the cold, hot fire's might, that he should rule with love over them.

5. Even thus it goes in the philosophic work; when the wrathful forms of the earthliness, viz. the outward Saturn, Mars, and Mercury, see the heavenly champion with the virgin's property among them, and perceive that he has far another desire than they, then they are angry in themselves; for the love-desire, when it casts a glimpse on the fire-flagrat, awakes their fire-flagrat, and then the wrath proceeds forth from the anxiety into love; from whence arises a death's flagrat in the love; but seeing there can be no death therein, the love condescends in the fire-flagrat, and gives forth [or diffuses] itself into their desire, and leaves its essence; so that in their desire they reach after its property in the death's flagrat; this is a poison to death, and a pestilence to hell; and in this property[1] death was deprived of its power in the humanity; for Christ, when he shed his heavenly blood in the flagrat of death, and left it in death, the wrath of God was driven to retain the heavenly love-essence in itself: Even there the fire-desire in the enkindled humanity was changed into a love-desire, and out of the anguish of death proceeded[2] a joy and strength of divine power.

6. But I will hereby give the well-wisher fundamentally to understand how it went with Christ, and how in like manner it goes with his philosophic work; both have wholly one process. Christ overcame the wrath of death in the human property, and changed the anger of the Father into love in the human property; the philosopher likewise has even such a will, he wills

---

[1] Manner, or condition.   [2] Was born, or begotten.

to turn the wrathful earth to heaven, and change the poisonful
Mercury into love; therefore observe us here right; we will not
write here parabolically, but wholly clear as the sunshine.

7. God would change the humanity (after it was become
earthly, and had awakened the poisonful Mercury in the love-
property, which [poisonful Mercury] had devoured the love, and
changed it into itself) again into the divine heavenly property,
and make heaven of the human earth, of the four elements only
one in *one* desire, and change the wrath of God in the human
property into love.

8. Now his anger was a might of the fire and wrath, and was
inflamed in man, and therefore there must be right earnestness
to withstand the same, and change it again into love: The love
must enter into the anger, and wholly give itself in unto the
wrath; it would not be enough that God should remain in
heaven, and only look upon the humanity with love; it could
not be, that the anger and wrath should thereby yield up its
might and strength, and freely give itself unto the love: As the
fire is not made better by the light, it still holds its wrath
notwithstanding in itself; but when a meek essence (as water)
comes into the fire, then the fire goes out.

9. Even so heavenly divine essentiality (understand heavenly
water, which the tincture of the fire and light changes into
blood) must enter into the wrathful fire of God, and become
the fire's food, so that the fire of God might burn from another
essence; for water could not have done it; the fire does not
burn in the water, but the meek oleous property of the fire and
light in the essence of divine meekness in the love-desire, that
did effect it.

10. The human fire-life consists in the blood, and therein
rules the wrath of God; now another blood, which was born out
of God's love-essence, must enter into the angry human blood;
they must go both together into the death of the wrath, and the
wrath of God must be drowned in the divine blood, and therefore
the outward humanity in Christ must die, that it might not any
more live in the wrath's property, but that the heavenly blood's
Mercury, viz. the speaking word, might alone live in the outward
humanity, and solely rule in peculiar divine power in the outward and inward humanity; that the self might cease in the
humanity, and God's Spirit might be all in all, and the self only
his instrument, whereby he makes what he pleases; that (I say)
the self-hood might be solely God's instrument, and wholly in
resignation; for God has not created man to be his own lord,

but his servant: He will have angels under obedience, and not devils in their own fire-might.

11. Now when his love would give itself into death, and deprive death of its might, then the two worlds, viz. the Father's fire-world, with the outward visible world, and also the divine love-world with the divine heavenly essentiality, that is, with heavenly flesh and blood, and also with corrupted flesh and blood, were formed into one person. God became man, and made man to God: The seed of the woman, viz. of the heavenly virginity, which disappeared in Adam, and also the corrupted man's seed in the anger, viz. Mary's seed, were formed into one person, which was Christ; and the seed of the woman, viz. of the virgin of God, understand the heavenly essentiality, should bruise the head of the serpent, understand, the wrath of God in the corrupted man; the head is the might of God's anger; the divine man, understand the divine property, should change the earthly into itself, and turn the earth to heaven.

12. Now when the person was born, heaven stood in the earth of man. Now the incarnation could not have done it alone, there must be yet after this another earnestness; for as long as Christ walked on the earth, the humanity which was from Mary's property was not almighty, but the humanity from God [was omnipotent], they were set opposite one against the other in two principles, yet not shut up, but both manifest in each other, the love against the anger, and the anger against the love.

13. Here now was the trial of the combat one with another, from whence also proceeded the temptation of Christ; and when the divine world overcame, then the great wonders broke forth through the outward human world; but all this could not accomplish it, there must yet be a greater earnestness, the human property, viz. the expressed word, was yet stirring in the inflameable anger: The human Sulphur must be changed into the heavenly, viz. into the heavenly part; and thereupon the human self, viz. the expressed Mercury was astonished, when upon the Mount of Olives the heavenly world in the love wrestles with the anger in the human world, viz. with the self-hood, so that the person of Christ did sweat bloody sweat; even there the one was dismayed at the other, the love at the horrible death, whereinto it should and must wholly yield and give in itself with the divine essentiality, and be swallowed up by the anger; and the anger [was dismayed] at its death, in that it must lose its might in the love.

14. Hence the whole person of Christ said, " Father, if it be

possible, let this cup pass from me; yet not as I will, but thy will be done." The love-world in Christ said, " Can it not be but that I must drink down the cup of thy anger? Then thy will be done." And the anger said, " If it be possible, let this cup of love pass from me," that I may revenge myself, and rage in the wrath of man for the sake of his disobedience; as God said to Moses, who stood in the spirit of Christ as a type of Christ before God, " Let me alone that I may devour this disobedient people: " But the name Jesus, which had incorporated itself in paradise with the promise of the woman's seed in the aim of the human and divine covenant, would not suffer him; for the humility of the name Jesus has always interposed against the wrath of the Father, against his fire's property, that his fire might not enkindle the half-poisonful Mercury in man, except only sometimes when Israel walked wholly in the wrath and disobedience; as is to be seen by Corah, Dathan, and Abiram, and by Elias.

15. So it was here on the Mount of Olives, the anger would live in the fire's might in man, and the name Jesus put itself into the anger; and here there was no other remedy, but that the name Jesus in divine love and heavenly essentiality must wholly resign up itself to be devoured by the anger: The Son must be, and was obedient to the angry Father, even to " the death of the cross; " as the Scripture says.

16. The dear love-humility and meekness suffered itself to be " scorned, mocked, spit upon," and judged by the anger; that is, the Jews must execute the justice of God; for by man's self-action sin was committed, and by man's self-action death and sin must be blotted out. Adam had introduced his will into the poison of the outward Mercury; so must Christ, viz. the love, freely give up its will also into the same poisonful Mercury. Adam did eat of the evil tree, Christ must eat of God's anger; and as it went inwardly in the spirit, so likewise outwardly in the flesh; and so also it goes in the philosophic work.

17. Mercury in the philosophic work denotes the Pharisees, he will not endure the love-child: When he sees it, he gives it trembling and anguish, and Venus also stands dismayed at the poison of the angry Mercury; they are in one another as if sweat did drop from them, as the artist shall see.

18. Mars says, I am the lord of fire in the body, Saturn is my strength, and Mercury is my life, I will have none of this love, I will devour it in my wrath; this denotes the devil in the anger of God; and seeing he cannot do it, he raises up Saturn, viz.

the impression, which signifies the worldly magistracy, and reaches therewith after Venus, and yet cannot get her into him, for she is to him a poison to death: This Mercury also can much less endure, for the love took away his dominion; as the high priests thought that Christ would take away their government, because he said that he was God's Son.

19. Thus Mercury is vexed at the child Venus, for Venus has wholly discovered herself, and freely given up herself; they may do now what they please, she will go even into the dragon's mouth, he shall only but open his jaws; and this Mars in Mercury does not understand, but they take the fair child, and shoot their venomous darts against it, and bind it with Saturn's might in their wicked bands, as the artist will see how they surround the colour of Venus.

20. Mars brings it first to Mercury, seeing he is the life, as before the high priest, who must examine and prove the fair child; but he hates it, he cannot reach into the heart after its love-will, he only judges it externally, because it is not of his property, that it stands forth with such a form as the Mercury himself, and yet has another power, virtue and will.

21. But seeing there is another Mercury which lives in its love in the child Venus, therefore he cannot kill it, but brings it to Saturn, as the Jews brought Christ from Caiaphas to Pilate, who signifies Saturn, who also takes the child: But seeing he is a lord of the impression, viz. of the darkness, therefore he cares not at all for the property of the child, but for the dominion only; he seizes on the child with the dark impression, and strips it of its fair Venus garment; and when Luna with the white splendour of the sun sees this, then she hides herself; as the disciples of Christ fled, and the enraged [rude] multitude also, who did highly presume to stand by him in the cross and persecution, but in the earnestness [1] they fly; for Luna is inconstant, she has not Sol's heart in the love-flame; and Saturn with his thorny impression puts the Sulphur upon the child, viz. the mother of all beings with the purple-coloured raiment of her own peculiar property, in which the wrath of Mars is contained and harboured.

22. When Mars, viz. the devil's crew, and Mercury also, viz. the self-pride of life, see that Venus has her royal garment on, understand the purple robe of Saturn and Mercury in Sol's colour mingled with fiery Mars, and adorned in Mercury's sulphur-colour in the open blaze as a shining lustre, for so is the materia according to the colour of the venereal property, which

[1] In the heat of his trial.

the artist must well observe, he then will clearly see as it is
mentioned.

23. When Mars, Mercury, and Luna also see this, then they
cry *Crucifige*, away with him, he is a false king in our garment;
he is a man as we are, and will be God, that is, they cast their
poisonful desire through the purple garment upon the child, and
so the artist will see that the child will appear in his own form,
as if it were full of streaks from the poisonful rays of Mercury
and Mars, which they lay upon the child through the impression
of Saturn; as Pilate whipped Jesus: The artist will see the
prickly crown of thorns standing very sharp with its point upon
the property of the child; also he will see that Venus does not
at all move herself, but stands still, and suffers herself to be so
done unto.

24. Further we are to understand, how that Adam had taken
on him a cold false love, and therewith so shewed himself before
God as if he were in peculiar dominion and will, and moreover
God's child, whereas he did but mock God therewith; for so the
love-desire appears when it is captivated in the impression of
death.

25. Thus must the second Adam Christ take all this upon
him, and enter into the same ignominy and scorn, and be
clothed with a purple garment as a king of this world, and be
mocked therein; for Adam had put on the purple garment of
the outward world's self-might in the splendour of the property
of self; and here it was made open shew of before the anger of
God: And the white garment which Herod put upon Christ to
mock him in signifies, and is the cold false love as a cloak of
falsehood, wherein man pranks up as if he were an angel, and
so puts upon himself Christ's purple mantle with his white robe,
and covers himself with Christ's pure snow-white garment, viz.
with his suffering and death, and yet holds and harbours the
man of falsehood, viz. the false love under a vail.

26. Now Christ must set forth this figure, and it was represented on his body; for he should overcome and stay the man
of falsehood which lay in the human property, and so it was
fully presented before God. Christ must be termed and reviled
for such an one as Adam was; the innocent must take the blame
upon him.

27. And thus it goes in the philosophic work, when the curse
of God's anger which is in the earth is to be changed into love;
for seeing Mercury sets the child of love before Saturn, and
Saturn cannot, and may not try it, therefore he puts upon it the

purple-coloured garment with stripes underneath, and sends it
before Sol's splendor, which glimmers in Mars, and the sun puts
upon it its white colour, viz. the lunar, and then the purple
colour vanishes, and the child stands in the lunar white simple
colour, very despicable without lustre: The sun would fain see
this child shew forth its golden colour, for it perceives there is a
solar virtue in the child, therefore it gives it the white colour
from the property of the eternal liberty; the child should but
give the power of the fire's centre thereunto, viz. the divine
might, and then it would be like the sun, and would be a lord over
the Sulphur of Mars and Mercury, yet only a lord over the outward world's essence, a governor in the wrath, as Sol is the like.

28. But Christ said to Pilate, " My kingdom is not of this
world," and would not answer Herod anything in this white
raiment when he put it on him, nor in the purple robe; for the
purple robe and the white raiment also were both false, and
were put upon him to disgrace and mock him, because Adam
had put them on, and proudly pranked up therein with falsehood;
Christ might not do any sign therein before Herod, though he
desired it. Hereby the shame of man, who was an image of
God, and yet had made himself a false king, was represented
before God's face; as the poor sinner confesses, and sets forth
his abominations before God, when he sets upon abstinence and
repentance.

29. Thus Christ represented to his Father the abominations
[or sins] of man in this false garment, and stood before him as
an ignominy, and confessed the sins of man to his Father in the
stead and place of all men: And when his Father beheld him
through his imagination in this garment, he would have none of
this robe; therefore Pilate must pull it off from him again, and
set him before the Jews in his own form; but they cry, " Away,
away with him, he must be put to death; " for so his Father
would, that he should give himself up to death in his wrath,
and drown the same.

30. And Pilate condemned him to death, for he would not
acknowledge him for a king: So it also goes in the philosophic
work, Saturn will not receive the child, for it is not of his
property; and Mars and Mercury likewise will not have it in
its property: But what do they do?   The child is among them,
they would fain be rid of it, but yet cannot: They grow angry
and enraged, as the Jews against Jesus, and take the child into
their arms,[1] viz. into their false poisonful angry desire, and

---

[1] Text, hold.

will murther it, and quite sting and pierce through the materia of the child with their sharp, fiery, and poisonful rays, viz. with three sharp nails.

31. One whereof is Saturn, viz. the impression of the dark world, denoting the wrath of the dark world. The other is Mars, which signifies the devil, viz. the serpent's property in the anger of God. The third is Mercury, which signifies the false life, viz. how the wrath of God is enkindled in the expressed word in the human property.

32. These three nails pierce through the property of the child. Thus Venus, viz. the essence of love wholly yields itself to the three murtherers, and wholly foregoes its jovial life as if it died; and the mercurial life of the human property, understand the child's power, falls also to the three murtherers in its mother's house, viz. into the corporeal essence, wherein the young man received his virgin, wherein God became man.

33. Now when the heavenly body, and also the earthly, do thus yield unto these three murtherers, then appears the image of John and Mary by the cross as a type; for the young man's life, and also the virgin's in the young man, has freely surrendered, and given forth itself: And now the two properties, viz. the divine and human, divide themselves in the form of each power, which the artist may see if he has the eyes and understanding thereunto.

34. And here, when Saturn with his impression and dark sharpness, and Mars with his wrath, and Mercury with his poison-life do powerfully enter into the property of Venus, then the wrath forces itself into the love, and the love into the wrath essentially mixed, as assimilating one with the other: Here the wrathful death is dismayed at the love, so that in dying he falls into impotence [or a swoon], for it loses the might of the wrath; and the love is, and stands also in the source of the wrath in death's flagrat as impotent [or in a swoon], and gives itself forth wholly into the flagrat [or stroke] of death, and even then the heavenly essence, viz. the heavenly blood flows forth from it into the property of the third principle, viz. of the young man. Here the virgin gives her pearl to the young man for a propriety, and God and man become one.

35. For the virgin's blood out of the divine essentiality does here now drown with its love-essence the young man's blood, viz. the self-hood, and the three murtherers surrender their life in the blood of the virgin, and then the red glee from the fire, and also the white from the life of the champion arise up

together, viz. from the wrath the life, and from the love the meekness: and both, viz. the life of the anger, and the life of the love, ascend together as one only life; for in death they become one: The death dies away in the love, and becomes in the love the life of the divine kingdom of joy; for it is not a dying, but a free surrendering of its power, might, and will, a transmutation; the virgin's blood changes the human, dead as to God, into an heavenly [blood], the life of the young man dies, and the life of the Deity remains fixed and steadfast, for it stands in its property in the nothing.

36. And here, thou dear seeker, when thou seest the crimson-coloured blood of the young man arise out of death with the virgin's white blood, then know that thou hast the arcanum of the whole world, and a treasure in this valley of misery, which surpasses the value of gold; take it and esteem it more excellent and sovereign than that which shall again arise from death: If thou beest born of God, then thou wilt understand what I mean.

37. For this is the type of Christ, [shewing] how Christ has drowned sin, and the enkindled anger of God in the human property; it is not only an offering, for then Moses had accomplished it; it is not a bare verbal forgiveness, as Babel teaches: No. The human will must from all its powers enter into this death, into this blood, viz. into the highest tincture.

38. The purple robe which Christ wore could not do it; the white hypocritical pharisaical priest's coat could also not effect it, no flattery or demure hypocrisy avails here; no comfortings, soothings, or giving God good words are effectual here; the crafty malignant man must be mortified in Christ's blood, he must be drowned in the virgin's blood: The seed of the woman must bruise the head of the serpent; the will must wholly disclaim and depart from its selfish property, and become as an ignorant child, and wholly enter into God's mercy, into the virgin-like blood of Christ, that sin and the poisoned Mercury may be drowned in its Mars, that the white lion may arise; for the lion which now appears in the white colour, in crimson red, is the Mercury of life, viz. the expressed word, viz. the soul, which before was a wrathful devil in its self-hood, ruling and domineering in the anger of God in the three forms of the poison-source, viz. in Saturn, Mars, and Mercury: Now it is the white scarlet-coloured lion from the house of David and Israel, fulfilled in the covenant of promise.

39. N.B.—But that we may give satisfaction to the well-wisher, we will further shew him the whole ground even to the

resurrection of Christ: When the Jews had hung Jesus upon the cross, and he had shed his human and heavenly divine blood, and drowned the turba in the human [blood], then Jesus said, " Father, forgive them, for they know not what they do."

40. When Jesus had broken death in the humanity, and took away self, he did not then wholly cast away the human property, wherein death and the anger of God were, but then he did first truly assume it; understand, he even then did truly take the outward kingdom into the inward; for the outward kingdom was begotten as a wonder out of the eternal wisdom in the speaking word, and spoken forth into a form, as a manifestation of the Deity in love and anger, in good and evil: So that Jesus would not that the outward type of the wonders in the likeness of God should perish [or quite vanish], but the wrath which had over-powered the love in man should be forgiven, that is, it should be given into the nothing, viz. into the liberty, that it might not be manifest in its own self-property; it must be servant, and only a cause of the fiery love and divine joyfulness; nothing should perish [or be lost] in man, for God had created him to his image.

41. Thus let the philosopher observe, that when the three murtherers, viz. Saturn, Mars, and Mercury, sink [1] in the crimson-coloured blood of the lion, they do not perish; but they are pardoned, that is, their wrath is changed into a love-desire, viz. out of Venus into Sol; for when the fiery desire enters into the watery desire, then a shining, viz. a glorious splendour, arises from and in the fire; for Venus is white, and the fire-desire is red.

42. Here now it is changed into one colour, which is yellow, that is, white and red both in one colour, which is the majestical [lustre]; for when Mercury is changed into the power of joy, then arises the multiplication; he changes his mother, wherein he lay shut up in death, into Sol; he makes the earthly heavenly in one property, as the virgin was: For here the virgin loses her name, for she has given her love and pearl to the champion, who is now called here the white lion, as the Scripture speaks of the lion of the house of Israel and David, who should demolish the devil's kingdom, and destroy hell, that is, break the anger of God, and change it into love.

43. This champion or lion is no man or woman, but he is both; the tincture of the fire and light must come into one, viz. of the essence which is Venus, and of the spirit which is Mars in

[1] Are drowned.

Mercury; the Father's love and anger must become one thing, and then this one thing is called the kingdom of joy; so long as it is separated, there is in the thing only anguish and torment, and mere desire; but when it burns in one will, it is a joyful proceeding forth from itself: And this egressive property is called the Holy Ghost, viz. the life of the Deity.

44. Therefore know that the virgin's and young man's blood must be both shed together, that the fire-lion might die; which was manifest in the human property, that the love of the virgin might change his wrath in her dear love-blood into her property, and obtain the soul from the young man; for in Adam the virgin disappeared, for the soul departed out of its love-will out of the resignation into its own, and became disobedient to God.

45. Here the virgin does again take the soul into herself, and gives it her crown of pearl, as to a noble champion, and calls him in his own name the white lion or champion. O ye children of men, observe it, I beseech you; open the gates of the world in your heart; Open them wide that the King of Glory may come in, even the great champion in battle, who hath deprived death of its might, and destroyed the hell in God's anger, and made of the world paradise.

46. O ye wise seekers, how does the Lord open his windows! Why do you sleep in the desire of much increase [in your covetousness], which is multiplied in the wrath? Do but enter only into the divine resignation; you may partake of that which the powers of heaven are able to afford: If you do but forsake your selfishness, then the earth shall become heaven to you, says the spirit of wonders; but you shall not obtain it in your wicked ways and covetous doings.

47. And when Jesus through the shedding of his blood had given the wrath of God in man to the love, that the Father had received the love in the human property into the wrath; then the kingdom of the devil in the wrath, and the kingdom of love did immediately part asunder; they were divided: And this figure did hang with Christ on the cross, viz. the wicked mocker at the left hand, who reviled Jesus, and was not capable of his blood-shedding; and the other at the right hand, who was converted from his sins to Jesus, and said, "Lord, remember me when thou comest into thy kingdom;" to whom Jesus answered, "Verily, to-day thou shalt be with me in paradise."

48. Thus we are rightly to consider, that when the wrath of God is drowned in the blood of Christ, so that it changes its might into love, that even then paradise is again open; for

when JESUS had tinctured the human blood which was corrupted in sin with the virgin's blood in the love, then the virgin
received the manhood, viz. the self-hood, into her virgin's love.
This was the paradise, and an habitation of God, with and in
man, where God dwells in the humanity, and is all in all in it.

49. Thus it falls out also in the philosophic work, when Mars
and Mercury die according to the property of the dark impression of Saturn, then Venus takes them into her love-blood, and
Venus gives her love into the poisonful fire-desire: She wholly
gives herself in unto the fire of MARS in MERCURY, and she yields
herself fully to be their own; but seeing Mars and Mercury
become impotent (as to the might of the fire and poison) in the
love, the love and anger thereupon change themselves into one
essence, into one desire; and here, when the fire, viz. the fire-
desire, gives in its desire to the love; then saith the love,
"To-day thou shalt be with me out of thy fire-anguish in
paradise," viz. in joy, that is, thou shalt be changed in me: And
here Venus gets the soul in the philosophic work, so that Mars
and Mercury become her soul, and the strife ceases; for the
enmity is appeased and quelled: And thus the child subsists in
the fire immoveably without any change; for Mars does not
at all annoy it, and so likewise Mercury and Saturn hurt it not,
for they are in the child at the end of nature, where there is no
turba any more.

50. Mercury is pure in Saturn, he has no more poison, whereby
to make soil [or rust] in the water, viz. in the salt of Saturn:
And let the philosopher and divine also well observe this, that
in paradise there is a perfect life without any shadow of change,
also without any false evil desire, and a continual day, where
the paradisical man is clear as a transparent glass, in whom the
divine sun shines through and through, as gold that is thoroughly
bright and pure, without any spot or foulness.

51. "And when Jesus knew that all was finished, he seeth his
mother and John his disciple standing by under the cross, and
saith unto his mother, Woman, lo! this is thy son; and to the
disciple, Behold thy mother, and forthwith the disciple took
her unto his own home."

52. This is an excellent type, how Christ has forsaken this
world, viz. the human self-hood, and is again gone to the
Father; for he saw his mother according to this world, and his
disciple, viz. his uncle, according to the outward humanity from
his mother's side, and yet said to his mother, "Woman, behold,
there is thy son," I am no more thy son according to my out-

ward humanity; it is changed into God's Son, and is no longer of the world, but it lives to God; But seeing thou art to be yet in the world, take John, who is not yet changed, to be thy guardian; and thou John take thy mother; and he presently took her to himself.

53. This is the type of the Christian Church upon earth: For we the poor children of Eve are not presently wholly changed according to the outward man; but we must also pass into death, and putrify, that the wrath also in the flesh may rot and putrify, and the spirit might rest in the death of Christ till the general resurrection and transmutation of the outward man; in which the earth of man shall be transformed into heaven, and the mirror [or type] of the wonders shall appear therein.

54. Thus he commanded his disciple to take care of his mother: His mother is the Christian Church upon earth, wherein the children of God are begotten according to the spirit, whom he should take care for, and guide and lead them, till the number of the humanity out of the flesh shall be accomplished, and then the spiritual body shall arise, and shall be proved in Christ's death, in his entrance into the anger, where he changed the anger into love; and the kingdom with the source of darkness shall be separated from it.

55. But in this life-time, though the spirit be changed [1] in the divine power, and the spirit be baptized with the virgin's baptism, and puts on the image of Christ internally, viz. Venus's body in the love; yet Adam is not capable of it till he also enters into the transmutation of Christ, which comes to pass in death [or in the dying to this mortal life].

56. But in the meanwhile, John, as the teacher of Christ in Christ's stead, must provide for the outward mother according to the outward man, and feed and teach the lambs of Christ with Christ's spirit: And it exactly shews us how the outward man is not God's mother; for Christ separates himself from his outward mother, and gives her to John; he has put on [2] the eternal mother, viz. the Father of the eternal birth, and therefore they do very ill that honour and worship the outward mother of Christ for God's mother.

57. The whole true Christendom is Christ's mother, which bears Christ in her: And John, viz. the servants of Christ are her nurses, which take care for the mother of Christ as John did; he presently received the mother of Christ and provided for her,

---

[1] Transformed.   [2] Taken, or received.

as her son, and not as her lord; for Christ said to him, "Behold, she is thy mother:" So should all the disciples and teachers of Christ do, and take care of the poor Christendom, as sons, with great humility towards the mother, provide for, and cherish her with diligence and circumspection, and serve her with all discreet modesty, courtesy, and humility; feed and comfort her with the spirit of Christ, not as the priests in Babel do, who ride over her as wealthy, rich, domineering masters, and will be lords over the mother, and only seek honours, and to fatten their bellies in pleasure, and live in strife and contention: These, one with the other, of what name or title soever they be, are not all Johannites, but they are the poisonful mercurial Pharisees, in whom there is nothing but mere anguish, vexation, pain, and torment, where one property does continually torment, envy, and hate the other, and hold it out for false; and yet they are all only out of one root, and have all only one will, except that one colour does not glister as the other.

58. For Saturn is not as Jupiter; Jupiter is not as Mars; Mars, viz. the fire-spirit, is not as the light of the sun; and the sun is not as Venus with her meek water-source; and Venus is not as Mercury with his sound; for she is meek and still, and Mercury sounds and sets up his note; and Mercury also is not as Luna, which as a simple body does give body to all the rest for manifestation; one is far otherwise than another, and has not one property and will; and yet they are in the centre of the essence, viz. in Luna and Saturn, in the property of the soul and body, all of them one and the same lump. Thus the partial sectarian Mercurialites, and Baal's servants, are divided in these properties; they are the Pharisees which judge and condemn Jesus in his members.

59. They wrangle and contend only about the church, and yet none will take care of the poor forsaken mother of Christ: They are mad in their martial and mercurial contest,[1] and are not Johannites, they enter not in Christ's spirit at the door of Christ into the sheepfold; they are wolves, lions, and bears, yea foxes and fearful hares, who fly from and forsake the mother; their rise and original is out of Babel, where they continually contend, wrangle, grin, and bite one another for the letter. Every one will be lord and master over the letter, and transpose and place it as he pleases, only for the honour, applause, and pleasure of this world: They consider not that the mother is a

---

[1] In war for their proud unrighteous mammon, and in bitter strife about their outward worship of Christ.

widow, and that Christ has left and ordained them that they should be such curates for her as John.

60. O thou dear mother of Christendom, let these wolves, bears, and lions go, and shelter themselves where they please, regard no longer these evil beasts; take the John, the disciple of Christ, who teaches the love and humility.

61. O thou dear and worthy mother, art thou not only one? Why dost thou suffer the lions to rend and tear thee in pieces? Christ is thy husband, all these are strangers and hirelings, unless they walk in thy filial love, and humble themselves towards the mother, and provide for her as ministers, else they be all wolves, bears, and tearing lions; though there were many thousands of them, yet one is not at all better than another, unless he comes forth in the line of John, and takes care of Christ's mother, and provides for the mother with earnestness in Christ's spirit: Which if he has not, he is not then called of Christ to be a guardian or curate to the mother; but he is a Mercurialite, a Pharisee, such as Christ called the seed of serpents, and generation of vipers, who crucify Jesus in his members.

62. And thus the philosopher must consider of, and well observe Christ's mother, whom he recommended to John to take care of: He must likewise be a John, and know that his business is about the mother, and that his work in this world is not wholly [1] heavenly: He will not so manifest paradise, that God will appear, and be manifest face to face in his work: No, he remains in the mother, yet he obtains the universal in the mother; for the mother of Christ obtained it also, for it was said to her, " Thou art the blessed among all women."

63. So likewise the philosopher reaches to the blessing in this valley of misery, that he is able to bless his corrupt body, that is, tincture it and free it from sickness, even to the limit of the highest constellation according to Saturn; and therefore let him take heed of covetousness, for so he introduces the turba.

64. By the type of John and the mother of Christ, he is to know, that the kingdom of God and the kingdom of this world are two in his work, and that God's kingdom lies shut up in the mother, viz. in his work, of which he must take care; and be a minister thereunto, and not a lord of the mother, but an alms-giver, and not a gatherer of treasure and wealth, not a covetous muck-worm; also none shall attain to it, or understand our meaning, that will not be a guardian of the mother: The Most High has laid a bar before the foolish understanding,[2] that it is

---

[1] Altogether.   [2] Understanding of folly.

blind, till it be weary with seeking; I speak in the ground of truth.

65. And when Jesus had commended his mother to John, he again turned his desire into the mother of the human property, and said, "I thirst;" he thirsted after the members of human property, and desired the salvation of mankind, viz. the health of his members, understand of his children, which should be begotten in him; and the Jews gave his humanity gall and vinegar to drink; and when he tasted it, he would not drink it.

66. Here is again the outward type, shewing how it went inwardly: The name Jesus, viz. the love of God which was entered into the humanity, and had espoused itself thereunto, did thirst in the love-desire after the corrupt humanity, and would fain taste the pure water of the humanity in itself; but the wrathful anger of God, which was enkindled in the human property, gave itself in with the human property to the thirst of the love-desire: And when the love-desire tasted of it, it would not drink it, but sunk down into it as wholly resigned, or freely yielded up, and did unite and very essentially incline itself into the anger of God as a full and perfect obedience, and as fully and freely given over as a peculiar propriety thereinto.

67. This was now the flagrat of the wrath, that the love should so come into it; whereupon the earth trembled, and the rocks clave asunder; for so the death was dismayed at the life: And here the awakened wrath's property did separate itself into the centre, viz. into the first principle, into the fire-root; and now from the centre there proceeded forth the hunger to the new-birth in the human property; of the hunger unto death was made a hunger to life; for the love tinctured the anger, that the fire-desire to the dark impression became a desire of life.

68. Understand it here right; God the Father, who gave his dear heart into the humanity to help mankind, did now thirst after the humanity, viz. after his heart or word of power; and the Deity in the humanity, viz. the heart of the Father, did thirst after the Father; and the love or the essence of the light did thirst after the fire's essence: For the fire's, or soul's essence in Adam was departed out of the love-essentiality (wherein the paradise did consist) into a selfishness, and was become disobedient to God; and thereupon the essence, life, and being of the light and love died in its growing, that is, it withered as to the vegetative life, or heavenly growth, blooming, and sense of the paradisical source, and awaked and arose to the earthly world.

K

69. Here the Father brought the soul, which was entered into his wrath, and had manifested itself in his anger, again into the love, viz. into the disappeared paradisical image: And here the dark world was dismayed in death's flagrat at the fire-flagrat, which arose up in love in the death as a joyful flagrat; which joy-flagrat entered into the dead bodies of those who had hope in Israel (who did hope upon the Messiah) as a sound of the power of God, and awakened them from death.

70. This flagrat rent in twain the veil in the Temple, viz. the veil of Moses, which hung before the clear face of God, so that man could not see God, and therefore he must serve him with an offering, and type of this final discovery, in which God did manifest himself again in the humanity: This flagrat broke the type in the offerings and sacrifices, and manifested the clear face of God, and united the human time with eternity.

71. All whatever the Jews did outwardly to Christ, the same was a type of the inward, viz. how it went between God and the humanity, viz. between the eternity and time: The Jews gave Jesus gall and vinegar in his thirst, both these properties are a Mercury in the Sulphur of Saturn, viz. in the impression; this is even the type and full resemblance of the soul's property, as it is in itself alone void of the other love-properties.

72. God gave this property of the soul again into his love, the death into the life, the disappeared love-essence (which the word of God had assumed to itself in the essence and seed of Mary, and quickened to life) into the anger's property, into the soul's essence, viz. into the centre of the fire and dark world; whereupon the soul-like fire and dark world became an exceeding triumphant joyful paradisical life: And here the champion upbraided death and hell, viz. the dark world in the soul, and said, " Death! where is thy sting " now in man? " Hell! where is now thy victory " in the wrath of the poison-source in the expressed word or Mercury? All is now dead: O death, I am to thee a death; Hell! I am to thee a conqueror; thou must serve me for the kingdom of joy: Thou shalt be my servant and minister to the kingdom of joy; thou shalt enkindle the flames of love with thy wrath, and be a cause of the spring in paradise.

73. Thus we give the philosopher to understand our sense and deep ground in nature, who desires to seek and open the disappeared essence of the earth, which lies shut up in death, viz. in the curse of God: The veil of Moses hangs also before him, and a very right earnestness is requisite to rend the veil in

twain, that he may be able to see the face of nature, otherwise he is not fitted for it.

74. And as it went in the humanity of Christ, betwixt God's love and anger, and both were transformed into one; so likewise it is in his work of nature, the poisonful Mercury in the Sulphur of Mars and Saturn gives its lunar menstruum, viz. the greatest poison of the dark source into Venus's property; when Venus thirsts after the fire of love, then Mercury gives his poison into the thirst of Venus, and Venus's thirst gives itself wholly to the poison, as if it died; it wholly yields up its desiring life, whereupon arises the great darkness in the philosophic work: For the materia becomes as black as a raven, for Venus has resigned its life, from whence the glance [or splendour] arises, as it is to be seen by Christ, that the sun lost its light, and there was a great darkness contrary to the common course of nature.

75. For when the inward sun gave in itself unto the anger, viz. into the darkness of God; then the outward sun, which receives its power and lustre from the inward, as a glass or resemblance of the inward, could not shine; for its root from whence it shines was entered into the darkness in the place of this world, and would turn the darkness in the curse of God into light, viz. it would make the place of this world again paradise.

76. Thus likewise the sun of the outward world, which is a figure of the inward all-essential sun, must stand still with its splendour in the darkness, from the sixth hour unto the ninth, which is even the time of Adam's sleep when he entered with the desire into the centre of the eternal nature, viz. into the birth, where the love and anger part themselves into two centres, and would prove the cold and hot fire, which took him, and did powerfully work in him. Here are three hours according to the ternary,[1] and in the grave three days according to the time, viz. according to the humanity.

77. When Adam was in the image of God, and was neither man nor woman, but both; he stood forty days in paradise without wavering, and when he fell he stood even till the third day, viz. forty hours in the sleep, even till God did make or build the woman out of him. Thus Israel must be tempted forty days on Mount Sinai, whether they would live in the obedience of God under the wonders and mighty acts; and when it could not be, God gave them the law of his covenant as a mirror of that which was promised in the covenant; therefore

[1] Or number three.

the temptation of the body was upon them forty years, that the body must eat manna to try whether man could be remedied: And when the body [or outward person] could not stand, then Joshua brought them through the water with the covenant of the type,[1] where Israel must serve with sacrifices in the covenant in the type of the final accomplishment, till the time of restitution came in: And then the valiant champion in battle stood forty days in the wilderness in the temptation, and stood out the first trial of Adam in paradise; and the three hours of darkness on the cross are the three hours of temptation of Christ, when the devil tempted him: And again the forty hours of Christ in the grave are the forty days of Adam in paradise, and the forty days of Moses upon the Mount; and the forty years in the wilderness, and the forty days after the resurrection before the ascension, are even one and the same: And now when the champion had stood out Adam's trial, the soul was tempted forty days in the human property, whether it would eat of God's word, and live in full resigned obedience in the will of God, and be a true image, likeness, and similitude of the divine power in the unsearchable eternity, according to the Trinity of the Deity.

78. In the like manner let the philosopher observe, that the essence of time does also stand in such a property, for man was created out of the essence of time into an image, as an extract of all essences, a complete image and likeness according to time and eternity, ruling and standing in the time and in the eternity as an instrument of the great infinite God, with whom, by and with his Spirit, he would make and do what he pleased.

79. Now man is the instrument of God, with [or by] whom he manifests his hiddenness both in his own human property, viz. in the essence and image of God; and then also through man, as with the instrument in the mother of all beings, as in the grand mystery, viz. in the soul of the great world.

80. Man has power so far as he goes, as an instrument of God in divine obedience, as his Spirit guides and leads him, that he can introduce the earth which stands in the curse of God into the benediction, and make of death's-anguish the highest triumphant joy in the outward pregnant mother; but he himself does it not, only his will labours with the understanding therein, and conjoins the compacta,[2] which belong together, as life and death which stand opposite to one another: These he must join together, and bring them into one by such an art as time and

---

[1] Mirror, resemblance.   [2] Things to be compacted.

eternity are united by and in the man Christ, and by him all those which give their will thereinto.

81. He will see in his work all whatever God did in the humanity; when he brought it again into the universal, viz. into paradise, he will see how the wrath devours and swallows up the fair Venus into his pricking thorny essence, and how Venus does fully yield in herself; and how the wrath also dies away in Venus, and becomes wholly dark and black as a coal; for death and life lie together both in death, viz. in the obedience of God: They both hold still to him, and suffer the Spirit of God to make of and with them what it pleases, who introduces them again into the eternal will of God to which he at first created them: And thus the essence stands again in the beginning in the order as God created it: It must only stand in its impression, in the verbum fiat, viz. in the divine making, till the day of God's separation, when God will change the time again into the eternity.

82. And when Jesus had drank the cup and tasted the vinegar mixed with gall in the outward [man], and inwardly in the love-property, viz. in the virgin, the wrathful anger of God; then said the whole man Christ, " My God, my God, why hast thou forsaken me? " For God's speaking word stood still now in the human property, and the new-born essentiality which was dead in Adam, and was again quickened in Christ, cried with the same, " My God, my God, why hast thou forsaken me? " For the anger of God was by the soul's property entered into the image of the divine essentiality, and had devoured the image of God.

83. Here now the image in the creature of the soul cried, " My God, my God, why hast thou forsaken me? " For the human image which disappeared in Adam, and was again revived in Christ's incarnation, should bruise the head of God's anger in the fire-soul, and change its fire-might into Sol: [1] And now the speaking word of God did here forsake it, and it fell into the soul's wrath, where it felt God's anger; for the speaking word did so bring it through the anger into death, and out of the death again into the solar life, understand into the eternal sun.

84. Like as the candle dies in the fire, and out of that death the light and power proceed, viz. the great painless life; so out of Christ's dying and death the eternal divine sun should and must arise in the human property; but the selfishness of the human property, viz. the soul's own self-will to live in the fire's might must here die and be drowned in the image of love, and

---

[1] Text, the sun.

the image of love must also resign and give itself in unto the wrath of death, that so all might fall down into death, and arise in God's will and mercy through death in the paradisial source in the resignation, that God's Spirit might be all in all. Hell's eye must see through the love, as the light shines out of the fire, and the fire from the darkness, and the darkness takes its original from the eternal desire.

85. And as Adam changed the likeness of God into the dark death's form, so God did again change the likeness through his fire-wrath out of death into the light; he drew forth the likeness again out of death, as a blossom grows from the harsh [1] earth.

86. Thus it goes likewise in the philosophic work; Venus is forsaken when she receives the three wrathful properties into herself in wrath; their wrath, viz. the death devours her life, whereupon she loses the colour, and yet becomes a death to the three forms in the wrath, for she drowns death with love. Thus the life is made a death to death, viz. to the wrath, and now they both lie in the will of the eternal nature, viz. in the verbum fiat, which proceeds [2] with them the divine way, in manner as it proceeded forth into essence in the beginning of the creation: For in the beginning paradise, viz. the universal was manifest, and the love shined through the death or anger. Even so it must be again, Venus must become the eye or sight in the wrath, and then of Saturn, Mars, and Mercury there will be a Jupiter: Mars becomes sun, and Saturn moon, and so Mars shines with the sun out of Saturn in Luna from Venus's eye, and all seven are only one: Thus the strife has an end, and all is accomplished till the resurrection of the body.

87. And when Jesus had drank the cup, and said, " My God, why hast thou forsaken me? " then he said, " All is finished," understand the work of man's redemption; and he said further, " Father, into thy hands I commit my spirit, and bowed his head, and gave up the ghost." Here the whole life of Christ resigned itself into the Father's desire, viz. into the will of the eternal nature, and fully gave in the will of his self-hood, viz. his creaturely will again into the centre, viz. into the first mother, from whence the soul-like creature was produced, that is, into the grand mystery of eternity: The self-will must again enter into nature's end, so that the selfishness may wholly die, that God's eternal will and spirit may be and do only all in all in the humanity, and that the creature might afterwards be alone his instrument, wherein he might do and work according to his

---

[1] Or wild.   [2] Goes out.

good pleasure: And thus God the Father has in Christ's death and entrance into our humanity again received our self-hood into his will; and that this might be, he first tinctured the humanity with the Deity, that the humanity might be a pleasant sweet savour and offering to him in his power, for before death lay before it.

88. Here the love destroyed death, and opened the fast seal, that the will might again enter into that which it was before [it was] the creature; and so we all must follow him upon the path which he has made open for us; none can see God, unless God become first man in him, which is brought to pass in faith's desire, and even then the corrupt will (which is apprehended in the death and anger of God, and which blooms in the earthly essence, and brings forth fruit unto death) be wholly mortified, and fall into the free resignation, into the will and mercy of God: And then the own will is with and in Christ at nature's end in the grand mystery of God, viz. in God's hands. God's hands are the eternal desire, or the eternal will, which is unchangeable; thus the creaturely self-will dies; it enters wholly into the nothing, that it might no more live to itself, but to God.

89. Thus it falls out also in the philosophic work; when the artist has first seen great wonders, which the creaturely and natural will has wrought in the power [of] Venus, insomuch that he supposes that he is nigh thereunto; even then nature does first die in his work, and becomes a dark night unto him; the property and power of all the forms must give forth themselves from their centre, and fall upon nature's end; all do freely yield over themselves as one dead essence, and there is no longer any effectual working therein, all is divided in the crown into the thousandth number, and then it is again in the mystery as nature's end as it was before it came into the creaturely being; understand, the essential desire, viz. the expressed Mercury, must again come unto the end of its selfishness, and resign itself into the speaking word.

90. The corporal essence remains in the centre of the four elements till the judgment of God, which now at death stands in the centre of Sol, viz. in the compaction of Venus and Mercury, which compaction at death falls wholly into one [thing], viz. into one power of Jupiter,[1] that is, into the centre of the liberty; for here the desire to cold and heat goes out, all earthly will and desire of the properties dies, and there is no more any hunger after the earthly, or death's property.

[1] Into the sole power and virtue of Jupiter.

CHAPTER XII

1. WE are not to think that when Christ died the natural death in the human property, that he died as to his creaturely soul,[1] much less as to the Deity; also he did not disappear or die in the heavenly essentiality and in the heavenly tincture: This cannot be; only the will and dominion of self, viz. of the outward world, which domineered in man unto the own will and own powers of the selfish creature (wherein man was disobedient to God), he gave that wholly into the Father's hands, viz. into the end of nature, into the Father's great mystery; not that it should be dead, but that God's Spirit might alone be the life thereof, that the divine dominion might be in Christ's person, that the Eternal Father might rule and reign with his Eternal Spirit in his image; and therefore God has determined to keep the last judgment by this Jesus.

2. Now the creature of Christ does it not alone, but God in his image through the creature in the dominion of his Eternal Spirit of all the three principles, which is the life and dominion of every being, in each thing according to its property.

3. And understand us right, when Christ died on the cross, the name Jesus did not also die, which destroyed death, and tinctured the expressed word, viz. the form of the Deity (or the formed word), viz. the soul with love: No, it cannot be, the eternity does not die, only the spoken word, which stands again in the desire of the speaking, viz. in the fiat, which changes itself in its own speaking, viz. in the self-desire, and brings its own sound into another form and source than the speaking word had spoken it, and set it forth with the verbum fiat into a form, signature, and will; as Lucifer with his royal throne, and Adam also did, when they both departed out of resignation into self-hood; the instrument would be master.

4. The outward working sensitive life wherein the anger of

[1] Soulish creature.

152

God was set on fire did wholly die away, not that it should be
a nothing, but it fell into the nothing, viz. into God's will, into
God's working and feeling, quite from the will of the outward
world, which is evil and good, so that it might no longer live to
the world, viz. to the astrum in the walm, the boiling or seething
power of the four elements; but to the Eternal Father's nature
in the walm of the pure divine element the life of the outward
world died.

5. Thus the true human life fell immediately again into that
place from whence Adam had brought it, viz. into paradise, upon
which Christ said to the thief, "To-day thou shalt be with me
in paradise;" it fell into Adam's death, whereby he died to
paradise, and sprang up in Adam's death as a new creature out
of the old, like as the branch springs from the corn: And this it
did from the might and power of the speaking word, which of
grace was entered with living essentiality into the disappeared
heavenly essentiality of man, and had freely given itself into
the centre of the soul-like nature, and also into the wrath of the
anger and death in the flesh, and changed the anger into love,
and tinctured the corrupt blood in the anger with the love.

6. The divine tincture tinctured the human; the divine sun
entered into the human; the divine sun entered into Adam's
night, viz. into Adam's sleep; God's sun with the name Jesus
entered with Adam's soul and humanity in Christ's person into
death, understand into Adam's sleep.

7. When Christ died, then Adam died also to his self-hood
in Christ's death; the name Jesus was in Christ the serpent-
destroyer in Adam's humanity; Christ entered into the image
of the first Adam, so that the first Adam in the humanity of
Christ became the same Christ, and serpent-destroyer, indeed
not in the same creature, but in the same soul's and body's
property.

8. The first Adam fell into sleep, viz. into the impotence of
the divine world, and died in the death of death; the second
Adam entered into the death of death; and took the death of
death captive in himself, viz. in the humanity of Adam: He
was a death to death, and brought forth the life out of death
into the eternal liberty: He arose in the divine omnipotence
in the essence of the first Adam: God's Spirit in the speaking
eternal word brought forth Adam out of death in Christ's
humanity. Adam arose in Christ's humanity, and all the
children of Adam, which are partakers of Christ's kingdom, arise
in Christ; all in Christ's flesh and blood, soul and spirit, but

every one in his creature which he has had here, and mortified in Christ's death.

9. Every one is a particular twig; but there is only one tree, which is Christ in Adam, and Adam in Christ, only one, not two; only one Christ in all Christians; so that I may say, " If I be dead in Christ to the world, I am the same Christ, viz. a branch on the same tree."

10. But seeing that I in the outward man do yet live in my self-hood, therefore I must also die with the outward man in Christ's death, and arise and live in him. Now therefore I live with the will of faith in the mind in Christ, and am a Christian in the will of the mind in the desire of faith, and receive Christ with his humanity into my will, and cast my will into his death; and thus my inward man is also dead in Christ's death, and lives no longer to self-hood; but I am resigned in him, and lie buried in his death: But seeing he is risen in God's will, I also live in his resurrection in him; but my earthliness in its selfish property lives to the earthly world, until it also dies quite to self-hood, and enters into the resignation and putrefaction, and then Christ will awaken it through my inward man, which now lives in him.

11. Like as he is risen from the dead, even so shall I, who shall die to the earthliness in him, viz. in my first father Adam, in the name Jesus as a Christian in Christ; my twig, withered in sin on the tree, shall obtain strength and sap in the name Jesus to life. I shall and must spring forth afresh with my humanity in him as in my stem who is become a heart and power in my father Adam, and bring forth fruit to the praise of God.

12. My will-spirit, which now is in Christ's humanity, and lives in Christ's Spirit, that shall in Christ's power give sap to the dry tree, that it shall again arise at the last day in the sound of the trumpet of the divine breath in Christ's voice, which also is my voice in his breath, and spring afresh in the tree Christ, viz. in paradise: The paradise shall be in me; all whatever God has and is shall appear in me as a form and image of the divine world's being; all colours, powers, and virtues of his eternal wisdom shall be manifest in me, and on me, as on his likeness: I shall be the manifestation of the spiritual divine world, and an instrument of God's Spirit, wherein he makes melody with himself, with this voice, which I myself am, as with his signature: I shall be his instrument, and organ of his expressed word and voice; and not only I, but all my fellow-members in the glorious tuned instrument of God: We are all strings in his joyful

consort; the spirit of his mouth strikes the tune and note on our strings.

13. And therefore God became man, that he might again repair his glorious instrument which he had made for his praise, which perished as to him, and would not sound according to the desire of his joy and love, and introduce again the true love-sound into the strings: He has introduced the voice which sounds in his presence again into us, viz. into his instrument, he is become that which I am, and has made me that which he is, so that I may say, that I am in my resignation in him his trumpet, and the sound of his instrument and divine voice,[1] at which now I rejoice in all my fellow-strings and voices, which with me are tuned and set as an eternal work, to the praise and glory of God.

14. Thus know ye now my fellow-voices in the praise of God, that I sound with my string played upon in the spirit upon and in your note, and thus sing I to you; that whatever Jesus has done through the Christ, viz. through his and my humanity, the same he does yet to-day in me and in all my fellow-members. He died to my self-hood in his death, and I also die to my self-hood in his death: He is given up to his resignation in God his Father, and God his Father has raised him up with the spirit of his mouth in him, and set him forth for the royal image according to the Holy Trinity, through and with whom God will judge all things in the place of this world.

15. Thus God also has awakened in him my spirit and soul through his spirit in the great name Jesus in Christ, so that I in my resignation in him need not to die, for he died in me and for me; his death, in that he is risen from death, is become my eternal life, so that now I live in his death, as one dying; and yet there is no more any death in him, but thus I die to myself and sin in him, seeing that my desire and will presses forth from my self-hood into it, so that I die daily to myself, till once I shall obtain the limit of my self-hood, and my self-hood with the earthly will and desire does wholly die to its selfishness; then shall my self-hood, and all whatever is in me which seeks and loves itself, fall into the death of Christ, viz. into the first mother, from whence God created me, and my self-hood shall become a nothing; and even then my self-hood lies in Christ's death in the resignation as an instrument of God, who then will make it his instrument as he pleases.

16. But seeing now my soul and spirit lives in his resurrection,

[1] Breath, air, tune.

and his voice [air or breath] is in me, according to the resignation in him, as St. Paul says, " Our conversation is in heaven, from whence we wait for the Saviour Jesus Christ; " therefore also his voice, which is in me in that I am [or live] no longer to my self-hood, but he alone [is and lives in me], shall raise up my dead body, which I resign to him, and bring it into his first image, to which he created it.

17. Thus now I live in God, and my self-hood does not know it, for it lives not in God, but in itself (God is indeed in it, but it does not apprehend him), and hides the pearl which I am in Christ; not I, but he in his humanity in my creature in himself: And thus I speak and write of the great mystery of all beings, not that I have apprehended it in my self-hood, but he strikes my signature in my desire, which presses into him, as he pleases.

18. I am known to myself, but not in my self-hood, but in his mirror which of grace he has put into me, thereby to allure my self-hood to him, viz. into the resignation; and so likewise, dear brethren, it shall again be represented to you out of his glass,[1] which he has set forth through my capacity in him, as his instrument.

19. Thus it goes also in the philosophic work; Sulphur, Mercury, and Sal are entered by the curse of God into their self-hood, viz. into a self-working and living; all does now work in the curse and anger of God according to the property of the first principle; if God had not placed the sun as a nature-god of the outward visible world therein, which tinctures every working life, even everything which grows and moves, all would be in the dark death's impression, viz. in the abyss of hell.

20. Now if anything shall be freed from this self-hood, viz. from the wrathful death, and be again brought into the universal, viz. into the highest perfection, then it must die wholly to its self-hood, and enter into the stillness, viz. into the death of the resignation at nature's end: Mars must wholly lose the might of the fire and wrath, and Mercury also his poison-life; Saturn must be a death to himself, insomuch that the artist sees nothing but the great darkness, and even then the light appears in the resignation; for St. John says, " The light shineth in the darkness, and the darkness apprehended it not; " that is, in its self-hood, viz. in its own will and working it cannot apprehend it; but in the resignation the nothing, viz. the liberty of God shines in it.

21. For the nothing manifests itself in its lubet out of the

[1] Mirror.

liberty in the darkness of death; for the nothing will not be a nothing, and also cannot be a nothing, and likewise it cannot otherwise manifest itself, but according to the property of the free lubet, which is now fixed [or steadfast], and in it also as a nothing, for there is no turba therein; the self-will and hunger is dead, and in the nothing, and the lubet of the eternal liberty is its life: Now seeing that the highest being has once moved itself, and come into a visible comprehensible essence, it does again figure [or form] that same essence, which departs from its self-hood, and enters into the nothing, into such a being [or essence] as it was before the times of the world: But seeing the verbum fiat stands yet to this day creating of the corporal essence, it does again make a fixed perfect essence; as the like is brought to pass in the philosophic work, where a new life arises out of death, as God does raise us up in himself in Christ, if we die to self-hood, and wholly resign up ourselves to him.

22. And thus when the expressed Mercury in the Sulphur of Saturn resigns its self-hood into Venus, then the verbum fiat changes it again into such an essence according to the lubet of the liberty; the death arises in a new body out of the darkness of death, in a white fair colour, but as an hidden lustre, wherein the colour is not rightly and distinctly known, till it dissolves itself, and the materia becomes desiring; then the sun arises in the centre, and Saturn in the property of Jupiter and Venus in all the seven forms (that is in the verbum fiat) as a new creation, and the desire of all the seven forms tend to Sol's lustre, viz. to the white and red colour from the fire and light, which is the majestical [colour, lustre, or glory].

23. CHRIST after his resurrection walked [1] forty days in the mystery of all the three principles at once, in the property of the first Adam after his creation before his sleep, and before his Eve was formed, and appeared to his disciples in his property which he had here from the outward world, and did eat with them, and shewed them his assumed humanity, and that he had in no wise wholly put it off.

24. Even so let the artist understand us, that in the philosophic work the first matter does not wholly pass away or vanish, but it enters into the death of the life of its wrathful property, and dies in the curse of God, but rises again in its former being, which it had before the curse of God: The curse only is destroyed therein, and the first life does again rise up therein, and therefore it is fixed, and subsists in the fire, for it

[1] Or conversed.

is dead to the dominion of the four elements, and lives in the fifth essence; not that it has that same life, but it stands still therein; yet the spirit of the new-born essence is a vegetative life with its growing therein; its lustre stands therein, it shews the first Adam in innocence, who stood likewise in such perfection.

25. And as Christ tinctured our corrupt humanity, in which Mercury was turned to poison, with the heavenly blood of the eternal divine virginity and essentiality, whereby the human self-hood died in the poison, and the resigned life did again arise; so the poisonful mercurial, martial, and saturnine will and desire die in the blood of Venus in the philosophic work, and both enter together into death, and arise both together in one love, in one will.

26. Therefore let the artist observe the tincture; it is more noble and precious for man's use in this valley of misery than the body which arises in the tincture; for the spirit is the life; the body is only a figure of the life, and the blood is a mansion of the spirit.

27. The artist must well observe this; in the blood of the young man, when his pearl[1] gives itself to the three murtherers, that it also sheds its blood in and with the young man's, then the champion stands in hell, and disclaims the human self-hood: Then the white lion appears upon his crimson-coloured beast; even there lies the cure of sickness, and the death of death.

28. The body is dissolved in the blood of love in the death out of the earthly into an heavenly [property]. The tincture gives itself into the new body; and afterwards, when the body rises in Sol's splendour, it also forsakes its will; it resigns itself wholly into the body's essence, and becomes its beauty, splendour, and colour, which the artist can never separate; for they are together in the fifth essence, viz. in the mystery of the verbum fiat, and belong to God's motion of the final day of separation; in this time to his own manifestation unto his honour, and deeds of wonder; but after this time to the crystalline world in the glassy sea before the ancient in the Apocalypse.

A Brief Summary of the Philosophic Work

29. Our meaning might seem very difficult to the reader, in that we go so far about and shew Christ all along therein; at which let no man wonder, we do not seek gold, or any temporal

[1] Or virgin.

goods thereby, and drive man into vain curiosities; we speak only with the children whom God has chosen thereunto; for the time is born, where that which is lost shall be again found; yea not only the universal for the body of this world, but also for the soul.

30. The process is very short in both, and it is only of one property which is thus: The tree, understand the life, is divided into seven forms; now the curse of God is come into the seven forms, so that they are in strife and enmity, and one form annoys the other, and can never agree unless they all seven enter into death, and die to the self-will. Now this cannot be, unless a death comes into them, which breaks all their will, and be a death to them; as the deity in Christ was a death to the human self-hood, and the seven forms in the human life; thus it is here also: The human will was changed in Christ into the eternal sun, viz. into the resignation in God; so must all the forms in the philosophic work be changed into one, viz. into Sol: Seven must become one, and yet remain in seven, but in one desire, where each form desires the other in love, and then there is no more any strife and contest.

31. Therefore let the artist but consider how he may give death to the death with the pure life, and how he may awaken the dead and disappeared life, which is heavenly, and lies hidden and captivated in the curse, so that it may again receive the fire-soul; and if he does but bring it so far, it works of itself.[1]

32. When the virgin again receives her bridegroom, who has been faithless, then he is prepared and fitted to the work; otherwise he is no way at all fitted; but all is in vain and to no purpose [which he attempts]. There is not any possibility for the heavenly image according to God's likeness in man to be otherwise helped and restored after that the fire-soul had entered into its self-hood, unless the Spirit of God introduced itself into the disappeared image, viz. into the heavenly essentiality, and gave itself in with the image awakened in it into the soul's fire, viz. into the wrath of death, and be a death to death, viz. to the wrathful anger of God, that it might be drowned in the love, in the blood of the heavenly essentiality; and though there could be no parting nor dying, yet there was a dying of the wrath, so that the wrath was changed into a joy and love.

33. Thus the artist's work is exactly and throughout no otherwise: For man was created out of all beings, out of the

[1] It makes itself, or it has its own faber in itself.

heaven and earth; but when he became wholly earthly, and the curse seized on him, the curse also came over the earthly being, from whence man was made: Thus the heaven was shut up from man, and the heaven also was shut up in the earth, as metals, trees, and herbs, in the food of man, and whatever belonged to his ornament and delight.

34. The soul of the earth, viz. the property of the fire of the first principle is entered into its self-hood, viz. into God's anger; now the heaven is hidden in it; therefore the artist must in his work reduce the soul in the curse and the heaven again into one: He must introduce the soul again into heaven, or else there is no possibility: Now he cannot bring the soul in its iniquity into heaven, for it will not, and therefore he must bring the heaven into the soul, and wholly give in the heaven to the soul, that the soul may eat of heaven, whether she will or no; the heaven must be as death[1] in the soul, so that the soul cannot get rid of it, how angry soever she be, and vehemently rages against it, till she be overcome in her wrath, and enters with the desire into heaven, viz. into the disappeared essence, and wills to murther it, as the Jews did Christ; and if she so enters into the heavenly essence, then the image of the heavenly essence falls into the jaws of the murtherer.

35. Thus when the heavenly essence gives its desire to the murtherer, the murtherer is dismayed at the dear love-life, and arises in the flagrat in the heavenly essentiality; thus the dis-appeared essence does again receive the fire flagrat into itself, and wholly unites itself with the fire-life; and so the fire must burn in love and meekness, and forego[2] its right in the centre, as the light which shines from the fire; thus and no otherwise the heavenly essence obtains its life; and as a fire does thoroughly heat an iron that it appears as if it were mere fire, and it is so, but the iron does still retain its substance; so the disappeared essence, viz. the heaven is manifest in the poisonful mercurial and martial fire-soul, and makes of seven wills only one, and yet seven remain, but the enmity ceases.

36. This is an universal, which also changes the enmity[3] or malignity of all diseases in the human body into one will [into unity]; so that the raging and raving, viz. the seven forms of life in their enmity become unanimous; and then the hunger of the disease ceases, and the process to the universal is as has been already mentioned. It is not my intention to mention a clear declaration thereof; it is clear enough; he that will not seek

---

[1] Or as dead.   [2] Or leave.   [3] Contrariety.

thereby a new man born in God, and apply himself diligently thereto, let him not meddle with my writings.

37. I have not written anything for such a seeker, and also he shall not be able to apprehend our meaning fundamentally, though he strives never so much about it, unless he enters into the resignation in Christ; there he may apprehend the spirit of the universal, otherwise all is to no purpose; and we faithfully warn the curious critic not to amuse himself, for he will not effect anything in this way, unless he himself enters thereinto, and then it will be shewn him without much seeking; for the way is child-like [plain and easy].

CHAPTER XIII

OF THE ENMITY[1] OF THE SPIRIT AND OF THE BODY, AND OF THEIR CURE AND REMEDY

1. EVERYTHING is in itself a senseless, and as a dead thing or being; it is only a manifestation of the spirit, which is in the body: The spirit is signed with the body;[2] whatever the spirit is in itself in an incomprehensible [imperceptible] operation, the same is the body in the comprehensible and visible working. There is one form of the seven forms of nature superior and chief; the other hang to it, and give their signs also, according as each of them is strong in the essence; and as the forms stand in their order in each thing, so they sign the body of every thing and creature in its generation [or kind]: This is the manifestation of the divine wisdom in the expressed word of love and anger.

2. There is not anything but it has its soul in it according to its property, and the soul is a kernel to another body: Whatever lives and grows has its seed in it; God has comprehended all things in his word, and spoken them forth into a form, as the will had formed[3] itself in the desire, the expressed word is a platform of the speaking, and has again the speaking in it; this same speaking is a seed to another image according to the first, for both work, viz. the speaking, and the spoken [word].

3. The speaking works in itself, viz. in the eternity, and the spoken also in itself, viz. in the time; the speaking is the master, and the spoken is the instrument; the speaking makes the nature of eternity, and the spoken makes the nature of time; each makes in its comprehension two properties, viz. light and darkness, wherein the element of all beings consists, which in the expressed word operates itself into four elements, but in the speaking word there is but one: The element in itself is neither hot nor cold, also neither dry nor moist; but it is a lubet, viz. a desiring will, wherein the divine wisdom makes the different[4]

---

[1] Contrary will, contrariety.   [2] Or signs and marks itself in the body.

[3] Or comprehended, or conceived.   [4] Colours of distinction.

and various colours; all according to the desire's property, in which[1] there is neither number nor end: But in the four elements there is number and end; for with the expressing (in that they are become self-full) they have taken a beginning, and have formed themselves into a model or platform of a time, which runneth as a watch-work; it forms, frames, and destroys.

4. This watch-work consists of seven forms, or properties (as is before mentioned), which make in themselves a threefold spirit, viz. a vegetative, sensitive, and rational: The vegetative consists in the four elements; the sensitive in the seven forms of nature, and the reasoning power in the constellation; but the understanding proceeds only from God, for it rises out of the eternal nature; all life whatever, which has its limit in the expressed word, consists in Sal, Sulphur, and Mercury; for therein consist the seven properties of every life of this world; and also the spirit of vegetation, sensation, and reason.

5. Sulphur is the mother of all spirituality and corporality; Mercury manages the dominion therein; and Sal is the house of its habitation, which Mercury itself makes in Sulphur: Reason arises in the oil of the Sulphur, whereinto the constellation gives its desire, viz. the essence of its property, from whence immediately the senses and thoughts arise; but the understanding proceeds from the oil of the element, viz. in the free lubet in the speaking Mercury.

6. Now then, seeing it is very necessary for us poor children of Eve to know from whence the disease and enmity of our life arise, and what that is in us which makes us our own enemies, and vex, perplex, and plague us in ourselves; much more necessary it is to know the cure, whereby we may cure ourselves in our self-hood, and bring ourselves into the limit of rest.[2]

7. This we will delineate and declare, if there be any one that has a mind to enter upon it, and truly prove and try it; and we will set forth from whence evil and good arise originally, and how they arise, and give occasion to the understanding searcher to seek: And we will shew how the will to evil and good arises, and how the evil is the death of the good, and on the contrary the good the death of the evil.

8. When we consider what the mercurial life is, then we find that it consists in Sulphur; for Sulphur is a dry hunger after matter, which makes an austere impression, and in its austere impression it has the fire, and also in its impression the oil, from whence the life burns. Now the impression makes coldness, and

---

[1] Element.   [2] Into the desired end or perfection of rest.

its compunction or attraction makes heat, so that [1] now there is a cold fire and an hot fire in one thing; the cold makes in itself hardness and darkness, and the heat makes in itself the light, and yet there could be no light, if the oil in the Sulphur did not die in hot anguish, as the candle in the fire.

9. Now there is a twofold dying in Sulphur, from whence also a twofold life is generated; First, the impression or desire does draw in, contract, enclose, make hard, cold, thick; and the hardness, viz. the enclosed, causes a death in the enclosed being, and yet in that spirit there is no death, but a pricking, raging, and anxious cold fire-life, which is generated with the impression, and is the life of the darkness.

10. Secondly, in the same anguish, in the austere desire, the hot fire is generated, which consumes the substance, which the coldness, viz. the impression of the desire to nature makes: Thus there remains in the fire the contention betwixt the cold and heat; the cold will have its life according to its property, and in that it strives for life, it enkindles the heat in its impression, and immediately the heat deprives the cold of its might, and consumes the cold substance, and then also the fire-spirit cannot subsist; for unless it has substance it goes out, therefore it must continually, and without intermission, die in itself in the fiery anxious desire: So long as it has the cold's substance to live upon, its life arises, and yet it is nothing but a constant dying and consuming, and in its devouring is the greatest hunger after substance; this same [hunger] passes forth through and with the devouring out of the dying of the fire, and dwells in the nothing, yet it may not be a nothing, and also it cannot be a nothing, therefore it draws the fire again into itself; for its own desire is bent towards its mother: But seeing it is once dead to the fire-source, it cannot die any more in the fire of the heat or cold, but it continually proceeds forth from the fire, and the fire draws it again continually into itself, and so it is the life of the fire; and this is the air, which in the fire is rightly called wind, by reason of the strength and force; and in that which is proceeded forth [2] it is properly called air, by reason of its life of meekness.

11. And in the dying of the fire we are to understand the oil, whence the fire receives its shining light, in which the true life is understood; for that which proceeds forth in the fire-death with the desire to be delivered and freed from the fire-source, that is

---

[1] Thus now.
[2] In the outward principle in the expressed formed word.

a desire of meekness, and takes its original in the first will to nature, in which the eternal nothing brings itself with its lubet into a desire.

12. This lubet brings forth itself through the cold and hot death (through both the dyings) again into the liberty, viz. into the NOTHING; and so it is manifested in the austere impression through the fire, and brought into a principle, and yet it is not either of the fire or of the cold, but so is its manifestation.

13. But seeing the eternal lubet to nature introduces itself with nature into a desire; thereupon this desire cannot die either in the cold or heat, for it takes its origin neither in the heat or cold, but in the nothing; and so it is, after it proceeds from the dying in the fire, again desiring, namely of its own property, and impresses itself, for in the fire it has taken the impression.

14. Now it cannot conceive anything in its impression but an essence according to its desire, which is now water; understand according to the dark impression's property it is water, and according to the fire it is oil; and that which in the cold impression is wholly enclosed in the hardness, as a conception according to the wrath's property, is earth.

15. Thus the wrathful fiery desire draws continually the same air, water, and oil into itself, and devours it, and so the fire-wrath is changed in the air, and oil, and water, into a shining light; for the nothing desires nothing else but power and lustre, and so it makes itself manifest, and brings itself into essence: And the spirit which proceeds forth out of the fire burning in the oil, viz. in the light from the fire and light, gives reason and understanding; for it has originally taken its rise in the nothing, and was the desire to nature; and has brought itself through all the properties of nature, through heat and cold, through the dying in the fire through the light, and dwells again in the nothing.

16. It is a prover and knower of all the properties, for it is generated through all, and proceeded forth from all; it is as a NOTHING, and yet has all things, and passes through heat and cold, and yet none of them apprehend it; as we see that the life of the creature dwells in heat and cold, and yet the right life is neither hot nor cold.

17. Now therefore understand us right: This birth in the eternity is spiritual, but in the time it is material; for I cannot say of God that he is darkness and fire, much less air, water, or earth; but in his eternal desire he has so formed himself with

the time in the place of this world into such an essence, which he formed in the speaking MERCURY according to the properties of the will, and brought with the expressed word into such a formation according to the properties of the desire in the eternal nature, viz. in the verbum fiat.

18. Now the expressed word, viz. the eternal nature's property is understood in Sulphur, for therein is the sevenfold wheel of the birth, which in the spirit, viz. in the first conception to nature, is a constellation, and divides itself out of the constellation in its own peculiar birth into seven properties, and out of the seven properties into four elements.

19. This constellation is a chaos, wherein all things lie, but hidden; and it is the first body, but spiritual; and the sevenfold wheel is the first explication [or working forth] of the chaos, and makes the second body, viz. the reason; the second manifests the first, and it is also a spiritual body; the third body is elementary, a cabinet of both the first, and is a visible tangible body.

20. The first body, viz. the chaos, or the first constellation, seeing it is spiritual, is the word expressed out of the eternal conception; the same has again its speaking in itself, which is the mercurial wheel in the Sulphur with the seven forms, which speaks forth again from itself the four elements.

21. Thus the one proceeds forth from the other; the first before the chaos is the lubet of eternity in the abyss, which takes in itself a will to its own manifestation; this is all God; and the will conceives in itself a desire in the lubet; this is the chaos, or first astrum,[1] wherein consists the eternal nature, which with the desire to nature introduces itself into seven forms, as is before mentioned, and so manifests the chaos, viz. the eternal hidden wisdom of God; and with the desire in the mercurial wheel the element is formed, being a spiritual body of the mercurial life.

22. Now all this is twofold, viz. the desire makes in itself in its impression the darkness, wherein is the strong might of the enkindling of nature, and it is painful; and the free lubet to the desire makes in itself through the enkindling of the desire light and pleasing motion; the light is the power and lustre, and the element is its body, or essence; whereas yet it is only spiritual: Thus the fire-desire is a joyfulness in the free lubet, and in the darkness it is an aching painful source.

23. Out of this whole essence man was created to the image

[1] Constellation.

of God, and understand us right, he stood after and in the
creation in the dominion of the element; the mercurial wheel [1]
in Sulphur stood in the light, and in the free lubet of eternity;
but he departed further with his desire into the four elements,
viz. into the centre of darkness, from whence heat and cold arise.

24. His desire in the beginning was bent [inclined] into the
liberty of God, viz. into the element, where he was resigned in
God; and then God's love-will ruled him with the free lubet's
property, but he departed out of the free lubet of God, out of
the resignation into a self-will, which he forged in the centre to
nature, from whence the pain and torture arise, viz. heat and
cold, so also astringency, sour bitterness, and all the properties
of the dark impression.

25. Even there he fell into the eternal death, viz. into the
dying source, in which the mercurial life in the Sulphur rules in
the poison, where one form in the mercurial sphere does envy,
hate, annoy, and destroy the other, where there is meer anguish,
aching, tormenting, and enmity; for the free lubet was quenched
in him, wherein the holy element, viz. the divine body consists,
and there arose in the same pure element the four elements of
the outward source; there the image of God was cursed, which is
nothing else but that God's love-will, which ruled in the image
of his likeness, withdrew from man, and so man fell into the
dominion of nature: And seeing the four elements have a
temporal beginning and end, and must again enter into the end,
therefore also the human body, which is now become wholly
earthly in the four elements, must fall again into the four
elements, and be destroyed therein: And therefore now we
are to consider of his cure and restoration, how he may again be
delivered from death, and be again introduced with the body
into the pure element, and with the spirit into the dominion of
God's will.

26. Now there is no other remedy but that he with the spirit
which arises in the chaos, and was inspired by God's will-spirit
into the created image, does again depart out of his self-hood,
viz. out of his natural will, and resign himself up fully and freely
into the first will, which in the beginning formed him into an
image: He must wholly die to his self-hood in himself in the
death of the dark impression (as far as he lives therein to his
own will in the self-desire of the outward life of the four elements)
and cast himself with total resignation into God's will, viz. into
God's mercy, that he may no longer live and will to himself, but

[1] Sphere.

to God, viz. to the first will of God, which created him in its image, whereby God manifested himself in an image; and so he is with the first astrum, viz. with the chaos of the soul, again in the same comprehension wherein God created him to his image.

27. But seeing the self-hood, viz. the self-will, strives against this, and will in no wise die to its self-hood (understand the will of the outward world, which is from the outward stars and four elements), therefore God's food must be given to the inward will of the spirit to eat of, that it may live without need and hunger as to the outward being, that it may continually mortify and break the will of the earthly self-hood, till the earthliness, viz. the earthly body, does freely unloose or dissolve itself in death, and also enter again into the mother, from whence it was created, and forsake its self-hood, that the pure body of the element (in which the true life in God's will-spirit does again enkindle the soul in the resigned will [1]) and the disappeared body from the pure element may become a mansion of the soul, viz. a paradisical budding [or bloomy renovation in the eternal spring-time of paradise].

28. And that the own will of the soul might be able to do this, viz. that it might break itself off from its self-hood, and willingly enter into the death of its self-hood, and become a nothing in its self-hood, the free will of God, viz. the eternal lubet to the chaos of the soul, which is the eternal Mercury in the power of the majesty, is again entered into the disappeared image of God proceeded from the pure element, viz. into the virgin-like life, and draws the will of the soul to itself, and gives it again out of love and grace the heavenly corporality of the pure element for food, and the water in that element in the tincture of the fire and light, viz. of the eternal life, for drink: And it has incorporated itself in the humanity, and freely tenders itself to all souls with full desire: That soul which dies to its self-hood, and brings its hunger again into God's mercy, may enjoy this food, whereby it again becomes the first creature in God's love.[2]

29. Now we are to consider how the poor soul captivated in God's anger, being void of the heavenly food, lives in mere anguish, and distress, and restless pain; as the outward earthly body in its properties lives in its hunger in mere anguish, distress, and oppressing pain, unless the soul with the pure element does so overpower and keep it under, that it does not fully domineer

---

[1] Or in which the soul in the resigned will does again enkindle by its desire the true life in God's will-spirit, viz. in the eternal light or liberty.
[2] Such a creature as it was at first, before it fell.

in its own dominion of the outward astrum and four elements in the poisonful mercurial wheel, according to the dark impression, by reason of the influence of the element: If the universal does withstand it, then it may stand in quiet rest, but yet no longer than the inward penetrates the outward [body], and tinctures it: There is in the four elements no perfection, till the body is changed again into the pure element; therefore it must enter again into that from whence the four elements arise.

30. Now in this time of the four elements there is mere pain and vexation;[1] the soul amuses itself on the outward astrum, which forces into it, from whence its false imagination arises, and the body stirs up the poisonful mercurial wheel, from whence sickness and pains befall it; therefore the soul must be cured with the inward perfection, viz. by the speaking word, wherein it stands in God's hand, which alone is able to tincture the soul, and bring it into rest: The outward body must be tinctured and healed with the expressed Mercury; and if the outward Mercury does also stand in the curse as a poison-wheel, then he must be tinctured with his own light in his mother in the body [or womb] of Sulphur: Mercury's own will and hunger must be broken, that the envious odious hunger may become a love desire.

31. And now to know how this may be brought to pass, we must consider the generation in Sulphur, from whence joy and sorrow do arise; for the poisonful Mercury may not otherwise be resisted, and also nothing can resist it, but its own mother which brings it forth, in whose womb it is couched: As nothing can resist the cold but the heat only, and yet the heat is the cold's son; so also the poisonful Mercury must be resisted with its own child, which he himself generates in his mother's womb out of heat and cold out of himself.

32. As the love proceeding from the heart of the Father, which is his Son, withstands the anger of the Father, whereby the Father is merciful; so likewise it is in the expressed word or Mercury.

33. Now understand it thus: I do not mean that the cold poison of Mercury should be, or could be resisted with the enkindled heat; no, but if the cold poison be enkindled, then the remedy must be from the same likeness; but it must be first freed from the coldness, viz. from the enflamed cold wrath, and brought into meekness, and then it does also still and appease the hunger of the cold's desire in the disease of the body: For if enkindled heat be administered to the enkindled

[1] Source.

cold, then the cold is dismayed at the heat, and falls into a swound, viz. into death's property; and so the heat becomes in this death's property a poison-life, viz. an anxious sting; and the mercurial wheel runs into sadness, viz. into sickness, or a crazy dotage, wherein all joy is forgotten.

34. For if the life shall subsist in its own right, then the heat and cold must stand in equality,[1] that so they may accord one with another, and no enmity or disaffection [2] be at all in any of them; the one must not exceed or over-top the other, but they must stand in one will; for the enkindled cold desires no heat, but only likeness: Every hunger desires only likeness for its food, but if the hunger be too strongly enkindled in the cold, such a cure is not to be given it which is so enkindled; indeed it must be in as high a degree in the cold; but the violent force must be first taken away from it; so that it may be only as the mother which generates it, not according to the enkindled poison-source, but according to the mother's joy; and so the sickness, viz. the poison in the anguish, will be likewise changed into such a joy, and so the life receives again its first property.

35. The raw opposite body does not belong to the cure, but its oil, which must be mollified with its own love, understand with a meek essence, which also belongs to the same property; for the seven forms of nature are only one in the centre: Therefore that oil must be brought so far in the wheel, till it enters into its highest love-desire, and then it is rightly fit for cure; for there is nothing so evil but it has a good in it, and that very good resists its evil [or poisonful malignity].

36. Thus also in the same sickness it may withstand the enkindled wrath in the body; for if the cold poison be enkindled in the body, then its good falls into faintness;[3] and if it cannot obtain the likeness of its essence for its help, it remains in faintness; and then the enkindled wrath also does immediately consume itself, and falls also into faintness; and so the natural death is in both, and the moving life in the body ceases; but if it attains the likeness,[4] then it gathers strength again, and the enkindled hunger of the disease must cease.

37. In like manner also we are to consider of the heat, which needs no cold property, but the likeness; yet it must be first freed from the wrath of the same likeness, and brought into its own highest joy and good, so that this likeness does not effectually [5] operate either in heat or cold, but in its own love-

---

[1] Equal essence.   [2] Or departure.   [3] Into a swoon, or impotency.
[4] Or assimilate.   [5] Or vehemently, by force.

desire, viz. in its best relish, and so it will bring the heat in the body into such a desire: All corruptions in the body proceed from the cold; if the brimstone be too vehemently enkindled by the heat, then the right and property of the cold dies, and enters into sorrow.

38. Mercury is the moving [1] life in all, and his mother is Sulphur; now the life and death lie in Sulphur, viz. in the wrestling mercurial wheel. In the Sulphur there is fire, light, and darkness; the impression causes darkness, coldness, and hardness, and also great anguish: and from the impression of the attraction Mercury takes his rise, and he is the sting of the attraction, viz. the motion or disquietude, and arises in the great anguish of the impression, where coldness, viz. a dark cold fire, by reason of the hardness, arises in the impression; and in the sting of anguish, viz. in the disquietude, an hot fire arises.

39. Now Mercury is the wheel of motion, and a stirring up of the cold and heat; and in this placeit is only a painful aching source in heat and cold, viz. a cold and hot fiery poison-anguish, and forces forward as a wheel, and yet it is a cause of joy, and all life and motion; but if it shall be freed from the anguish, and introduced into the joy, then it must be brought forth through death.

40. Now every sickness and malady is a death's property; for Mercury has too much enkindled and enflamed himself either in heat or cold, whereby the essence or flesh, which he has attracted to himself in his desire, viz. in his mother in the Sulphur, is burnt, whereby the earthliness arises both in the water and flesh: Even as the matter of the earth and stones, viz. the grossness of the same, is nothing else but a burnt Sulphur, and water in Mercury is his property, where the salniter in the flagrat of the mercurial wheel, from whence the manifold salts arise, is burnt [or too vehemently enflamed], from whence come the stink and evil taste.

41. Otherwise if the Mercury did so effectually operate therein in the oil of Sulphur, that he might be brought through the death of the impression from the heat and cold, then the earth would be again in paradise, and the joy-desire would again spring [or bloom afresh] through the anguish of the cold's impression: And this is the cause that God laid the curse upon the earth; for the mercurial wheel was deprived of its good (viz. the love-desire, which arises in the eternal liberty, and manifests itself with this mercurial wheel through cold and heat,

[1] Stirring, active.

and proceeds forth through the fire, and makes a shining of the light) and the curse was brought thereinto, which is a withdrawing of the love-desire.

42. Now this Mercury, being a life in the Sulphur of its mother, stands in the curse, viz. in the anguish of heat and cold, and makes in his flagrat, or salnitral walm, continually salts, according to such property as he is in each place, and as he is enkindled in each body; these salts are only the taste in the seven properties.

43. Now if the Mercury be too vehemently enkindled in the cold, then he makes in the salnitral flagrat in his mother in the Sulphur a cold hard impressive salt, from whence melancholy, darkness, and sadness arise in the life of Sulphur; for observe what salt is in each thing, such a lustre of the fire, and such a vital shining from the fire is also therein; but if Mercury be enkindled in immoderate heat, he then burns up the cold essence, and makes raging pains and achings according to the impression, and according to the sting's property, from whence arises in the Sulphur great heat and inflammation; he dries up and consumes the water, so that the desire's hunger or sting has then no food to satisfy its wrathful hunger, upon which he rages and tears in the salt, as it is the poison's property [so to do], from whence the painful distemper in the flesh arises.

44. But if he obtains the likeness again in the property as he stands in the centre of his mother, viz. in the Sulphur, understand as she has generated him in the beginning, viz. as he at first came forth to the natural life in both tinctures of man and woman, understand in the child where his life did enkindle, then he is freed from all anguish, and enters again into the likeness of the heat and cold; and though the strife arises in many even from the very womb, yet the combat is first raised up after the beginning of the life: In the life's beginning the life enters into its highest joy; for the gates of the three principles are opened in equal accord; but the strife soon begins about the conquest between the darkness and light.

45. But now we are to consider what is to be done to Mercury, if he be enkindled [1] either in heat or cold, whereby he raises up sickness and pains: Now it were very good that men had the right cure; but alas! it will remain hidden and covered by reason of the curse of the earth, and the abominations and sins of men, because they awaken this poison in Mercury with their immoderate bestiality.[2]

---

[1] Enraged.   [2] With their bestial lustful excess or disorder.

46. Yet the poor captive has need of deliverance; and though men have not the high universal, which reaches the centre, and brings the wheel of life into its first property, yet men must take from the mercurial walm [1] of the earth its fruits thereunto, seeing the body is also become earthly: A man must accord (or assimulate) one likeness with another, one salt with another, according as the inflammation is in the salt of the body: For observe, in what property the brimstone is enkindled, either in heat or cold, in melancholy or falling sickness (whether the brimstone be burnt too in the body and putrified, or whether it be yet fresh and burning), even such an herb, such a brimstone belongs to the cure, lest the heat or cold be terrified in the salniter, where the salt arises, by a strange might which comes into it, and generates a mort [2] salt, and sets open more and more the house of sadness: But it is not sufficient and powerful enough in its wild nature and property as it grows out of the walm [3] of the earth; it is not able to master the root of the enkindled Mercury in the brimstone, but it does more vehemently enkindle it in such a source and property.

47. That which thou desirest should happen to the body, the same must first happen to that which shall cure the body: To the cure of a foul sickness there belongs a foul brimstone, and so to a cold or hot sickness the like is to be understood; for look in what degree of the fire or cold Mercury is enkindled, and in what form among the seven properties of nature; that is, what salt soever among the seven salts is enkindled, such a salt belongs to the cure: For sickness is nothing else but an hunger; now the hunger desires nothing else but its likeness; but now the property of that life, which in its beginning of its rise stood in joy, is the root; and the sickness is its immoderate enkindling, whereby the order [or temperature] is broken and divided: Thus the root desires in its hunger the likeness, but the inflammation has taken it away; now the inflammation is stronger than the root, therefore the hunger of the inflammation must be appeased, and that which itself is must be administered to it.

48. But as God cured us with his love, and restored to us the salvation of the soul, when we had enkindled the same in the poisonful Mercury of his anger; in like manner also this likeness must be first cured and circulated in the mercurial wheel, and freed from the heat and cold; indeed not taken away from them (this cannot be, and it were also unprofitable), but it must be brought into his highest joy, and then it will make such a

---

[1] Seething.   [2] Mortifying.   [3] Seething.

property in the body in the Mercury of the brimstone and salt; for the root of life does again quicken itself therein, and lifts up the first desire, so that now the hunger vanishes in the fall of the inflammation.

49. Now it behoves the physician to know how he may deal with the medicaments in the likeness, so that he does not enrage them, and bring them into another property; for in their property they are even as a man's life is: He must take care that they remain in their degree, as they are originally brought forth in their mother; for nothing can come higher than it is in the centre of its original according to the hiddenness; but if it shall come higher, then it must assume another property to itself; and so it is not in its own degree, and has not its proper virtue, but an improper one; which indeed may very well be, but it has lost its nature-right, wherein it stands in joy, and is not able to effect any proper operation in the assimulate of its own nature.

50. Therefore there is nothing better than to let everything remain in its innate genuine virtue; only its wrath must be changed into its own joy, that so its own virtue according to the good part may be advanced into its dominion, and then in the likeness it is powerful enough in all sicknesses without any other mixture: For the original in the life desires no other multiplicity, but only its likeness, that it may stand, live, and burn in its own power and property.

51. The power of the Most High has given to all things (to every one according to its property) a fixed perfection; for "all was very good," as Moses says, but with the curse the turba is introduced, so that the properties stand in the strife of Mercury; yet in each property, in every herb, or whatever is, in whatever grows or arises out of the walm [1] of the four elements, there is a fixity hidden; for all things which are in the four elements are originally sprung forth out of the eternal element, in which there is no strife, neither heat nor cold, but all things were in equal weight of all the properties in a love-play, as it is so now in paradise; and the same [paradise] sprung forth in the beginning of this world before the curse through the earth: Thus it is also yet hidden in all things, and may be opened by understanding and art, so that the first virtue may overcome the enflamed malignity.

52. Though we men have not full power to do it in self-might, yet it may be done in God's permission, who has again turned

[1] Seething.

his mercy towards us,[1] and again opened paradise and its comprehension in man: Hath God given us power to become his children, and to rule over the world? Why then not over the curse of the earth? Let none hold it for impossible; there is required only a divine understanding and knowledge thereunto, which shall blossom in the time of the lily, and not in Babel, for whom we also have not written.

[1] Or put his mercy into us.

CHAPTER XIV

OF THE WHEEL OF SULPHUR, MERCURY, AND SALT; OF THE
GENERATION OF GOOD AND EVIL; SHEWING HOW THE ONE
IS CHANGED INTO THE OTHER, AND HOW ONE MANIFESTS ITS
PROPERTY IN THE OTHER, AND YET BOTH REMAIN IN THE
FIRST CREATION IN THE WONDER OF GOD TO HIS OWN
MANIFESTATION AND GLORY

1. THIS is an open gate of the foregoing description: Every
one says, "Shew me the way to the manifestation of the good."
Hear and observe well, dear reason; thou must thyself be the
way, the understanding must be born in thee, otherwise I cannot
shew it thee; thou must enter into it, so that the understanding
of the work in its practic art, wherein I deal not, may be opened
to thee; I write only in the spirit of contemplation; how the
generation of good and evil is, and open the fountain: He
shall draw the water whom God has appointed thereunto; I will
here only describe the wheel of life as it is [1] in itself.

2. When I speak of Sulphur, Mercury, and Salt, I speak of
one only thing, be it either spiritual or corporeal; all created
things are that one thing, but the properties in the generation
of this only thing make a difference [or give various gradual
distinctions]; for when I name a man, or lion, bear, wolf, hare,
or any other beast; yea also a root, herb, tree, or whatever may
be named, it is the same only thing.

3. All whatever is corporeal is the same being; the herbs and
trees, and also the animals, but each thing in its difference of
the first beginning: According as the property in the verbum
fiat has imprinted itself in each thing, so is that kind in its
propagation, and all things stand in the seed and procreation;
and there is not anything but has a fixity in it, be it either
hidden or manifest, for all shall stand to the glory of God.

4. Whatever is risen from the eternal fixity, as angels and the
souls of men, remains indestructible in its fixt being; but whatever is risen in the unfixt being, viz. with the motion of time,
that does again enter into the first motion from whence it has
taken its original, and is a map of its form which it had here,

[1] Or what it is.

like a picture, or as an image in a glass without life; for so it was from eternity before the times of this world, which the Most High has introduced into an image, into the comprehensible natural life in time, to behold the great wonders of his wisdom in a creaturely being, as we plainly see.

5. Now we are to consider the only mother, how the same is in her property, from whence the innumerable multiplicity arises, and has continually risen; and how she generates life and death, evil and good; and how all things may be brought into their first [*ens*], viz. into the place where they originally arise, to which the death, or the dying, is the greatest mystery.

6. For nothing, which is departed out of its first order, as the mother brought it forth, can go back again, and enter with its assumed order into its root, unless it dies again with its assumed order in its mother; and even then it is again in the end, and in the place whence it was created, and so it stands again in the verbum fiat, viz. in the bound of its order in the expressed word, and may enter again into that which it was in the beginning before it was corporeal; and there it is good, for it stands again in that from whence it proceeded.

7. Now therefore we are to consider the beginnings of all things, for we cannot say that this world was made out of something, it was only and barely a desire out of the free lubet, that the abyss, viz. the highest good or being, viz. the eternal will, would behold itself in the lubet as in a glass; therefore the eternal will has conceived the lubet, and brought it into a desire, which has impressed itself, and figurised, and corporised itself both to a body and spirit according to the same impression's property, according as the impression has introduced itself into forms, whereby the possibilities [or powers] are risen in the impression as a nature.

8. This impression is the only mother of the manifestation of the mystery, and it is called nature and essence, for it manifests what has been from eternity in the eternal will; yet we are to conceive that there was in eternity a nature in the eternal will, as an eternal mind in the will; but it was only a spirit in the will, and the essence of its ability was not made manifest, but only in the looking-glass [1] of the will, which is the eternal wisdom, wherein all things which are in this world were known in two centres, viz. according to the fire and light, and then according to the darkness and essence; all which came with the motion of the eternal will through the desire in the will into

[1] Mirror.

a manifest mystery, and so introduced itself into a manifest possibility.

9. This is now the essence expressed or made manifest out of eternity into a time, and consists in the fore-mentioned forms in Sulphur, Mercury, and Salt, where the one is not divided or parted asunder from the other: It is one eternal essence, and shapes [1] itself into the properties of the desire according to the possibility of the manifestation; and we are to understand that one property is not, nor cannot be without the other; they are altogether the same only possibility: And now we will speak of their differences, viz. how this only possibility introduces itself into good and evil, viz. into still peace and constant unquietness.

10. We find seven especial properties in nature, whereby this only mother works all things, which are these, viz. First, the desire, which is astringent, cold, hard, and dark. Secondly, bitter, which is the sting of the astringent hard enclosure; [2] this is the cause of all motion and life. Thirdly, the anguish, by reason of the raging in the impression, where the impressed hardness falls into a tearing anguish and pain by reason of the sting.

11. Fourthly, the fire, where the eternal will in this anxious desire introduces itself into an anxious darting flash [or twinkling lightening], viz. into strength and devouring of the darkness, with which the hardness is again consumed, and introduced into a corporeal moving spirit.

12. Fifthly, the egress [3] of the free will out of the darkness and out of the fire, and dwelling in itself, where the free will has received the lustre, so that it enlightens and shines as a light out of the fire, and the potent desire of the free will, which it has sharpened in the fire (in that it is dead in the fire to the essence of the darkness of the first form, and consumed) does now in the light's desire draw into itself the essence from the dying of the fire, according to its hunger, which is now water; and in the lustre it is a tincture from the fire and light, viz. a love-desire, or a beauty of colours; [4] and here all colours arise; as we have fully set it down in our other books, but especially in the *Threefold Life of Man*.

13. Sixthly, the voice or sound, which in the first form is only a noise from the hardness, and is dead or mortified as to that [hardness] in the fire, and yet in the fifth form, in the love-desire, viz. in the pleasant property, it is again received as a clear

sound out of the dying of the fire in the lustre of the light in the tincture, wherein all the five senses, viz. Hearing, Seeing, Feeling, Smelling, and Tasting, arise in the tincture of the light from the fire.

14. Seventhly, the menstruum, or the seed of all these forms which the desire impresses into a comprehensive body or essence wherein all lies; whatever the six forms are spiritually, that the seventh is essentially.

15. Thus these are the seven forms of the mother of all beings, from whence all whatever is in this world is generated; and moreover the Most High has, according to this mother, introduced and created such properties as this mother is in her wrestling forms (understand, as she brings herself with the wrestling into properties) into a wheel,[1] which is as a mind of the mother, from whence she continually creates and works; and these are the stars with the planetary orb according to the platform of the eternal astrum, which is only a spirit, and the eternal mind in the wisdom of God, viz. the eternal nature, from whence the eternal spirits are proceeded and entered into a creaturely being.

16. And moreover the Most High has introduced the property of this wheel in the motion, as a life into the four officers, which manage the dominion in the pregnant mother; and these are the four elements to which the wheel of the mind, viz. the astrum affords will and desire; so that this whole being is but one only thing, and yet is so proportioned [or composed] as a mind of a man: Even as he is in soul and body, so also is this only essence; for it[2] was created out of this whole essence into an image according to eternity and time; out of eternity according to the soul, and out of time according to the outward essence, as a similitude and image of eternity and time, both according to the eternal will and mind and its essence, and also according to the mind of time and its essence: And therefore now we are rightly to consider of the sulphurean wheel of all essences, how the properties introduce themselves into good and evil, and again bring themselves out of good and evil.

17. The impression or desire, viz. the first form to nature, which is called, and is also the fiat, receives the desire's property according to the property of all the seven forms into itself, and impresses them, so that out of the nothing proceeds forth an essence according to the properties of the will: Now its own property, seeing it is only a desire, and impresses itself, is dark,

---

[1] Orb, or rotation.   [2] Or he.

and causes hardness, viz. a strong pulsation,[1] which is a cause of the tone or sound, which becomes yet more hard in the fire, viz. in the fourth form, where then the grossness dies away, and it is received again in the fifth form, viz. in the love-desire; and again it proceeds forth in its own property in the love-desire, and makes the sixth form, viz. the sound, voice, or tone out of the fire and water.

18. Now this tone or sound, which is called Mercury, arises in the first form, viz. in the impression, by reason of the will and attractive desire; for the attraction makes the motions and the compunction in the hardness, which we distinguish, and call the second form, but it is a son of the first, and in the first.

19. This second form or property is the raging, stinging, and bitter pain; for the first is astringent, and the second is drawing, viz. the desire into an essence; this same essence is the property of the first,[2] and the attraction makes therein the second property, viz. a bitter stinging which the hardness cannot endure; for it would be still, and thereupon it does more vehemently impress itself to withhold the sting, and yet the sting does thereby only grow the greater: Now the hardness, viz. the astringency draws inwards, and the sting from the hardness[3] upwards: Hence arises the first enmity and opposition; for the two forms, which yet are but one, make themselves their own enemies; and yet if this were not, there would not be any essence, neither body nor spirit, also no manifestation of the eternity of the abyss.

20. But now seeing the bitter sting cannot ascend, and the hardness also cannot hold or enclose it, they fall into a turning or breaking through like a wheel, which runs into itself as an horrible essence, where both properties are known only as one, and yet each remains in itself unaltered, and produce the third property between both, viz. the great anguish; out of which the will, understand the fixt will to nature, desires to go forth again into the liberty, viz. into the nothing, into the eternal rest; for here it has thus found itself, and manifested itself, and yet there is no separating or departing: and this anxious form is the mother of Sulphur, for the sting makes it[4] painful, and the hardness impresses it, that it is as a dying source, and yet it is the true original to life.

21. It has two properties in itself, viz. according to the

---

[1] Or noise.   [2] Or the first property.
[3] Or the sting in the hardness, viz. the hardness itself.
[4] Understand the mother of Sulphur.

impression or desire it is dark and hard; and according to the desire of the will, which wills to be free from the anguish, and enters again into the liberty, it is spiritual and light; and the sting breaks in pieces its conceived essence which the astringent desire conceives in itself, so that its essence is hard and spalt, and wholly darting as a flash of lightning from the darkness, and from the desire of the light, understand to the liberty.

22. Now these three forms are in one essence as a raging spirit; and the desire impresses these properties, so that an essence is made according to their property, viz. according to the astringent dark desire, viz. according to the first original: There is an earthly essence, out of which in the beginning of the great motion the earth was made, and according to the bitter raging spirit there is the instigation in the essence, viz. a poison, and it also imprints [or impresses] itself in the essence, from whence the earthliness is so wholly loathsome and bitter; and the third form, viz. the anguish gives a fiery property thereinto; and yet here there cannot be as yet any essence, but it is only a spiritual essence, and the mother to the essence.[1]

23. The fourth form in this essence is the fire, which as to one part takes its original out of the dark hard impression, viz. from the hardness, and from the raging sting in the anguish, which is the cold black fire, and the pain of the great anguish; and as to the other part it takes its original in the will's spirit to nature, which goes again out of this hard dark coldness into itself, viz. into the liberty without the nature of the austere motion, and enkindles the liberty, viz. the eternal lubet to the desire of nature, with its sharpness, which it has conceived in the impression, whereby it is a moving and stirring lustre: For the liberty is neither dark nor light; but by reason of the motion it is light, for its lubet brings itself into the desire to light, that it may be manifest in the light and lustre; and yet it cannot be otherwise brought to pass but through darkness, so that the light might be made known and manifest, and the eternal mind might find and manifest itself; for a will is only one thing and essence, but through the multiplicity its form is made manifest, that it is infinite, and a mere wonder, of which we speak with a babe's tongue, being only as a little spark out of these great infinite wonders.

24. Now understand us thus; the liberty is, and stands in the darkness (and inclining to the dark desire after the desire

[1] Prima materia.

of the light[1]), it attains with the eternal will the darkness; and
the darkness reaches after the light of the liberty, and cannot
attain it; for it encloses itself with the desire in itself, and makes
itself darkness in itself; and out of both these, viz. out of the
dark impression, and out of the desire of the light or liberty
towards the impression, there is a twinkling [or darting] flash
in the impression, viz. the original of the fire; for the liberty
shines in the impression, but the impression in the anguish
comprehends it into itself, and so it is now as a flash: But seeing
the liberty is incomprehensible, and as a nothing, and moreover
without and before the impression, and abyssal,[2] therefore the
impression cannot conceive or hold it; but it gives itself into the
liberty, and the liberty devours its dark property and essence,
and rules with the assumed mobility in the darkness, unapprehensible to the darkness.

25. Thus understand us right: There is in the fire a devouring;
the sharpness of the fire is from the austere impression of the
coldness and bitterness, from the anguish; and the devouring is
from the liberty, which makes out of the something again a
nothing according to its property.

26. And understand us very exactly and well: The liberty
will not be a nothing, for therefore the lubet of the liberty introduces itself into nature and essence, that it might be manifest
in power, wonder, and being; it likewise assumes to itself
through the sharpness in the cold and dark impression the
properties, that it might manifest the power of the liberty: For
it consumes the dark essence in the fire, and proceeds forth out
of the fire, out of the anguish of the impression, with the spiritual
properties in the light; as you see, that the outward light so
shines forth out of the fire, and has not the source and pain of
the fire in it, but only the property; the light manifests the
properties of the darkness, and that only in itself; the darkness remains in itself dark, and the light continues in itself
light.

27. The liberty (which is called God) is the cause of the light;
and the impression of the desire is the cause of the darkness
and painful source: Now herein understand two eternal beginnings, viz. two principles, one in the liberty in the light, the other
in the impression in the pain and source of the darkness, each
dwelling in itself.

---

[1] Or opposite to the dark desire, or dark impression, which is after the
light's desire.
[2] Or without any ground.

28. And understand us farther concerning their opening essence and will, how nature is introduced into seven properties; for we speak not of a beginning, for there is none in eternity; but thus the eternal generation is from eternity to eternity in itself; and this same eternal generation has according to the property of eternity through its own desire and motion intro-duced itself with this visible world (as with a likeness of the eternal spirit into such a creaturely being which is a type or platform of the eternal being) into a time, of which we will speak afterwards, and shew what the creature is, namely a similitude of the operation of eternity, and how it has also this same working temporally in itself.

29. Now concerning the fire understand us thus: The fire is the principle of every life; to the darkness it gives essence and source, else there would be no sensibility in the darkness, also no spirit, but mere hardness, a hard, sharp, bitter, galling sting, as it is really so in the eternal darkness; but so far as the hot fire may be obtained,[1] the dark compunctive property stands in the aspiring covetous greediness like to a horrible madness, that it may be known what wisdom and folly is.

30. Now the fire gives also desire, source, and properties to the light, viz. to the liberty; yet know this, the liberty, viz. the nothing, has no essence in itself, but the impression of the austere desire makes the first essence, which the will-spirit of the liberty (which has manifested itself through the nature of the desire) receives into itself, and brings it forth through the fire, where the grossness, viz. the rawness, does then die in the fire.

31. Understand it thus: When the flash of fire reaches the dark essentiality, then it becomes a great flagrat, where the cold fire is dismayed, and does as it were die, falls into a swoon,[2] and sinks down: And this flagrat is effected in the enkindling of the fire in the essence of the anguish, which has two properties in it; viz. the one goes downwards into the death's property, being a mortification of the cold fire, from whence the water arises, and according to the grossness [3] the earth is risen; and the other part ascends in the will of the liberty, in the lubet, as a flagrat of joyfulness; and this same essence is also mortified in the flagrat in the fire, understand the cold fire's property, and gives also a water-source, understand such a property.

32. Now the flash, when it is enkindled by the liberty, and by the cold fire, makes in its rising a cross with the comprehension

---

[1] Or reached. [2] Becomes impotent. [3] The *caput mortuum*.

of all properties; for here arises the spirit in the essence, and it stands thus: ☿

If thou hast here understanding, thou needest ask no more; it is eternity and time, God in love and anger, moreover heaven and hell.

33. The lower part, which is thus marked ☽, is the first principle, and is the eternal nature in the anger, viz. the kingdom of darkness dwelling in itself; and the upper part, with this figure ☿ is the salniter: The upper cross above the circle is the kingdom of glory, which proceeds forth in the flagrat of joy, in the will of the free lubet in itself out of the fire in the lustre of the light into the power of the liberty; and this spiritual water, which also arises in the flagrat of joy, is the corporality, or essentiality, in which the lustre from the fire and light makes a tincture, viz. a budding and growing, and a manifestation of colours from the fire and light.

34. And this form of separation between the living and the dead essentiality is the fifth form, and is called the love-desire; its original is from the liberty, which in the fire has introduced itself into a desire, viz. out of the lubet of the liberty into the fair and fiery elevation of joy, being a flame of love, which also imprints in its love-desire the property of that which it has conceived in the will of the eternal mind, which brings itself through the fire's sharpness again into itself, viz. into the first properties, which arise in the first impression, viz. from the motion and stirring; and the joyfulness arises out of the anguish: For this is joy, that the will to nature is delivered and freed from the dark anguish, for else there would be no knowledge of what joy was, if there was not a painful source; and in its love-desire it conceives the first properties in the first impression, which divide themselves in this desire into five forms; viz. from the fire-flash into seeing, for the water of love reaches the lustre of the tincture, wherein the sight consists; and from the hardness, viz. from the penetration of the sting in the hardness, into hearing, so that in this same nothing, viz. in the liberty, there is a sound, which the tincture catches, and brings it forth in the water of the desire: and from the raging sting into feeling, so that one property feels another; for if all properties were only one, there would be no seeing, hearing, or feeling, also no under-standing: And from the assimulation, that one property arises in the other, but with another property, comes the taste; and

from the egressive spirit of the properties (in that the egress of each property enters into the other) arises the smell.

35. Now these five forms do all of them together make in the love-desire, viz. in the fifth form, the sixth, that is, the sound or voice, as a manifestation of all the forms in the spirit's property, which the fiery light's desire encloses with the spiritual water as one only essence, which is now the fiery will's own essence, which has brought itself forth in the light, wherein it works and makes the seventh form, as an habitation of the sixth, from whence the essence and dominion of this world were generated, and introduced into a form according to the right[1] of the eternal birth.

36. Now understand us right; we do not hereby understand a beginning of the Deity, but the manifestation of the Deity: The Deity is herein known and manifested in Trinity; the Deity is the eternal liberty without all nature, viz. the eternal abyss; but thus it brings itself into byss for its own manifestation, eternal wisdom, and deeds of wonder.

37. The Eternal Father is manifested in the fire, and the Son in the light of the fire, and the Holy Spirit in the power of the life and motion proceeding from the fire in the light of the kingdom of joy, being the egressive power in the love-flame; we speak only by parts of the universal as a creature.[2]

38. The Deity is wholly everywhere all in all; but he is only called God according to the light of love, and according to the proceeding spirit of joy; but according to the dark impression he is called God's anger and the dark world; and according to the eternal fire-spirit he is called a consuming fire.

39. We give you only to understand the Being of all beings, whose original in itself is only one eternal essence; but with its own manifestation it comes into many beings, to its own honour and glory; and now we will shew you what the creature's life and dominion is in this all-essential Being.

40. Now therefore understand us right what we mean by these three words, Sulphur, Mercury, and Sal: In the eternity all is spirit; but when God moved himself with the eternal nature, wherein his own manifestation consists, he produced out of the spiritual essence a palpable and manifest essence, and introduced it into a creaturely being according to the eternal properties, which also consists of spirit and essence, according to the right[3] [or law] of eternity.

---

[1] Law, or appointment.   [2] Or in a creaturely manner.
[3] Or genuine property.

41. And now I will speak of the outward kingdom, viz. of the third principle or beginning; for in this world there is also light and darkness in each other as in the eternity: God has given this world a sun, as a nature-god of the outward powers, but he rules therein as Lord; the outward [kingdom] is only his prepared work, which he rules and makes with the assimulate, as a master makes his work with an instrument.

42. Sulphur is in the outward world, viz. in the mystery of the great God's manifestation, the first mother of the creatures; for it arises out of darkness, fire, and light; it is on one part, according to the dark impression, astringent, bitter, and anxious; and on the other part, towards the Deity, as a similitude of the Deity, it is fire, light, and water, which in the fire separates itself into two forms, viz. according to the mortification into water, and according to the life into oil, in which the true life of all the creatures of the outward world consists.

43. Mercury is the wheel of motion in the Sulphur; he is on one part according to the dark impression the stinging rager, and the great unquietness, and separates itself also in the fire in its mother, viz. in the Sulphur, into two properties, viz. into a twofold water; for in the mortification of the fire all is turned to water, understand into a living pleasant water according to the light, which produces silver in the brimstone, viz. in the seventh property of nature, which is the powerful body, and in the fire its water is quicksilver, and in the astringency, viz. in the anguish of the darkness, it is a rust or smoke; therefore if its outward water-body be cast into the fire, understand [that body] which it receives in Sulphur from the watery property, then it does evaporate,[1] for in the fire every property separates itself again into the first essence, from whence it came originally, where all things were only a spirit.

44. And then secondly it separates itself according to the water of the dark impression into a poison-source, which yet cannot be understood to be a water, but only a corporeal essence of the spirit; for as the spirit's property is, so is also its water; and even so it is in the fire-flagrat.

45. Further understand us in the fiery flagrat concerning the salniter, from whence the manifold salts and powers arise; for all the properties of the spirit are become corporeal in the great motion of the essence of all essences, and entered into a visible and comprehensible being: This flagrat is effected in the enkindling of the fire; and in the mortification of the fire it

---

[1] Or fly from thence as a smoke.

impresses into itself from the water's original a water, according to the property of the flagrat, which yet is rather fire than water, but its mortal essence is water according to the property of the flagrat; it is the comprisal of all properties, it brings forth in its comprehension, viz. in the fiery flagrat all properties in itself, and apprehends the property of the light in its powers, and also the property of the dark impression in its powers, and makes all fiery; one part according to the coldness, and one part according to the heat; but the most part according to the endless Mercury, which is the life of all essences in evil and good, in light and darkness.

46. This salniter is the mother of all salts in vegetables and animals, viz. in herbs and trees and everything; he is in all things, which give a taste and smell, the first root according to each thing's property; in the good (which grow in the love-desire in the oil of brimstone) he is good, powerful, and pleasant; and in the evil he is evil in the anguish of brimstone; and in the darkness he is the eternal horror and despair, continually desiring in the flagrat to aspire above the gates in the fire, from whence arises the will of all devils, and of all pride, to ascend above the humility of the love-desire; and in the fire is the trial of his essence, as we see how he clashes and consumes himself in the flash as a sudden thought.

47. For its essence arises not in the essence of eternity, also it cannot inherit it, but in the enkindling of the temporal fire, yet it is perceived in the eternal spirit by reason of the elevation of the joy; but according to the essence of mortification, viz. according to the salt of the fire it subsists in the fire: For this property arises out of the first desire, viz. in the essence of the first impression, which property the philosophers call Saturn, therefore the salt is manifold: All sharpness in the taste is salt, the good taste arises out of the oleous salt, and so also the smell, which is the egressive spirit in which the tincture appears as a lustre [or fair complexion] of colours.

48. Thus understand us right; the salniter in the fire-flagrat is the separation of the properties, where death and life separate themselves, viz. the life which enters with the love-desire into an essence and dominion; and then the life which in the flagrat of death, according to the property of the cold, sinks down in the mortification of the flagrat as an impotency, and gives weight; and according to the subtility it gives water, and according to the grossness of the austereness earth; and according to Sulphur and Mercury, sand and stones; and according to

the subtility in Sulphur and Mercury, understand according to the water of the same, it makes flesh, and according to the anxious darkness a smoke or rust; but according to the oleous property, viz. according to the love-desire, a sweet spiritual essence; and according to the spirit a pleasant smell; and according to the moving of the fire and light the [one] element; and from the lustre in the fire-flagrat with aspect of the light the precious tincture, which tinctures all oily salts, from whence the pleasant taste and smell arise.

49. The salnitral flagrat is the sude [1] in the essence, from whence the growth and pullulation arise, that there is a growing in the impression of the essence; the salt is the preservation, or upholding of the essence, so that a thing subsists in a body or comprehension; it holds the Sulphur and Mercury, else they would part from each other in the fire-flagrat.

50. All things consist of Sulphur, Mercury, and Salt: In the salnitral flagrat the element separates itself into four properties, viz. into Fire, Air, Water, and Earth, which in itself is none of these, but only a moving and gentle walming,[1] not as the air, but as a moving of the will in the body, a cause of life in the essence; for as the eternal Spirit of God proceeds from the Father, who is a spirit from the fire and light, and is the motion and life of the eternity; so likewise the air proceeds forth continually out of all the properties in the salnitral flagrat in the fire, from the anguish in Sulphur in the forcing mercurial wheel, as an impetuous aspiring motion; it is a son of all the properties, and also the life of the same; the fire of all the forms affords it, and also receives it again for its life; the water is its body, wherein it makes the seething in the salniter, and the earth is its power, wherein it enkindles its strength and fire-soul.

51. There is but one only element, and that unfolds itself in the salnitral flagrat into four parts, viz. with the enkindling it gives a consuming fire of the darkness, and its essence; and in the flagrat of the dying of the cold and the darkness it parts itself into essences, viz. according to the subtility into water, and according to the grossness into earth; and then according to the motion in the flagrat's walming into air, which does most resemble the element, but not wholly essentially; for the [one] element is neither hot nor cold, also not forcing or compulsive, but gently moving.

[1] Seething.

OF THE DESIRE OF THE PROPERTIES

52. Every property keeps its own desire; for a property is nothing else but an hunger, and the hunger forms itself into such an essence as itself is, and in the salnitral sude it gives such a spirit into the four elements; for the original of the sude is in the element, from whence four elements proceed in this flagrat.

53. Each body stands in the inward motion [1] in the element, and in the growth and life in the four elements; but every creature has not the true life of the element, but only the high spirits, as angels and souls of men, which stand in the first principle; in them the element is incitable: In the life of the third principle it stands still, and is as a hand of God, where he holds and governs the four elements as an exit, or instrument with which he works and builds.

54. Now every property of nature does in its hunger take its food out of the four elements; as the hunger is, so it takes a property out of the elements; for the four elements are the body of the properties, and each spirit eats of its own body.

55. First, there are the sulphurean properties according to the first and second impression, viz. according to the dark, astringent, and anxious impression; and then according to the love-impression in the light, viz. according to evil and good.

56. The dark hunger desires essence according to its property, viz. earthly things, all whatever resembles the earth; and the bitter hunger desires bitter raging, stinging, and pain; it receives into itself such an essence (as the poison-source) out of the elements: And the hunger of anguish desires anxious hunger, viz. the anguish in the brimstone; also the melancholy [takes] the desire to die, and continual sadness; and the fire-flash receives into it anger, aspiring, ambition, pride, a desiring to destroy all, and make it subject to it, a desire to domineer in and above all, to consume all, and to be peculiar; and it takes the bitterness from whence the flash arises to envy and hatred, and the astringency to covetousness, and the fire to anger and indignation.

57. Here is the true desire of God's anger and all devils, and of all whatever is against God and love; and this hunger draws such an essence into self; as it is to be known and searched out in the creatures, and also in the herbs.

58. Now the fire-flash is the end of the first desire, viz. of the

---

[1] Or as to its inward motion.

dark nature, and in the fire the dying of the first hunger and will begins; for the fire consumes all grossness of the first forms, and casts them into death; and here is the separation of both wills, viz. the one which enters back again into the property of death, and is a will in the life of the dark desire; as the devils have done, who would domineer in the fire-flash in the salnitral sude over time and eternity; but they were driven back by the Spirit of God, and spewed forth out of the love-desire as an abomination: And thus also it happens here to the wicked soul of man, upon which the election follows. Here is the [aim] or scope of the election of grace, of which the Scripture speaks, that God knows his; and here the eternal lubet of God's liberty apprehends the will-spirit, which is arisen in the dark centre, and brings it through the dying in the fire into the element.

59. In the salnitral flagrat lies the possibility backwards and forwards; if the will of the desire goes back, then it is as to the kingdom of this world [earthly], and as to the kingdom of the eternal world it is in God's anger, and cannot see God unless it be converted, and enters into the dying in the fire, and wholly dies to its selfness, and enters into the resignation of the eternal will in the salnitral flagrat into the element, viz. into the heavenly essentiality and corporality, so that the hunger may eat of the pure element; and then it has further no other desire; for it is in the fire dead to the austere dark hunger, which is evil; thus from the dying in the fire arises the light, for here the liberty is enkindled, that it becomes also an hunger, and a desire; this is now a love-desire, a love-hunger.

60. In the outward world it is the light of the sun in the four elements; and it is the bestial love-desire, viz. after the sulphurean body and essence, from whence the copulation and multiplication arise, viz. the vegetative life; and from the Mercury in the salniter (in which the sensible life is) therein the astrum gives the reason in the animals from the properties of the salniter.

61. For the whole astrum is nothing else but a salniter in the verbum fiat in the motion of the Being of all beings in the fiery flagrat, comprehended in the properties of the salts, wherein all the powers of the element stand as an external birth, which continually boil [1] in the four elements as a salnitral salt, and introduce their property in their desire in the four elements into the essence of bodies, as is to be seen in trees, herbs, grass, and all growing things.

[1] Or seethe.

62. Thus understand us farther concerning the second centre, which is manifest in the dying of the fire in the light, whereby the abyss of God's liberty introduces itself into the byss of nature, both with the inward world in the kingdom of heaven in the eternity; and then also with the outward kingdom in the time.

63. Now all this has also the properties of the desire, and takes its original from the first principle, viz. from the first centre, and there is yet no right dying in the fire; the dark essence only dies, and the will-spirit goes forth with the eternal will to nature again out of the fiery death in the light; it is only a transmutation of the spirit, so that an hunger arises out of the liberty, and this hunger is a love-desire; as to the soul of man it draws essence from the element of God, viz. in the divine salniter it [takes] the divine salts or powers into itself; and as to the outward world's desire it draws the oil out of the Sulphur into itself, in which [oil] the outward life burns; and so it is likewise in the vegetables and metals, and other things.

64. The sun makes the outward transmutation, and the divine light in the soul's property makes the inward; according as each thing stands in its degree, so does its hunger reach a property: those which are in the time [receive a property] from the time, and those in eternity likewise out of eternity: The hunger which proceeds from eternity eats of the eternity, and that which is of the time eats of the time. The true life of all creatures eats of the spiritual Mercury, viz. of the sixth form, where all salts are essentially; the spirit eats of the five senses, for they are the spirit's corporality; and the body, viz. the vegetable life, eats of the essence of the Sulphur and Salt; for Christ says in like manner, " Man liveth not by bread only, but by every word which proceedeth out of the mouth of God."

65. Now the sixth form of nature is the expressed spiritual word; and the speaking word therein is the eternal word: In the first impression in the darkness it is the word of God's anger; and in the outward world it is the poisonful Mercury, viz. a cause of all life and stirring, of all tones and sounds; now every property eats of its likeness in its degree; the hunger of time [eats] of time, and the hunger of eternity [eats] of eternity, both the spirit of Mercury and the spirit of Sulphur; whereas yet there are not two [spirits] but only two properties; all whatever does only take its original in one principle, as the creatures of the outward world, they have only one region, but a twofold inclination from the good and evil; but whatever takes its

original out of two principles, as man, he has also a twofold food and dominion, viz. from the dark centre, and from the outward centre; but if he dies to his self-hood, and brings his hunger into God's kingdom, then he may eat of the divine Mercury, viz. of the five divine sense with the soul, and of the element in the divine essence; and yet the outward man apprehends not in this life-time the divine essence corporeally, but only through the imagination, where the inward body penetrates the outward; as the sun shines through the water, and yet the water continues still water, for here is our fall in Adam.

66. The element will wholly penetrate the four elements, and it was wholly one in man, but in the curse the element separated from the soul, so that the poor soul now lives only in the vessel of the four elements unless it again enters in the death of its earthly will into the divine desire, and springs forth in the element.

67. Thus also the outward body is in the curse, and eats of the cursed earth's property, viz. only of the earthly salniter, where one hunger of the earthly properties continually opposes another; for the curse is a loathsome abominate in all salts, and from thence it comes that a constant contrariety arises in the outward body; for one hunger of the properties receives [or catches] from the other the abominate: [1] Now to help the body that it may be freed from the abominate, it must take the assimulate of the lothing abominate, which is risen in the body as a sude or seething, and introduce it into the dying of the fire, and bring it out in the love-desire from the curse of the vanity; now this is no otherwise effected but as the true life dies to the dark vanity.

68. The abominate of the outward life arises from a property of the salt which is contrary to the oil of the life: Thus the abominate does forth with enkindle itself in the four elements, and begins to seethe in the salniter as a strange life: This strange life does at last darken and destroy the first true life, if it be not resisted; and it can have no better help than with the assimulate of the introduced abominate, which the life has taken into itself; *therefore that must be done to the cure, which is to be done to the life*, that it might be freed from the abominate.

69. The cure must be freed from the same abominate, which it has received in the four elements from the like false insinuation [influence, or impression], it must be brought into the death of the four elements, and its spirit must also be tinctured in the fifth form with the venus desire, viz. with a pleasant essence,

Nauseate, abomination.

nothing else but a strife and a contrary will, a self-envying,[1] a desire of the abominate, a lust of death.

3. For the lust which arises out of the desire must die; if the will (which proceeded out of the great mystery of eternity, which the Spirit of God breathed into the image of man, viz. into the likeness) will be freed from the abominate and contrary will, then the desire of the four elements must die, and the will must enter again into the one only element, it must again receive the right of eternity, and act and go forth in one element, in manner also as God created him, whom he himself has opposed, and brought himself into the dominion of the four elements, in which he has inherited death, and also the strife in the forms of life, from whence arises his sickness, loathing, and enmity: For all whatever lives in God's will, that is not risen in the self-will, or if it be risen therein, it is again dead to the own [or selfish] desire.

4. Every will which enters into its self-hood, and seeks the ground of its life's form, the same breaks itself off from the great mystery, and enters into a self-fulness, it will be its own [or of its own selfish jurisdiction], and so it is contrary to the first mystery, for the same is alone all: And this child is accounted evil, for it strives in disobedience against its own mother which has brought it forth; but if the child does again introduce its will and desire into that, from whence it is generated and risen originally, then it is wholly one with the same, and cannot be annoyed by anything; for it enters into the nothing, viz. into the essence, from whence it proceeded.

5. Thus, O man! understand what thou art to do; behold thyself in thyself, what thou art, whether or no thou standest in the resignation of thy mother (out of which thou wert generated and created in the beginning), whether thou art inclined with the same will; if not, then know that thou art a rebellious, stubborn, disobedient child, and hast made thyself thine own enemy, in that thou art entered into self-desire and will, and hast made thyself thy own self-ful possession, so that thou canst not dwell in the first mother, but in thyself: For thy will is entered into self-hood; and all that does vex, plague, and annoy thee, is only thy self-hood; thou makest thyself thy own enemy, and bringest thyself into self-destruction or death.

6. Now if thou wilt get again out of death, then thou must wholly forsake thy own self-desire, which has introduced itself into strange essence, and become in self-hood, and the self-desire, as a nothing, so that thou dost no longer will or desire to thyself,

[1] Our own enemies.

but wholly and fully introduce thy desire again with the resignation into the eternal, viz. into God's will, that the same will may be thy will and desire.

7. Without this there is nothing but misery and death, a continual dying and perishing; for hence arises the election of grace. If the human will (which is departed out of the unity of eternity, and entered into a self-fulness, viz. into a selfish lust and desire) does again break itself off from self-hood, and enter into the mortification of self-will, and introduce its desire again only into the first mother, then the first mother does again choose it to be its child, and makes it again one with the only will of eternity: But that [will or person] which continues in self-hood, he continues in the eternal dying, viz. in an eternal selfish enmity; and this also is only called sin, because that it is an enmity against God, in that the creature will be at its self-ful command and government.

8. Thus in its self-hood, viz. in a dominion full of contention and strife, it cannot either will or do anything that is good; and as it does impose, awaken, and powerfully stir up to its self nothing else but the dying and death, so likewise it can do nothing else to its fellow-members; for hence also arises the falsehood [or lyes], that the creature denies the union with [or in] the will of God, and sets his self-hood in the place; so that it goes forth from the unity into desires and self-lusts: If it did but truly know that all beings were its mothers, which brought it forth, and did not hold the mother's substance for its own, but for common, then the covetousness, envy, strife, and contrary will and enmity would not arise; from which the anger, viz. the fire of destruction does arise.

9. All sins arise from self; for the self-hood forces itself with the desire into its self-fulness; it makes itself covetousness and envy, it draws in its own desire strange essence into itself, and makes the possessor of the strange essence also an enemy against itself, so that sin is wrought with sin, vileness with vileness, and all run confusedly in and among one another, as a mere abomination before the eternal mother.

10. In like manner also we are to consider of the regenerate will, which goes out of its selfishness or self-hood again into the resignation; the same becomes also an enemy and an abominate to self-hood; as sickness is an enemy to health, and on the contrary, health an enemy to sickness: Thus the resigned will, and also the self-will are a continual enmity, and an incessant lasting war and combat.

11. Self-will seeks only what serves to its self-hood; and the resigned will is not at all careful, but brings its desire only into its eternal mother, that it might be one with her: It will be a nothing, that the mother might be alone all in it. Self-will says to the resigned will, Thou art foolish, in that thou givest thyself to death, and yet mightest well live gloriously in me; but the resigned will says, Thou art my abomination, pain, and enmity, and bringest me out of eternity into a time only into perplexity and misery; thou plaguest me a while, and then thou givest my body to the earth, and the soul to hell.

12. True real resignation is the mortification of the abominate against God; he that wholly forsakes his self-hood, and gives himself up with mind and desire, senses and will, into God's mercy, into the dying of Jesus Christ, he is dead to the earthly world with the will, and is a twofold man; where the abominate works only in itself to death, but the resigned will lives in Christ's death, and rises up continually in Christ's resurrection in God: And though the self-desire sins, which indeed can do nothing else but sin, yet the resigned will lives not in sin, for it is mortified to the desire of sin, and lives through Christ in God in the land of the living; but self-hood lives in the land of death, viz. in the continual dying, in the continual enmity against God.

13. The earthly man is the curse of God, and is an abominate before God's holiness; he can do nothing else but seek his self-hood, for he is in the wrath of God: And though he does some thing that is good, yet he does it not from his own self-will, but the will resigned in God compels him that he must do what his self would not willingly do: And now if he does it, he does it as an instrument of the resigned will, not from his own desire, but from God's will, which guides the resigned will in the desire as an instrument.

14. Therefore now whoever will see the kingdom of God, and attain thereunto, he must educe [or bring forth] his soul out of self-hood, out of the earthly desire, as the physician brings forth the cure of the disease from the painful [tormenting] desire, and introduces it into a love-desire; and then the cure also brings forth the sickness in the body out of the painful desire, and sets it into a love-desire: Sickness becomes the servant of the physic; and so likewise the evil earthly will, when the soul's will is cured, is the resigned will's servant.

15. The elemental and sidereal man must only be the instrument wherewith man's soul labours in the resigned will; for thereto God has also created it; but the soul has made and set

up itself in Adam for lord and master, and is entered into his prison, and given its will thereinto; but if it will be acknowledged for God's child, then it must again die to the same, and be wholly mortified to the earthly self-hood and desire in God's will in Christ's death, and be wholly regenerated anew in God's will, and deprive the earthly will in self-hood of its power, and rule over it, and guide it in subjection and command, as a master does his instrument, and then self-hood loses the power and prevalence, and the lust of self-hood arises as a continual longing; self-hood does then continually long after the forms of its own life, viz. after self-glory, and after earthly abundance, also after envy and anger, whether it may be able to attain that abundance; and also after the cunning lyes of falsehood: These are the vital forms of the earthly self-hood.

16. But the resigned will does as a potent champion continually bruise the head of this serpent, and says, "Thou art arisen from the devil, and God's anger, I will have none of thee, thou art an abomination before God." And though the resigned will is sometimes captivated with false lust, when it overwhelms and overpowers it with the devil's desire and insinuation of its imagination, yet the resigned will does forthwith cry to the word [1] of God, that God's will does again bring it out of the abomination of death.

17. The resigned will has no rest here in this cottage, but must always be in combat, for it is lodged in a false house: It is indeed in itself in God's hand; but, without itself it is in the jaws and throat of the abyss of God's anger in the kingdom of devils, which continually pass up and down with it, and desire to try and tempt the soul, viz. the centre.

18. In like manner also the good angels stand by him in the resigned will, viz. in the divine desire, and defend him from the poisonful imagination of the devil; they keep off the fiery darts of the wicked one, as St. Peter says.

19. For all do work and desire in man, God's love and anger: He stands while he is in this tabernacle in the gate either to go out or in: Both eternal principles are stirring in him; to which the soul's will gives itself, of that it is received, and thereto it is chosen; he is drawn of both, and if the will of the soul remains in self-hood, then he is in the hand of God's anger.

20. But if he departs out of his self-hood, and forsakes his own damnation, and continually casts himself only into God's mercy, viz. into the suffering and death of Christ, and into his

[1] Voice or breath.

resurrection and restoration, and wills nothing of himself, but what God wills in him, and by him, then the will is dead to the life and desire of God's anger; for it has no own life, but lies in the death of self-hood and the desire of the devil; and the anger of God cannot reach him; for he is as a nothing, and yet is in God, and lives in the divine essence wholly, but not to himself, but to his first mother of eternity: He is again in the limit or place where he was before he was a creature, and in the will wherein God created him, and is an instrument in the voice of God, upon which only the will-spirit of God does strike, to its honour and deeds of wonder.

21. All self-ful seeking and searching in self-hood is a vain thing; self-will apprehends nothing of God, for it is not in God, but without God in its self-hood; but the resigned will apprehends it; for it does not do it, but the spirit in whom it stands still, whose instrument it is, he manifests himself in the divine voice in it as much as he pleases: And though it may apprehend much in self-hood by searching and learning (which is not wholly to no purpose), yet its apprehension is only without in the expressed word, viz. in a form of the letter; and it understands nothing of the form of the expressed word, how the same is in its ground; for it is only born in the form from without, and not in the power of the universal pregnatress, whose ground has neither beginning, comprehension, or end.

22. Now that he is born from within out of the speaking voice of God in God's will-spirit, he goes in the byss and abyss everywhere free, and is bound to no form; for he goes not in self-hood, but the eternal will guides him as its instrument, according as it pleases God: but he that is born only in the letter, he is born in the form of the expressed word, and goes on in self-hood, and is a self-ful voice; for he seeks what he pleases, and contends about the form, and leaves the spirit which has made the form.

23. Such a doctor Babel is; it contends, wrangles, and rages about the form of the word, and continually introduces the self-ful spirit and understanding in the form, and cries out, Here is the Church of Christ; and it is only a self-ful voice, understanding nothing of the spirit of the form which is incomprehensible, and strikes upon its prepared instrument without limit and measure as it pleases. For conjecture, opinion, or the self-ful own imagination, which arises in the expressed voice [or literal outward word], is not God's word; but that which arises in God's Spirit in the wholly resigned will in divine power in the eternal

speaking word, that takes its original out of God's voice, and makes the form in the heart, viz. a divine desire, whereby the soul's will is drawn into God.

24. He is a shepherd, and teacher of Christ, who enters in through the door of Christ, that is, who speaks and teaches by Christ's spirit; without this there is only the form, viz. the history[1] that was once brought to pass, and that a man need only accept of it, and comfort himself therewith: but this will remains without, for it will be a child of an assumed grace, and not wholly die to its self-hood in the grace, and become a child of grace in the resigned will.

25. All whatever teaches of Christ's satisfaction, and comforting oneself with Christ's suffering, if it teaches not also the true ground how a man must wholly die to self-hood in the death, and give himself up in the resigned will wholly into the obedience of God, as a new child of a new will, the same is without, and not in the speaking voice of God, viz. in Christ's door.

26. No flattering or comforting avails anything, but to die to the false will and desire in Christ's death, and to arise in the wholly resigned will in Christ's resurrection in him, and continually mortify the earthly self-hood, and quench the evil which the earthly will introduces into the imagination, as an evil fire which would fain continually burn.

27. Comforting and setting the suffering of Christ in the forefront is not the true faith; no, no, it is only without, and not within: But a converted will, which enters into sorrow for its earthly iniquity, and will have none of it any more; and yet finds that it is kept back by the self-ful earthly lust, and with his converted will departs sincerely out of this abomination and false desire into God's mercy, and casts himself with great anxious [earnest] desire into Christ's obedience, suffering, and death, and in the converted will wholly dies to the earthly lust in Christ's death, which will not depart out of Christ's death, and continually cries Abba, loving Father! take thy dear Son's obedience for me; let me only in his death live in his obedience in thee; let me die in him, that I may be nothing in myself, but live and be in his will, in his humanity in thee; receive me, but wholly in his resurrection, and not in my unworthiness; but receive me in him; let me be dead in him, and give me his life, that I may be thy obedient son in him, that his suffering and death may be mine, that I may be before the same Christ in

[1] That Christ once died and suffered for us, etc.

him who has deprived death of its might, viz. a branch or twig of his life.

28. Thus, and no otherwise, is the true Christian faith; it is not only a comforting, but an incessant desire; the desire obtains the suffering of Christ, which [desire] would continually fain be obedient, if it knew but how it should behave itself before him, which continually does fall down before him, and dives itself into the deepest humility before him; it suffers and does all things readily, only that it might but receive grace; it is willing to take the cross of Christ upon itself, and regards not all the scorn of all the world in its self-hood, but continually presses forward into Christ's love-desire: This desire does only grow out of Christ's death, and out of his resurrection in God, and brings forth fruit in patience which is hidden in God, of which the earthly man knows nothing, for it finds itself in its self-hood.

29. A true Christian is a continual champion, and walks wholly in the will and desire in Christ's person, as he hath walked up and down upon the earth. Christ, when he was upon the earth, desired to overcome death, and bring the human self-hood in true resignation into divine obedience: And this likewise a right Christian desires to do; he desires continually to die to the iniquity of death and wrath, and give himself up to obedience, and to arise and live in Christ's obedience in God.

30. Therefore, dear brethren, take heed of putting on Christ's purple mantle without a resigned will; the poor sinner without sorrow for his sins, and conversion of his will, does only take it in scorn to Christ: Keep you from that doctrine which teaches of self-ful abilities, and of the works of justification.

31. A true Christian is himself the great and anxious work which continually desires to work [1] in God's will, and forces against the self-ful lusts of self-hood, and wills continually so to do, and yet is many times hindered by self-hood: He breaks self-hood, as a vessel, wherein he lies captive, and buds forth continually in God's will-spirit, with his desire resigned in God (as a fair blossom springs out of the earth), and works in and with God, what God pleases.

32. Therefore let the true Christendom know, and deeply lay to heart, what is now told and spoken to her, viz. that she depart from the false conjecture [or opinion] of comforting, without conversion of the will; it is only an outward [expressed] form

[1] Or works desire.

of the new-birth; a Christian must be one spirit with Christ, and
have [1] Christ's will and life in him; the form does not renew
him, neither comforting, or giving good words does at all help
or avail, but a mortifying of the evil inbred will, which is God's
child, and born out of Christ's death, no other will attains
Christ's inheritance; my much knowing doth not also do it;
the herdsman in the field is as near to it as the doctor; no wit
or subtle art in disputation about the way of God does help or
avail anything thereto, it is only a let and hinderance; the true
will enters into the love of God and his children; it seeks no
form, but falls down before its creator, and desires the death of
its false self-hood; it seeks the work of love towards all men; it
will not flourish in the world's scorn, but in its God; its whole
life is a mere repentance, and a continual sorrow for the evil
which cleaves to it: It seeks no glory or applause to shew itself,
but lives in humility: It acknowledges itself always as unworthy and simple; its true Christianity is always hidden in its
self-hood. He says, " I am in my self-hood an unprofitable
servant, and have not as yet begun to do or work repentance
right." He is always in the beginning to work repentance, and
would always fain reach the gates of the sweet grace; he labours
for that purpose as a woman in travail labours to bring forth,
and knows not how it fares with him; the Lord hides his face
from him, that his working may be great towards him: He sows
in anguish and tears, and knows not his fruit, for it is hidden
in God; as a painful traveller goes a long way, aiming at his
wished-for journey's end, so also he runs after the far mark of
his rest, and finds it not; unless his pearl does appear to him
in its beauty, and embraces him in its love: If it again departs
from his self-hood, then arises sighing and sorrowing again with
continual desire; and one day calls another, the day the night,
and the night the morning; and yet there is no place of rest in
the earthly self-hood, but only in the fair solar lustre of his
precious pearl; when the sun arises to him in the darkness,
then the night departs, and all sorrow and anguish fly
away.

33. Therefore, dear brethren, learn to take heed and beware
of contention, where men contend about the literal form: A
true Christian has nothing to contend for, for he dies to his
reason's desire; he desires only God's knowledge in his love and
grace, and lets all go which contends and strives about the form,
for Christ's spirit must make the form in himself; the outward

[1] Bear, or carry.

form is only a guide: God must become man, or else man becomes not God.

34. Therefore a Christian is the most simple [or plainest] man upon the earth, as Isaiah says, " Who is so simple as my servant? " All heathens desire self-hood, and tear and devour one another for the authority and honours: But a true Christian desires to die to them; he seeks not his own, but Christ's honour. All whatever contends about self-hood, viz. about the self-ful honour and pleasure of this life, the same is heathenish, and far worse than heathenish; yea like the devil, who departed from God into self-fulness: Let it cover itself with Christ's mantle as much as ever it will, yet the man of false self-hood is lodged under it; if he will be a Christian, then he must quite die to self-hood, that the same may only hang to him from without as a garment of this world, wherein he is a stranger and pilgrim, and always consider and think that he is but a servant in his high office, and serves God therein as a servant, and not be his own lord and master.

35. All whatever does lord itself without God's call and appointment, the same is from the devil, and serves the devil in his own power and form: Defend and flatter thyself as much as thou wilt, it does not avail before God; thy own heart accuses thee that thou art a false branch; thy nobility and highness do not at all avail or help thee in the sight of God, if thou dost not thereby drive in God's order; thy office is not thine, but God's; if thou walkest falsely therein, then thy own judgement is upon thee, and condemns thee to death; thou art a servant; and though thou art a king, yet thou servest, and must enter with the poorest into the new birth, or else thou shalt not see God.

36. All self-ful assumed [or arrogated] laws and authority, wherewith the poor are vexed and oppressed, do all come from self-hood, whose original is in the expressed form, which has with the form introduced itself into a self-hood, and brought itself out quite from God: Whatever does not serve in a servant's office before God, the same is all false, let it be either high or low, learned or unlearned: We are altogether servants of the great God; nothing brings itself into a self-fulness, unless it be born in God's anger in the impression of nature: And though a Christian possesses an own-hood, which is not false, yet he is only but a servant therein, viz. a distributer for his Master, a steward and overseer of his Master's work: He deals for his Master therein, and not for his self-hood only; all whatever he

plots and devises to bring into self-hood, and brings it, that he brings into the anxious cabinet of covetousness, envy, and self-ful pleasure of the flesh, viz. into a vessel that is separated from God, viz. into the impression of nature, and steals from his Lord and Master who has set him up for a steward; he is a sacrilegious person,[1] let him excuse himself, and pretend what he pleases.

37. A true Christian acknowledges himself for a servant of God, to whom it is given in charge to deal right with God's works. He is not his own, for he is also not at home in this earthly work of this tabernacle: Let him seek, search, plant and build, traffic and trade; and whatever else he does, he must always know that he does it to God, and shall give an account thereof, and that he is a stranger and servant in this work, and serves his Master; and not at all look upon the course of his forefathers who have walked therein in the pleasure of the earthly life; whoever does so is far from the kingdom of God, and can with no conscience and ground call himself [or think himself to be] a Christian; for he stands only in the form of Christianity, and not in the spirit of Christ; the form shall be destroyed, and cease with time, but the spirit remains steadfast for ever.

38. A true Christian is in the spirit a Christian, and in continual exercise to bring forth its own form, not only with words in sound and shew, but in the power of the work, as a visible palpable form, not weening, conjecturing, and giving good words out of the self-ful self-hood, and yet remaining in self-hood; but a dying to self-hood, and a growing forth in the will of God in the love-self-hood as a servant of God in God's deeds of wonder; a helping to strike his instrument in God's will, and be a true sounding string in God's harmonious concert; a continual making word in God's voice, viz. in the verbum fiat, which makes and works in and with God what God makes, forms, and works, as an instrument of God.

39. Therefore, O thou dear Christendom, behold thyself, whether thou workest in the working word of God in his will, or whether thou standest only in the form of Christendom, and workest thy own self-fulness in falsehood: Thou wilt find, how thou art become an abomination before the Most High, and thy casting forth [2] from the Most High out of this form (which thou in thy self-hood hast introduced into his expressed form) shall presently follow; and that because thou coverest thyself with the true form, and art a false child therein: Therefore thou

---

[1] Text, a pilferer from God and his substance.   [2] Spewing out.

art sought, and found with a false veil [or covering] in thy own form.

40. And as thou hast brought thyself into a false self-ful form under the true form, so thou shalt also destroy thyself, whereto the heaven helps thee, which thou hast a long time served in obedience, and from this there is no withholding; thy work is found to be in the turba, which shall well satisfy and satiate itself in destroying, as thou hast built up thyself in thy apostate falsehood in thy own form under the name of the true form, and hast played the hypocrite before God with the shew and ostentation of holiness, and only served the earthly man: But the servant of the Lord shall be sought and found; the Lord feeds his lambs in his own form, and brings them into his pasture; all the haughty and wealthy of the world shall find by experience what judgment the Lord will bring upon the face of all the earth, and all wicked hope shall be destroyed; for the day of the harvest draws near: "A terror from the Lord shaketh the earth, and his voice soundeth in all the ends of the earth;" and the star of his wonders arises, no one hinders it, for it is concluded of in the counsel of the watchmen in the gates of the deep.

41. Therefore let every one seek and find himself; for the time of visitation is at hand, that he may be found in his love; for the turba has found all false lust in it, and the Most High worker of all essences manifests the turba; and then all false lust or imagination becomes manifest, and each thing enters into its eternal keeper, for all things are generated out of imagination: So also it shall receive its property in the imagination, and every imagination [1] reaps its own work which it has wrought; for to that end all things have appeared, that the eternity might be manifest in a time: With deeds of wonder it brought itself into the form of time, and with deeds of wonder it carries itself forth again out of the time into its first place.

42. All things enter again into that from whence they proceeded; but they keep their own form and model, as they have introduced themselves in the expressed word; and everything shall also be received of its likeness, and the end is always; [2] and as all things generate themselves in the expressed word, so also they are signed in their inward form, which also signs the outward.

43. The self-ful will makes a form according to its innate nature; but a form is made in the resigned will according to the platform or model of eternity, as it was known in the glass

---

[1] Lubet or longing desire.   [2] Or, this is always the end.

of God's eternal wisdom before the times of this world; so the eternal will figures and forms it into a model of its likeness to the honour and wonderful acts of God; for all whatever goes on in its self-hood, the same forms itself; but what resigns itself freely, that is formed of the free will: Now no self-ful form with its own self-will can inherit the only Eternal Being; for where there are two wills in one, there is enmity.

44. Seeing then God is one only God, then all whatever will live in him must be like his will and word: As a concert of music must be tuned into one harmony, though there be many strings, and manifold voices and sounds therein; so must the true human harmony be tuned with all voices into a love melody, and that will-spirit which is not tuned unto the only concert in the divine voice, the same is cast forth out of this tune, and brought into its self-ful tune, viz. into its true fellow-voices of its own likeness; for every likeness shall receive its own.

45. Has any been here an evil spirit? Then he shall be introduced into the root of his likeness; for every hunger receives its like into itself; now the whole manifestation of eternity with this time is nothing else but an hunger and generation; as the hunger is, so is also the essence of its satiating; for with the hunger the creature took its beginning, and with the hunger it enters into its eternal [being].

46. In the hunger the spirit with the body is generated, and in the same hunger it goes into its eternal being, unless it breaks its first hunger, and brings itself into another by mortification, else all is at its end as soon as it is born; but death is the only means whereby the spirit may enter into another source and form: If it dies to its self-hood, and breaks its will in death, then a new twig springs forth out of the same, but not according to the first will, but according to the eternal will; for if a thing enters into its nothing, then it falls again to the creator, who makes that thing as it was known in the eternal will, before it was created to a creature; there it is in the right aim or limit of eternity, and has no turba, for it is in nature's end.

47. Whatever runs on in nature torments itself, but that which attains nature's end, the same is in rest without source, and yet works, but only in one desire: All whatever makes anguish and strife in nature, that makes mere joy in God; for the whole host of heaven is set and tuned into one harmony; each angelical kingdom into a peculiar instrument, but all mutually composed together into one music, viz. into the only love-voice of God:

Every string of this melody exalts and rejoices the other; and it is only a mere ravishing lovely and delightful hearing, tasting, feeling, smelling, and seeing: Whatever God is in himself, that the creature is also in its desire in him; a God-angel, and a God-man, God all in all, and without him nothing else. As it was before the times of this world in his eternal harmony [or voice], so also it continues in the creaturely voice in him in his eternity; and this is the beginning and the end of all things.

CHAPTER XVI

CONCERNING THE ETERNAL SIGNATURE AND HEAVENLY JOY;
WHY ALL THINGS WERE BROUGHT INTO EVIL AND GOOD

1. THE creation of the whole creation is nothing else but a manifestation of the all-essential, unsearchable God; all whatever he is in his eternal unbeginning generation and dominion, of that is also the creation, but not in the omnipotence and power, but like an apple which grows upon the tree, which is not the tree itself, but grows from the power of the tree: Even so all things are sprung forth out of the divine desire, and created into an essence, where in the beginning there was no such essence present, but only that same mystery of the eternal generation, in which there has been an eternal perfection.

2. For God has not brought forth the creation, that he should be thereby perfect, but for his own manifestation, viz. for the great joy and glory; not that this joy first began with the creation, no, for it was from eternity in the great mystery, yet only as a spiritual melody and sport in itself.

3. The creation is the same sport out of himself, viz. a platform or instrument of the Eternal Spirit, with which he melodises: and it is even as a great harmony of manifold instruments which are all tuned into one harmony; for the eternal word, or divine sound or voice, which is a spirit, has introduced itself with the generation of the great mystery into formings, viz. into an expressed word or sound: And as the joyful melody is in itself in the spirit of the eternal generation, so likewise is the instrument, viz. the expressed form in itself, which the living eternal voice guides, and strikes with his own eternal will-spirit, that it sounds and melodises; as an organ of divers and various sounds or notes is moved with one only air, so that each note, yea every pipe has its peculiar tune, and yet there is but one manner of air or breath in all notes, which sounds in each note or pipe according as the instrument or organ is made.

4. Thus in the eternity there is only one spirit in the whole work of the divine manifestation, which is the manifestator in the expressed voice and also in the speaking voice of God, which

is the life of the grand mystery, and of all that is generated from
thence; he is the manifestator of all the works of God.

5. All the angelical kingdoms are as a prepared work, viz.
a manifestation of the eternal sound of the voice of God, and
are as a particularity out of the great mystery, and yet are only
one in the divine eternal speaking word, sound, or voice of God;
for one only spirit rules them; each angelical prince is a property
out of the voice of God, and bears the great name of God; as we
have a type and figure of it in the stars of the firmament, and
in the kingdoms and dominions upon the earth among all
generations, where every lord bears his high title, respective
name and office: So likewise do the stars in the firmament,
which are altogether one only dominion in power under them,
where the great stars bear the name and the office of the forms
in the mystery of the seven properties, and the other after them,
as a particularity of houses or divisions, where every one is a
peculiar harmony or operation, like a kingdom, and yet all
proceeds in one harmony; like a clock-work, which is entirely
composed in itself, and all the pieces work mutually together
in one; and yet the great fixed stars keep their peculiar property
in the essence of operation, especially the seven planets according
to the seven properties of nature, as an under pregnatress of the
eternal mystery, or as an instrument of the spirit out of the
eternal mystery.

6. This birth of the astrum begets in the four elements, viz.
in its body or essence, joy and sorrow, and all is very good in
itself; only the alteration of the creature proceeds from the
lustful imagination, whereby the creature elevates the wrath of
the fire in the properties, and brings them forth out of the
likeness of their accord: Nothing is evil which remains in the
equal accord; for that which the worst causes and makes with
its coming forth out of the accord, that likewise the best makes
in the equal accord; that which there makes sorrow, that makes
also in the likeness joy; therefore no creature can blame its
creator, as if he made it evil; all was very exceeding good;
but with its own elevation and departure out of the likeness it
becomes evil, and brings itself out of the form [or property] of
the love and joy, into a painful tormenting form and property.

7. King Lucifer stood in the beginning of his creation in
highest joyfulness, but he departed from the likeness, and put
himself forth out of the accord [or heavenly concert] into the
cold, dark, fiery generation, out of which the hot fiery generation
arises; he forsook his order, and went out of the harmony,

wherein God created him; he would be lord over all, and so he entered into the austere fire's domination, and is now an instrument in the austere fire's might, upon which also the all-essential spirit strikes and sounds upon his instrument, but it sounds only according to the wrathful fire's property: as the harmony, viz. the life's-form is in each thing, so is also the sound or tone of the eternal voice therein; in the holy [it is] holy, in the perverse it is perverse: All things must praise the Creator of all beings; the devils praise him in the might of wrath, and the angels and men praise him in the might of love.

8. The Being of all beings is but one only Being, but in its generation it separates itself into two principles, viz. into light and darkness, into joy and sorrow, into evil and good, into love and anger, into fire and light, and out of these two eternal beginnings [or principles] into the third beginning, viz. into the creation, to its own love-play and melody, according to the property of both eternal desires.

9. Thus each thing goes into its harmony, and is guided [or driven] by one only spirit, which is in each thing according to the property of the thing; and this is the clock [or watch-work] of the great mystery of eternity in each principle according to the property of the principle, and then according to the innate form of the composed instrument of the same creatures, even in all these beginnings [or principles].

10. Death is the bound-mark of all whatever is temporal, whereby the evil may be destroyed; but that which arises out of the eternal beginnings, and in its harmony and life's-form enters into another figure, that departs out of God's harmony, out of the true order wherein God created it, and is cast out of the same harmony into its likeness, as a dissonant discording melody or sound in the great excellent well-tuned harmony; for it is an opposite contrary thing, and bears another tone, sound, and will, and so it is introduced into its likeness; and therefore hell is given to the devil for his house and habitation, because he introduced his life's-form into the anger of God, and into the fiery wrath of the eternal nature, so that now he is the instrument in the eternal fire of God, and the anger-spirit strikes his instrument, and yet it must stand to the honour and admiration of God, and be the sport and play in the desire and property of the wrathful anger.

11. The anger and wrath of God are now his joy, not as if he feared, sorrowed, and lived in impotency; no, but in great strength and fiery might, as a potent king and lord, yet only

in the same property of which he himself is, viz. in the first
principle in the dark world.

12. The like also we are to know concerning the angelical
world, viz. the second principle, where God's light and glorious
beauty shine in every being [or thing], and the divine voice or
sound rises up in all creatures in great joyfulness; where the
spirit proceeding from the divine voice makes a joyfulness, and
an incessant continual love-desire in those creatures, and in all
the divine angelical beings: As there is an anguish-source and
trembling in the painful fire, so in like manner there is a trembling
joyfulness in the light and love-fire, viz. a great elevation of the
voice of God, which makes in the angels and in the like creatures,
as the souls of men, a great manifestation of the divine joyfulness.

13. The voice [or breath] of God continually and eternally
brings forth its joy through the creature, as through an instrument; the creature is the manifestation of the voice of God:
What God is in the eternal generation of his eternal word out of
the great mystery of the Father's property, that the creature is
in the image as a joyful harmony, wherewith the Eternal Spirit
plays or melodises.

14. All properties of the great eternal mystery of the pregnatress of all beings are manifest in the holy angelical and humane
creatures; and we are not to think thereof, as if the creatures
only stood still and rejoiced at the glory of God, and admired
only in joy; not, but it is as the Eternal Spirit of God works
from eternity to eternity in the great mystery of the divine
generation, and continually manifests the infinite and number-
less wisdom of God; even as the earth brings forth always fair
blossoms, herbs, and trees, so also metals and all manner of
beings, and puts them forth sometimes more sovereign, powerful,
and fair, than at other times; and as one arises in the essence,
another falls down, and there is an incessant lasting enjoyment
and labour.

15. Thus likewise is the eternal generation of the holy
mystery in great power and reprocreation [or paradisical pullula-
tion] where one divine fruit of the great love-desire stands with
another in the divine essence; and all is as a continual love-
combat or wrestling delight; a blooming of fair colours, and a
pleasant ravishing smell of the divine Mercury, according to the
divine nature's property, a continual good taste of love from
the divine desire.

16. Of all whatever this world is an earthly type and

resemblance, that is in the divine kingdom in great perfection in the spiritual essence; not only spirit, as a will, or thought, but essence, corporeal essence, sap and power; but as incomprehensible in reference to the outward world: For this visible world was generated and created out of the same spiritual essence in which the pure element is; and also out of the dark essence in the mystery of the wrath (being the original of the eternal manifest essence from whence the properties arise) as an out-spoken breath out of the Being of all beings: Not that it was made of the eternal essence, but out of the breathing forth or [expression] of the eternal essence; out of love and anger, out of evil and good, as a peculiar generation of a peculiar principle in the hand of the Eternal Spirit.

17. Therefore all whatever is in this world is a type and figure of the angelical world: not that the evil, which is alike manifest with the good in this world, is also manifest in heaven; no, they are separated into two principles; in heaven all is good which is evil in hell; whatever is anguish and torment in hell, that is good and a joy in heaven; for there all stands in the light's source; and in hell all stands in the wrath in the dark source.

18. Hell, viz. the dark world has also its generation of fruits; and there is even such an essence and dominion in them as in heaven, but in nature and manner of the wrathful property; for the fiery property makes all evil in the darkness, and in the light it makes all things good; and in sum, all is wholly one in both eternal worlds; but light and darkness separates them, so that they stand as an eternal enmity opposite one to another, to the end that it may be known what is evil or good, joy or sorrow, love or anger: There is only a distinction between the love-desire of the light, and the anger-desire of the darkness.

19. In the original of the eternal nature, in the Father's property in the great mystery of all beings, it is wholly one: for the same only fire is even in the angelical world, but in another source, viz. a love-fire, which is a poison, and a fire of anger to the devils, and to hell; for the love-fire is a death, mortification, and an enmity of the anger-fire; it deprives the wrath of its might, and this the wrath wills not, and it also cannot be; for if there were no wrath, there would be no fire, and also no light: If the eternal wrath were not, the eternal joy also would not be; in the light the wrath is changed into joy; the wrathful fire's essence is mortified as to the darkness in the wrathful fire, and out of the same dying the light and love-fire arise; as the light

burns forth from the candle, and yet in the candle the fire and light are but one thing.

20. Thus also the great mystery of all beings is in the eternity in itself only one thing, but in its explication and manifestation it goes from eternity to eternity into two essences, viz. into evil and good; what is evil to one thing, that is good to another. Hell is evil to the angels, for they were not created thereunto; but it is good to the hellish creatures : So also heaven is evil to the hellish creatures, for it is their poison and death, an eternal dying, and an eternal captivity.

21. Therefore there is an eternal enmity, and God is only called God according to the light of his love; he is indeed himself all, but according to the darkness he saith, " I am an angry jealous God, and a consuming fire."

22. Every creature must remain in its place wherein it was apprehended in its creation and formed into an image, and not depart out of that same harmony, or else it becomes an enemy of the Being of all beings.

23. And thus hell is even an enemy of the devil, for he is a strange guest therein, viz. a perjured fiend cast out of heaven: he will be lord in that wherein he was not created; the whole creation accuses him for a false perjured apostate spirit, which is departed from his order; yea even the nature in the wrath is his enemy though he be of the same property; yet he is a stranger, and will be lord, though he has lost his kingdom, and is only an inmate in the wrath of God; he that was too rich, is now become too poor; he had all when he stood in humility, and now he has nothing, and is moreover captivated in the gulf: this is his shame, that he is a king, and yet has fooled away his kingdom in pride; the royal creature remains, but the dominion is taken away; of a king he is become an executioner; what God's anger apprehends, there he is a judge, viz. an officer of God's anger, yet he must do what his Lord and Master wills.

24. This reason most ignorantly gainsays, and says, " God is omnipotent, and omniscient, he has made it: Even he hath done with his work as he hath pleased, who will contend with the Most High? " Yes, dear reason, now thou thinkest thou hittest it right; but first learn the A B C in the great mystery: All whatever is risen out of the eternal will, viz. out of the great eternal mystery of all beings (as angels and the souls of men are), stands in equal weight[1] in evil and good in the free will as God himself; that desire which powerfully and predominantly

[1] Counterpoised.

works in the creature, and quite overtops the other, of that property the creature is. As a candle puts forth out of itself a fire, and out of the fire the wind, which wind the fire draws again into itself, and yet gives it forth again; and when this spirit is gone forth from the fire and light, then it is free from the fire and light; what property it again receives, of that it is: The first mystery wherein the creature consists is the all-essential mystery, and the other in the forth-going spirit is its propriety, and a self-ful will. Has not every angel its own peculiar spirit, which is generated out of its own mystery, which has its original out of eternity? Why will this spirit be a tempter of God, and tempt the mystery, which immediately captivates it in the wrath, as happened to Lucifer? It has the drawing to God's wrath and to God's love in it; why does not the spirit (which is generated out of both) which is the similitude of the Spirit of God, continue in its place in obedience, as a child before the mother in humility?

25. Thou sayst it cannot; It is not so: [1] Every spirit stands in the place where it was created in equal weight, and has its free will; it is a spirit with the all-essential Eternal Spirit, and may take to itself a lubet in the all-essential Eternal Spirit as it wills, either in God's love or anger; whereinto it introduces its longing imagination, the essence and property of that it receives in the great mystery of all beings.

26. In God the birth is manifest in love and anger; why not also in the creature which is created out of God's essence and will, out of his voice and breath into an image? What property [or note] of the voice the creature awakes in itself, the same sounds in, and rules the creature: God's will to the creature was only one, viz. a general manifestation of the spirit, as each [creature] was apprehended in the property of the eternal mystery; yet, Lucifer was apprehended in the good angelical property, which plainly testifies that he was an angel in heaven; but his own incorporised will-spirit forced itself into the wrathful mother, to awaken the same in it, and thereby to be a lord over every created being. Now the will-spirit is free, it is the eternal original, let it do what it will.

27. Therefore we are to know this, and it is no otherwise, that the will-spirit which takes its original out of love and anger, out of both eternal principles, has given itself into the wrath, whereby the wrath has powerfully got the upper hand and dominion, and put itself out of the equal harmony into a dissonance or discord,

---

[1] Or, This is spoken without any ground or foundation.

and so he must be driven into his likeness; this is his fall, and so it is also the fall of all evil men.

28. Now self-reason alledges the Scripture, where it is written, "Many are called, but few are chosen:" Also, "I have loved Jacob and hated Esau;" also, "Hath not a potter power to make of one lump [of earth] what he pleaseth?" I say the same also, "That many are called, but few are chosen;" for they will not; they give their free will into God's anger, where they are even apprehended, and so are chosen to be "children of wrath;" whereas they were all called in Adam into paradise, and in Christ into the regeneration; but they would not, the free will would not, it exalted itself into the wrath of God which apprehended it, and so they were not chosen children; for God's love chooses only its likeness, and so likewise God's anger; yet the gate of the regeneration stands open to the wicked, whom the anger of God has apprehended. Man has the death in him, whereby he may die to the evil; but the devil has not, for he was created to the highest perfection.

29. Thus it is also with Jacob and Esau: In Jacob the line of Christ got the upper hand in the wrestling wheel; and in Esau the fall of Adam; now Christ was therefore promised into the humanity, that he might heal the fall of Adam, and redeem Esau, which was captivated in the wrath, from the wrath; Jacob denotes Christ; and Esau Adam; now Christ is to redeem Adam from death and wrath, wherein he was captivated: But did Esau continue [1] in sin? That I know not; the Scripture also does not declare it; the blessing belonged to Esau, that is, to Adam, but he fooled it away in the Fall, and so the blessing fell upon Jacob, that is upon Christ, who should bless Adam and Esau, so that the kingdom and blessing might be given of free grace again to Adam and Esau; though he was apprehended in the curse, yet the door of grace stood open in Jacob, that is, in Christ; therefore Jacob said afterward, that is Christ, when he was entered into Adam's soul and flesh, "Come unto me all ye that are weary and heavy laden with your sins, and I will refresh you:" Also, "I am come to call the sinner to repentance;" not Jacob, who needs it not, but Esau, who needs it; and when he (viz. Esau) is come, then says Christ, "There is more joy in heaven for him, than for ninety-nine righteous ones, which need no repentance;" [viz. for one Esau that repents] there is more joy than for ninety-nine Jacobs, who in the centre of the life's original are apprehended in the line of

[1] Or die.

Christ: There is more joy for one poor sinner, whom the anger has apprehended in the centre of God's wrath in the life's original, and chosen to condemnation, if he brings the sins of death again into the mortification or death of sin, than for ninety-nine righteous ones that need no repentance.

30. But who are the righteous, for we are all become sinners in Adam? Answer, They are those whom the line of Christ in the humanity apprehends in the life's rise [or at the first point of opening of life in them], not that they cannot fall as Adam, but that they are apprehended in Christ's will-spirit in the wrestling wheel, where love and anger are counterpoised, and chosen to life; as happened to Jacob, so also to Isaac, and Abel: But this line should be the preacher and teacher of Cain, Ishmael, and Esau, and exhort them to repentance, and to turn out of the anger: And this line did give itself into the anger which was enkindled in Adam, Cain, Ishmael, and destroyed the devil's sting with love, that Cain, Ishmael, and Esau had an open gate to grace; if they would but turn and die in Jacob, that is, if they would enter into Christ's death, and die to sin in Abel, Isaac, and Jacob, and Christ, then they should be received into the election of grace.

31. Jacob took Esau's place in the blessing: Why did that come to pass? In Jacob was the promised seed of Abraham and Adam; from this line the blessing should come upon the sinful Adam and Esau; Jacob must be filled with God's blessing, that he might bless the first-born of angry Adam and Esau; for the blessing, that is, Christ must be born in our flesh and soul, that the seed of the woman might bruise the head of the serpent.

32. The anger must be drowned and appeased in the humanity; an offering did not do it, but this resigning into the wrath, that the love might drown the wrath. Jacob in Christ must drown Esau in the love-power in his blood, that Esau might also become a Jacob in Christ: But Esau was not willing to receive his brother Jacob, and contended about the first birth;[1] that is, Adam in sin will not, cannot receive [or accept of] Christ, he shall and must die to the sinful flesh and will.

33. Therefore Esau has ever fought against Jacob; for Jacob should drown him in Christ in his blood; this the evil Adam in Esau would not have, he would live in his self-hood, therefore he strove with the earthly Adam against Jacob; but when Jacob met him with his gifts, that is, when Christ came with his free love-gift into the humanity, then Esau fell upon his brother

[1] Or birthright.

Jacob's neck and wept; for when Christ entered into the humanity, Adam wept in Esau, and repented him of his sins and evil intent, that he would kill Jacob: For when God's love in the humanity entered into God's anger, the angry Father bewailed our sins and misery, and Jacob with his humility drove forth mournful tears out of his brother Esau; that is, the love in the humanity brought forth the great compassion out of and through the angry Father; so that the angry Father in the midst of his enkindled wrath in the humanity did set open a gate of mercy for Adam and all his children; for his love broke the anger, which [love] put itself into death, and made an open gate for poor sinners in the death to his grace.

34. Now it is commanded the poor sinner, whom the anger has chosen to the condemnation of eternal death, that he enter into this same death, and die in Christ's death to sin, and then Christ drowns it in his blood, and chuses him again to be God's child.

35. Here is the calling: Christ calls us into his death, into his dying; this the sinner will not have: Here is now strife in the sinner between the seed of the woman and the seed of the serpent; which now overcomes, that conceives the child: Now the free will may reach to which it pleases; both gates stand open to him. Many who are in Christ's line are also brought through imagination and lust, as Adam was, into iniquity; they are indeed called, but they persevere not in the election, for the election is set upon him who departs from sin; he is elected that dies to sin in Christ's death, and rises in Christ's resurrection, who receives God in Christ, not only in the mouth, but in divine desire in the will and new-birth, as a new fiery generation: Knowledge apprehends it not, only the earnest desire and breaking of the sinful will, that apprehends it.

36. Thus there is no sufficient ground in the election of grace as reason holds it forth: Adam is chosen in Christ; but that many a twig withers on the tree, is not the tree's fault, for it withdraws its sap from no twig, only the twig gives forth itself too eagerly with the desire; it runs on in self-will, viz. it is taken by the inflammation of the sun and the fire, before it can draw sap again in its mother, and refresh itself.

37. Thus also man perishes among the evil company in evil vain ways: God offers him his grace that he should repent; but evil company and the devil lead him in wicked ways, till he be even too hard captivated in the anger; and then it goes very hardly with him; he indeed was called, but he is evil; God

chuses only children: Seeing he is evil, the choice passes over him; but if he again reforms and amends, the eternal choice [or election] does again receive him.

38. Thus says the Scripture, "Many are called;" but when the choice in Christ's suffering and death comes upon them, then they are not capable of the same, by reason of the self-ful evil will which they had before embraced, and so they are not the elected, but evil children; and here it is then rightly said, "We have piped unto you, but you have not danced; we have mourned unto you, and ye have not lamented unto us:[1] O Jerusalem, how often would I have gathered thy children together, as a hen gathereth her chickens under her wings, and thou wouldest not:" It is not said, "thou *couldest* not," but "thou *wouldest* not;" and while they remain in the iniquity of sin, they also cannot: God will not cast his pearl before swine; but to the children which draw near to him he gives the pearl and his bread.

39. Therefore whoever blames God, despises his mercy, which he has introduced into the humanity, and brings the judgement headlong upon his body and soul.

40. Thus I have truly warned the reader, and set before his eyes what the Lord of all beings has given me: He may behold himself in this looking-glass both within and without, and find what and who he is: Every reader shall find his profit therein, be he either good or evil: It is a very clear gate of the mystery of all beings. With glosses and self-wit none shall apprehend it in its own ground; but it may well embrace the real seeker, and create him much profit and joy, and even be helpful to him in all natural things, provided he applies himself right, and seeks it in the fear of God, seeing it is now a time of seeking; for a lily blossoms upon the mountains and valleys in all the ends of the earth: He that seeketh findeth. Amen.

[1] Text, comforted us.

HALLELUJAH

POSTSCRIPT BY THE TRANSLATOR

THE preceding book is a brief signature, or character of natural and divine knowledge. But it will seem strange and simple to the proud self-conceited sophisters, the wiselings of pedantic reason, who will carp and cavil at anything but what dances to their pipe, or agrees with their conceits. But their censures are not to be valued; and their letter-learned mock productions of science are to be pitied, being only the courted shadows of their own amused fancy. Such as these being captivated in the mystery of Babel, wonder only after their beast Mammon, upon which they ride in pride, and scorn anything but what pleases and flatters them in their admired works of covetous iniquity, gilded over with seeming holiness. But the Babylonish structure of their turba-magna-performances will fall, when it has attained the highest limit of its constellation, and no wit of man shall be able to prop it up. In the meantime the Antichrist in Babel will rage and tyrannise, and execute the sentence of wrath, or his own dismal doom, upon himself.

But not to transgress by too large a digression from the intent of this postscript; the principal design of it is to explain some words which are used in the translation, as

FLAGRAT, LUBET, SOURCE, SUDE

FLAGRAT

The word in the German is *Schra'ck*, which signifies properly a fright, sudden astonishment, or dismay. In the other books it is translated terror, or crack, but I have put it *flagrat*, from the Latin word *flagro*, though I mean not by it only a burning, but even the powerful opening of the life or death of the enkindling of the fire in nature. For the fire is the dividing boundmark, in which the life of both principles is opened and separated; the life of the first is the dying death in the darkness, and the life of the second is the living life in the light. You may perceive a resemblance of this flagrat in thunder and lightening, as also in gunpowder, and the like. Take for instance divers sulphureous salnitral minerals exactly mixed, now their powers are as I may say contracted, or shut up in the astringent dark desire or death; but touch them rightly with the true fire, and you will see how they will soon open, disclose, and flash forth, and will even display and stream themselves forth into divers properties, colours, and virtues. It is even the bursting forth of the ardent desire in nature. It is, as I may term it, the magical fire-breath, whereby the powers either of light or darkness are dismayed. In short, it is the pregnant echo of the sound of eternity everywhere speaking, working, and opening itself in love or anger, in each thing according to its will and desire: In some it is the horrible flagrat to death; and in others it is the pleasant triumphant flagrat to life.

LUBET

The word in the Dutch is *lust*, which signifies a longing desire or will to a thing; also a delight, or contented joy; sometimes imagination and lust. But because our word lust is commonly used in the worst sense (a longing after evil and vanity) and would not properly agree to, or fully express the German word lust in all places, I have generally translated it *lubet*, from the Latin word *lubitum*, whereby is meant the divine *beneplacitum*, or good pleasure. By it is understood the origin to a desire in the eternal nothing, or pregnant magic, God's free well-liking to the desire of the manifestation of nature and creature, without which all had been an eternal stillness in the nothing. This lubet in man is the moving will to good or evil, light or darkness, love or anger.

SOURCE

By this are meant the first original qualities or properties of both the inward principles, as they break forth in the sude of the fire in the flagrat of love or anger in nature or creature. For in the darkness the love-*ens*, or paradisical light, is shut up in death, and causes an austere dark source, pain, horror, torment, or disquietude; and so it is the radical property of the contentious elements and stars in the curse of God: And in the light the life of love breaks forth, and swallows up this wrathful source of darkness and death, and turns it into joy or a divine source. So that by *source* is understood the original quality, property, or qualification of evil, darkness, anger, sorrow, cursing, damnation, death, hell; or the contrary to these in their divine source, or essential working property; both according to time and eternity.

SUDE

The word *sude* is German, and signifies a boiling or seething. It is the stirring of the seven properties in nature, arising from the assimilation or essential co-influence of the outward and inward Sol in Sulphur, from whence the blooming vegetation of the earth proceeds; also the generation of metals and minerals lies therein.

These are some uncommon words which are used in rendering this book into English. Words are *vehicula rerum,* they are formed to express things, not bare sounds, or empty airs. Now he who rightly understands the ground of the *cabala* and *magia,* and knows how the language of nature speaks in every tongue, might well translate this author. But the bare letter of his writings, though ever so exactly translated, will not give the understanding of them, but the spirit of regeneration in Christ, in whom the fulness of the Deity dwells corporeally.

N.B.—There is ONE CHARACTER by which God has characterised both himself, and all the creatures, and shewn that his presence is in all things; yet so that each creature has its wonder, either of the heavenly or of the earthly mystery. This peculiar mark, shape, and figure, that it may appear as a peculiar is the ⊩ in the sphere and mercurial wheel of nature, which goes through all the three principles, and in the third through all the kingdoms of minerals, vegetables, and animals, through heaven and earth; the wonderful depth of which is shewn in this book to the enquirer after the divine mysteries.

A DIALOGUE

BETWEEN

A SCHOLAR AND HIS MASTER

CONCERNING

THE SUPERSENSUAL LIFE

SHEWING

How the Soul may attain to Divine Hearing and Vision, and
what its Childship in the Natural and Supernatural Life is;
and how it passeth out of Nature into God, and out of
God into Nature and Self again; also what its Salvation
and Perdition are.

1 Cor. ii. 7, 8, 9, 10, 11, 12, 13, 14, 15.

" We speak the hidden mystical wisdom of God, which God ordained before the world unto our glory: Which none of the princes of this world knew: For had they known it, they would not have crucified the Lord of glory. But, as it is written, Eye hath not seen, nor ear heard, neither hath it entered into the heart of man to conceive the things which God hath prepared for them that love him. But God hath revealed them unto us by his Spirit: For the Spirit searcheth all things, yea, the deep things of God. For what man knoweth the things of a man, save the spirit of a man which is in him? Even so the things of God knoweth no man, but the Spirit of God. Now we have received, not the spirit of the world, but the spirit which is of God; that we might know the things that are freely given us of God. Which things also we speak, not in the words which man's wisdom teacheth, but which the Holy Ghost teacheth; comparing spiritual things with spiritual. But the natural man receiveth not the things of the Spirit of God: For they are foolishness unto him; neither can he know them, because they are spiritually discerned. But he that is spiritual judgeth, or discerneth all things."

OF THE SUPERSENSUAL LIFE

OR

THE LIFE WHICH IS ABOVE SENSE

IN

A DIALOGUE between a Scholar or Disciple and his Master

DIALOGUE I

DISCIPLE. MASTER

THE disciple said to his master: Sir, how may I come to the supersensual life, so that I may see God, and may hear God speak?

The master answered and said: Son, when thou canst throw thyself into THAT, where no creature dwelleth, though it be but for a moment, then thou hearest what God speaketh.

Disciple. Is that where no creature dwelleth near at hand; or is it afar off?

Master. It is in thee. And if thou canst, my son, for a while but cease from all thy thinking and willing, then thou shalt hear the unspeakable words of God.

Disciple. How can I hear him speak, when I stand still from thinking and willing?

Master. When thou standest still from the thinking of self, and the willing of self; " When both thy intellect and will are quiet, and passive to the impressions of the Eternal Word and Spirit; and when thy soul is winged up, and above that which is temporal, the outward senses, and the imagination being locked up by holy abstraction," then the eternal hearing, seeing, and speaking will be revealed in thee; and so God heareth " and seeth through thee," being now the organ of *his* Spirit; and so God speaketh in thee, and whispereth to thy spirit, and thy spirit heareth his voice. Blessed art thou therefore if that thou canst stand still from self-thinking and self-willing, and canst stop the wheel of thy imagination and senses; forasmuch as hereby thou mayest arrive at length to see the great salvation of God, being made capable of all manner of divine sensations and heavenly communications. Since it is nought indeed but thine own hearing and willing that do hinder thee, so that thou dost not see and hear God.

Disciple. But wherewith shall I hear and see God, forasmuch as he is above nature and creature?

Master. Son, when thou art quiet and silent, then art thou as God was before nature and creature; thou art that which God then was; thou art that whereof he made thy nature and creature: Then thou hearest and seest even with that wherewith God himself saw and heard in thee, before ever thine own willing or thine own seeing began.

Disciple. What now hinders or keeps me back, so that I cannot come to that, wherewith God is to be seen and heard?

Master. Nothing truly but thine own willing, hearing, and seeing do keep thee back from it, and do hinder thee from coming to this supersensual state. And it is because thou strivest so against that, out of which thou thyself art descended and derived, that thou thus breakest thyself off, with thine own willing, from God's willing, and with thine own seeing from God's seeing. In as much as in thine own seeing thou dost see in thine own willing only, and with thine own understanding thou dost understand but in and according to this thine own willing, as the same stands divided from the divine will. This thy willing moreover stops thy hearing, and maketh thee deaf towards God, through thy own thinking upon terrestrial things, and thy attending to that which is without thee; and so it brings thee into a ground, where thou art laid hold on and captivated in nature. And having brought thee hither, it overshadows thee with that which thou willest; it binds thee with thine own chains, and it keeps thee in thine own dark prison which thou makest for thyself; so that thou canst not go out thence, or come to that state which is supernatural and supersensual.

Disciple. But being I am in nature, and thus bound, as with my own chains, and by my own natural will; pray be so kind, sir, as to tell me, how I may come through nature into the supersensual and supernatural ground, without the destroying of nature?

Master. Three things are requisite in order to this. The first is, Thou must resign up thy will to God; and must sink thyself down to the dust in his mercy. The second is, Thou must hate thy own will, and forbear from doing that to which thy own will doth drive thee. The third is, Thou must bow thy soul under the cross, heartily submitting thyself to it, that thou mayest be able to bear the temptations of nature and creature. And if thou dost thus, know that God will speak into thee, and will bring thy resigned will into himself, in the supernatural ground; and then thou shalt hear, my son, what the Lord speaketh in thee.

Disciple. This is a hard saying, master; for I must forsake the world, and my life too, if I should do thus.

Master. Be not discouraged hereat. If thou forsakest the world, then thou comest into that out of which the world is made; and if thou losest thy life, then thy life is in that for whose sake thou forsakest it. Thy life is in God, from whence it came into the body; and as thou comest to have thine own power faint and weak and dying, the power of God will then work in thee and through thee.

Disciple. Nevertheless as God hath created man in and for the natural life, to rule over all creatures on earth, and to be a lord over all things in this world, it seems not to be at all unreasonable, that man should therefore possess this world and the things therein for his own.

Master. If thou rulest over all creatures but outwardly, there cannot be much in that. But if thou hast a mind to possess all things, and to be a lord indeed over all things in this world, there is quite another method to be taken by thee.

Disciple. Pray, how is that? And what method must I take, whereby to arrive at this sovereignty?

Master. Thou must learn to distinguish well betwixt the thing, and that which only is an image thereof; betwixt that sovereignty which is substantial, and in the inward ground or nature, and that which is imaginary, and in an outward form, or semblance; betwixt that which is properly angelical, and that which is no more than bestial. If thou rulest now over the creatures externally only, and not from the right internal ground of thy renewed nature; then thy will and ruling is verily in a bestial kind or manner, and thine at best is but a sort of imaginary and transitory government, being void of that which is substantial and permanent, the which only thou art to desire and press after. Thus by thy outwardly lording it over the creatures, it is most easy for thee to lose the substance and the reality, while thou hast nought remaining but the image or shadow only of thy first and original lordship; wherein thou art made capable to be again invested, if thou beest but wise, and takest thy investiture from the supreme lord in the right course and manner. Whereas by thy willing and ruling thus after a bestial manner, thou bringest also thy desire into a bestial essence, by which means thou becomest infected and captivated therein, and gettest therewith a bestial nature and condition of life. But if thou shalt have put off the bestial and ferine nature, and if thou hast left the imaginary life, and quitted the low imaged condition of it; then art thou come into the super-imaginariness, and into the intellectual life, which is a state of living above images, figures, and shadows: and so thou rulest over all creatures, being re-united with thine original, in that very ground or source, out of which they were and are created; and henceforth nothing on earth can hurt thee. For thou art like all things; and nothing is unlike thee.

Disciple. O loving master, pray teach me how I may come the shortest way to be like unto all things.

Master. With all my heart. Do but think on the words of our Lord Jesus Christ, when he said, " Except ye be converted, and become as little children, ye shall not enter into the kingdom of heaven." There is no shorter way than this; neither can there be a better way found. Verily, Jesus saith unto thee, Unless thou turn and become as a child, hanging upon him for all things, thou shalt not see the kingdom of God. This do, and nothing shall hurt thee; for thou shalt be at friendship with all the things that are, as thou dependest on the author and fountain of them, and becomest like him, by such dependence, and by the union of thy will with his will. But mark what I have further to say; and be not thou startled at it, though it may seem hard for thee at first to conceive. If thou wilt be like all things, thou must forsake all things; thou must turn thy desire away from them all, and not desire or hanker after any of them; thou must not extend thy will to possess that for thy own, or as thine own, which is something, whatsoever that something be. For as soon as ever thou takest something into thy desire, and receivest it into thee for thine own, or in pro-priety, then this very something (of what nature soever it is) is the same with thyself; and this worketh with thee in thy will, and thou art thence bound to protect it, and to take care of it, even as of thy own being. But if thou dost receive nothing into thy desire, then thou art free from all things, and rulest over all things at once, as a prince of God. For thou hast received nothing for thine own, and art nothing to all things; and all things are as nothing to thee. Thou art as a child, which understands not what a thing is; and though thou dost perhaps understand it, yet thou understandest it without mixing with it, and without sensibly affecting or touching thy perception, even in that manner wherein God doth rule and see all things; he comprehending all, and yet nothing comprehending him.

Disciple. Ah! how shall I arrive at this heavenly understanding, at this sight of all things in God, at this pure and naked knowledge which is abstracted from the senses; at this light above nature and creature; and at this participation of the divine wisdom which oversees all things, and governs through all intellectual beings? For, alas, I am touched every moment by the things which are about me; and overshadowed by the clouds and fumes which rise up out of the earth. I desire therefore to be taught, if possible, how I may attain such a state and condition as no creature may be able to touch me to hurt me; and how my mind, being purged from sensible objects and things, may be prepared for the entrance and habitation of the divine wisdom in me?

Master. Thou desirest that I would teach thee how thou art to attain it; and I will direct thee to our master, from whom I have been taught it, that thou mayest learn it thyself from him, who alone teacheth the heart. Hear thou him. Wouldest thou arrive at this; wouldest thou remain untouched by sensibles; wouldest thou behold light in the very light of God, and see all things thereby; then consider the words of Christ, who is that light, and who is the truth. O consider now his words, who said, " Without me ye can do nothing " (John xix. 5), and defer not to apply thyself unto him, who is the strength of thy salvation, and the power of thy life; and with whom thou canst do all things, by the faith which he worketh in thee. But unless thou wholly givest thyself up to the life of our Lord Jesus Christ, and resignest thy will wholly to him, and desirest nothing and willest nothing without him, thou shalt never come to such a rest as no creature can disturb. Think what thou pleasest, and be never so much delighted in the activity of thine own reason, thou shalt find that in thine own power, and without such a total surrender to God, and to the life of God, thou canst never arrive at such a rest as this, or the true quiet of the soul, wherein no creature can molest thee, or so much as touch thee. Which when thou shalt, by grace, have attained to, then with thy body thou art in the world, as in the properties of outward nature; and with thy reason, under the cross of our Lord Jesus Christ; but with thy will thou walkest in heaven, and art at the end from whence all creatures are proceeded forth, and to which they return again. And then thou canst in this END, which⁷is the same with the BEGINNING, behold all things out-wardly with reason, and inwardly with the mind; and so mayest thou rule in all things and over all things, with Christ; unto whom all power is given both in heaven and on earth.

Disciple. O master, the creatures which live in me do withhold me, that I cannot so wholly yield and give up myself as I willingly would. What am I to do in this case?

Master. Let not this trouble thee. Doth thy will go forth from the creatures? Then the creatures are forsaken in thee. They are in the world; and thy body, which is in the world, is with the creatures. But spiritually thou walkest with God, and conversest in heaven; being in thy mind redeemed from earth, and separated from creatures, to live the life of God. And if thy will thus leaveth the creatures, and goeth forth from them, even as the spirit goeth forth from the body at death; then are the creatures dead in it, and do live only in the body in the world. Since if thy will do not bring itself into them, they cannot bring themselves into it, neither can they by any means touch the soul. And hence St. Paul saith, " Our conversation is in heaven; " and also, " Ye are the temple of God, and the Spirit of God dwelleth in you." So then true Christians are the very temples of the Holy Ghost, who dwelleth in them; that is, the Holy Ghost dwelleth in the will, and the creature dwelleth in the body.

Disciple. If now the Holy Spirit doth dwell in the will of the mind, how ought I to keep myself so that he depart not from me again?

Master. Mark, my son, the words of our Lord Jesus Christ; " If ye abide in my words, then my words abide in you." If thou abidest with thy will in the words of Christ; then his word and spirit abideth in thee, and all shall be done for thee that thou canst ask of him. But if thy will goeth into the creature, then thou hast broken off thereby thyself from him: And then thou canst not any otherwise keep thyself but by abiding continually in the most resigned humility, and by enter-ing into a constant course of penitence, wherein thou wilt be always grieved at thine own creaturely will, and that creatures do live still in thee, that is, in thy bodily appetite. If thou dost thus, thou standest in a daily dying from the creatures, and in a daily ascending into heaven in thy will; which will is also the will of thy Heavenly Father.

Disciple. O my loving master, pray teach me how I may come to such a constant course of holy penitence, and to such a daily dying from all creaturely objects; for how can I abide continually in repentance?

Master. When thou leavest that which loveth thee, and lovest that which hateth thee; then thou mayest abide continually in repentance.

Disciple. What is it that I must thus leave?

Master. All things that love and entertain thee, because thy will loves and entertains them: All things that please and feed thee, because thy will feeds and cherishes them: All creatures in flesh and blood; in a word, all visibles and sensibles, by which either the imagination or sensitive appetite in men are delighted and refreshed. These the will of thy mind, or thy supreme part must leave and forsake; and must even account them all its enemies. This is the leaving of what loves thee. And the loving of what hates thee, is the embracing the reproach of the world. Thou must learn then to love the cross of the Lord Jesus Christ, and for his sake to be pleased with the reproach of the world which hates thee and derides thee; and let this be thy daily exercise of penitence to be crucified to the world, and the world to thee. And so thou shalt have continual cause to hate thyself in the creature, and to seek the eternal rest which is in Christ. To which rest thou having thus attained, thy will may therein safely rest and repose itself, according as thy Lord Christ hath said: In me ye may have rest, but in the world ye shall have anxiety: In me ye may have peace, but in the world ye shall have tribulation.

Disciple. How shall I be now able to subsist in this anxiety and tribulation arising from the world, so as not to lose the eternal peace, or not enter into this rest? And how may I recover myself in such a temptation as this is, by not sinking under the world, but rising above it by a life that is truly heavenly and supersensual?

Master. If thou dost once every hour throw thyself by faith beyond all creatures, beyond and above all sensual perception and apprehension, yea, above discourse and reasoning, into the abyssal mercy of God, into the sufferings of our Lord, and into the fellowship of his interceding, and yieldest thyself fully and absolutely thereinto; then thou shalt receive power from above to rule over death, and the devil, and to subdue hell and the world under thee: And then thou mayest subsist in all temptations, and be the brighter for them.

Disciple. Blessed is the man that arriveth to such a state as this. But, alas! poor man that I am, how is this possible as to me? And what, O my master, would become of me, if I should ever attain with my mind to that, where no creature is? Must I not cry out, " I am undone!"

Master. Son, why art thou so dispirited? Be of good heart still; for thou mayest certainly yet attain to it. Do but believe, and all things are made possible to thee. If it were that thy will, O thou of little courage, could break off itself for one hour, or even but for one half hour, from all creatures, and plunge itself into that where no creature is, or can be; presently it would be penetrated and clothed upon with the supreme splendour of the divine glory, would taste in itself the most sweet love of Jesus, the sweetness whereof no tongue can express, and would find in itself the unspeakable words of our Lord concerning his great mercy. Thy spirit would then feel in itself the cross of our Lord Jesus Christ to be very pleasing to it; and would thereupon love the cross more than the honours and goods of the world.

Disciple. This for the soul would be exceeding well indeed: But what would then become of the body, seeing that it must of necessity live in the creature?

Master. The body would by this means be put into the imitation of our Lord Christ, and of his body: It would stand in the communion of that most blessed body, which was the true temple of the Deity; and in the participation of all its gracious effects, virtues, and influences. It would live in the creature not of choice, but only as it is " made subject unto vanity," and in the world, as it is placed therein by the ordination of the Creator, for its cultivation and higher advancement; and as groaning to be delivered out of it in God's time and manner, for its perfection and resuscitation in eternal liberty and glory, like unto the glorified body of our Lord and his risen saints.

Disciple. But the body being in its present constitution, so " made subject to vanity," and living in a vain image and creaturely shadow, according to the life of the undergraduated creatures or brutes, whose breath goeth downwards to the earth; I am still very much afraid thereof, lest it should continue to depress the mind which is lifted up to God, by hanging as a dead weight thereto; and go on to amuse and perplex the same, as formerly, with dreams and trifles, by letting in the objects from without, in order to draw me down into the world and the hurry thereof; whereas I would fain maintain my conversation in heaven, even while I am living in the world. What therefore must I do with this body, that I may be able to keep up so desirable a conversation; and not to be under any subjection to it any longer?

Master. There is no other way for thee that I know, but to present the body whereof thou complainest (which is the beast to be sacrificed) " a living sacrifice, holy and acceptable unto God: " And this shall be thy " rational service," whereby this thy body will be put, as thou desirest, into the imitation of Jesus Christ, who said, his kingdom was not of this world. Be not thou then conformed to it, but be transformed by the renewing of thy mind; which renewed mind is to have dominion over the body, that so thou mayest prove, both in body and mind, what is the perfect will of God, and accordingly perform the same with and by his grace operating in thee. Whereupon the body, or the animal life would, being thus offered up, begin to die, both from without and from within. From without, that is, from the vanity and evil customs and fashions of the world: It would be an utter enemy to all the pomps thereof, and to all the gaudery, pageantry, pride, ambition, and haughtiness therein. From within, it would die as to all the lusts and appetites of the flesh, and would get a mind and will wholly new, for its government and management; being now made subject to the spirit, which would continually be directed to God, and so consequently that which is subject to it. And thus thy very body is become the temple of God and of his Spirit, in imitation of thy Lord's body.

Disciple. But the world would hate it and despise it for so doing; seeing it must hereby contradict the world, and must live and act quite otherwise than the world doth. This is most certain. And how can this then be taken?

Master. It would not take that as any harm done to it, but would rather rejoice that it is become worthy to be like unto the image of our Lord Jesus Christ, being transformed from that of the world: And it would be most willing to bear that cross after our Lord; merely that our Lord might bestow upon it the influence of his sweet and precious love.

Disciple. I do not doubt but in some this may be even so. Nevertheless for my own part, I am in a straight betwixt two, not feeling yet enough of that blessed influence upon me. O how willingly should my body bear that, could this be safely depended upon by me, according to what is urged! Wherefore pardon me, loving sir, in this one thing, if my impatience doth still further demand " what would become of it, if the anger of God from within, and the wicked world also from without, should at once assault it, as the same really happened to our Lord Christ? "

Master. Be that unto it, even as unto our Lord Christ, when he was reproached, reviled, and crucified by the world; and when the anger of God so fiercely assaulted him for our sake. Now what did he under this most terrible assault both from without and from within? Why: He commended his soul into the hands of his Father, and so departed from the anguish of this world into the eternal joy. Do thou likewise; and his death shall be thy life.

Disciple. Be it unto me as unto the Lord Christ; and unto my body as unto his; which into his hands I have commended, and for the sake of his name do offer up, according to his revealed will. Nevertheless I am desirous to know what would become of my body in its pressing forth from the anguish of this miserable world into the power of the heavenly kingdom.

Master. It would get forth from the reproach and contradiction of the world, by a conformity to the passion of Jesus Christ; and from the sorrows and pains in the flesh, which are only the effects of some sensible impression of things without, by a quiet introversion of the spirit, and secret communion with the Deity manifesting itself for that end. It would penetrate into itself; it would sink into the great love of God; it would be sustained and refreshed by the most sweet name JESUS; and it would see and find within itself a new world springing forth as through the anger of God, into the love and joy eternal. And then should a man wrap his soul in this, even in the great love of God, and clothe himself therewith as with a garment; and should account thence all things alike; because in the creature he finds nothing that can give him without God the least satisfaction; and because also nothing of harm can touch him more, while he remains in this love, the which indeed is stronger than all things, and makes a man hence invulnerable both from within and without, by taking out the sting and poison of the creatures, and destroying the power of death. And whether the body be in hell or on earth, all is alike to him; for whether it be there or here, his mind is still in the greatest love of God; which is no less than to say, that he is in heaven.

Disciple. But how would a man's body be maintained in the world; or how would he be able to maintain those that are his, if he should by such a conversation incur the displeasure of all the world?

Master. Such a man gets greater favours than the world is

able to bestow upon him. He hath God for his friend; he hath all his angels for his friends: In all dangers and necessities these protect and relieve him; so that he need fear no manner of evil; no creature can hurt him. God is his helper; and that is sufficient. Also God is his blessing in everything: And though sometimes it may seem as if God would not bless him, yet is this but for a trial to him, and for the attraction of the divine love; to the end he may more fervently pray to God, and commit all his ways unto him.

Disciple. He loses, however, by this all his good friends; and there will be none to help him in his necessity.

Master. Nay, but he gets the hearts of all his good friends into his possession, and loses none but his enemies, who before loved his vanity and wickedness.

Disciple. How is it that he can get his good friends into his possession?

Master. He gets the very hearts and souls of all those that belong to our Lord Jesus to be his brethren, and the members of his own very life. For all the children of God are but ONE in Christ, which one is Christ in all: And therefore he gets them all to be his fellow members in the body of Christ, whence they have all the same heavenly goods in common; and all live in one and the same love of God, as the branches of a tree in one and the same root, and spring all from one and the same source of life in them. So that he can have no want of spiritual friends and relations, who are all rooted with him together in the love which is from above; who are all of the same blood and kindred in Christ Jesus; and who are cherished all by the same quickening sap and spirit diffusing itself through them universally from the one true vine, which is the tree of life and love. These are friends worth having; and though here they may be unknown to him, will abide his friends beyond death, to all eternity. But neither can he want even outward natural friends, as our Lord Christ when on earth did not want such also. For though indeed the high-priests and potentates of the world could not have a love to him, because they belonged not to him, neither stood in any kind of relation to him, as being not of this world; yet those loved him who were capable of his love, and receptive of his words. So in like manner, those who love truth and righteousness will love that man, and will associate themselves unto him, yea, though they may perhaps be outwardly at some distance or seeming disagreement, from the situation of their worldly affairs, or out of some certain respects; yet in their hearts they cannot but cleave to him. For though they be not yet actually incorporated into one body with him, yet they cannot resist being of one mind with him, and being united in affection, for the great regard they bear to the truth, which shines forth in his words and in his life. By which they are made either his declared or his secret friends; and he doth so get their hearts, as they will be delighted above all things in his company, for the sake thereof, and will court his friendship, and will come unto him by stealth, if openly they dare not, for the benefit of his conversation and advice; even as Nicodemus did unto Christ, who came to him by night, and in his heart loved Jesus for the truth's sake, though outwardly he feared the world. And thus thou shalt have many friends that are not known to thee; and some known to thee, who may not appear so before the world.

Disciple. Nevertheless it is very grievous to be generally despised of the world, and to be trampled upon by men as the very offscouring thereof.

Master. That which now seems so hard and heavy to thee, thou wilt yet hereafter be most of all in love with.

Disciple. How can it be that I should ever love that which hates me?

Master. Though thou lovest the earthly wisdom now, yet when thou shalt be clothed upon with the heavenly wisdom, then thou wilt see that all the wisdom of the world is folly; and wilt see also that the world hates not so much thee, as thine enemy, which is the mortal life. And when thou thyself shalt come to hate the will thereof, by means of an habitual separation of thy mind from the world, then thou also wilt begin to love that despising of the mortal life, and the reproach of the world for Christ's sake. And so shalt thou be able to stand under every temptation, and to hold out to the end by the means hereof in a course of life above the world, and above sense. In this course thou wilt hate thyself; and thou wilt also love thyself; I say, love thyself, and that even more than ever thou didst yet.

Disciple. But how can these two subsist together, that a person should both love and hate himself?

Master. In loving thyself, thou lovest not thyself as thine own; but as given thee from the love of God thou lovest the divine ground in thee: By which and in which thou lovest the divine wisdom, the divine goodness, the divine beauty; thou lovest also by it God's works of wonders; and in this ground thou lovest likewise thy brethren. But in hating thy-self, thou hatest only that which is thine own, and wherein the evil sticks close to thee. And this thou dost, that so thou mayest wholly destroy that which thou callest thine; as when thou sayest I or MYSELF do this, or do that. All which is wrong, and a downright mistake in thee; for nothing canst thou properly call thine but the evil self, neither canst thou do anything of thyself that is to be accounted of. This self therefore thou must labour wholly to destroy in thee, that so thou mayest become a ground wholly divine. There is, there can be no selfishness in love; they are opposite to each other. Love, that is, divine love (of which only we are now discoursing), hates all EGOITY, hates all that which we call I, or IHOOD; hates all such restrictions and confinements, even all that springs from a con-tracted spirit, or this evil self-hood, because it is an hateful and deadly thing. And it is impossible that these two should stand together, or subsist in one person; the one driving out the other by a necessity of nature. For love possesses heaven, and dwells in itself, which is dwelling in heaven; but that which is called I, this vile self-hood possesses the world and worldly things; and dwells also in itself, which is dwelling in hell, because this is the very root of hell itself. And therefore as heaven rules the world, and as eternity rules time, even so ought love to rule the natural temporal life; for no other method is there, neither can there be of attaining to that life which is supernatural and eternal, and which thou so much desirest to be led into.

Disciple. Loving master, I am well content that this love should rule in me over the natural life, that so I may attain to that which is supernatural and supersensual; but pray tell me now, why must love and hatred, friend and foe thus be together? Would not love alone be better? Wherefore, I say, are love and trouble thus joined?

Master. If love dwelt not in trouble, it could have nothing to love: But its substance which it loves, namely, the poor soul, being in trouble and pain, it hath thence cause to love its own substance, and to deliver it from pain; that so itself may by it be again beloved. Neither could any one know what love is, if there were no hatred; or what friendship is, if there were no foe to contend with: Or in one word, if love had not something which it might love, and manifest the virtue and power of love, by working out deliverance to the beloved from all pain and trouble.

Disciple. Pray what is the virtue, the power, the height and the greatness of love?

Master. The virtue of love is NOTHING and ALL, or that nothing visible out of which all things proceed; its power is through all things; its height is as high as God; its greatness is as great as God. Its virtue is the principle of all principles; its power supports the heavens and upholds the earth; its height is higher than the highest heavens; and its greatness is even greater than the very manifestation of the Godhead in the glorious light of the divine essence, as being infinitely capable of greater and greater manifestations in all eternity. What can I say more? Love is higher than the highest. Love is greater than the greatest. Yea, it is in a certain sense greater than God; while yet in the highest sense of all, God is LOVE, and love is God. Love being the highest principle, is the virtue of all virtues; from whence they flow forth. Love being the greatest majesty, is the power of all powers, from whence they severally operate: And it is the holy magical root, or ghostly power from whence all the wonders of God have been wrought by the hands of his elect servants, in all their generations successively. Whosoever finds it, finds nothing and all things.

Disciple. Dear master, pray tell me but how I may understand this.

Master. First then, in that I said, "its virtue is nothing," or that nothing which is the beginning of all things, thou must understand it thus: When thou art gone forth wholly from the creature, and from that which is visible, and art become nothing to all that is nature and creature, then thou art in that Eternal One, which is God himself: And then thou shalt perceive and feel in thy interiour, the highest virtue of love. But in that I said, "Its power is through all things," this is that which thou perceivest and findest in thy own soul and body experimentally, whenever this great love is enkindled within thee; seeing that it will burn more than the fire can do, as it did in the prophets of old, and afterwards in the apostles, when God conversed with them bodily, and when his Spirit descended upon them in the oratory of Zion. Thou shalt then see also in all the works of God, how love hath poured forth itself into all things, and penetrateth all things, and is the most inward and most outward ground in all things: Inwardly in the virtue and power of everything; and outwardly in the figure and form thereof.

And in that I said, "Its height is as high as God;" thou mayest understand this in thyself; forasmuch as it brings thee to be as high as God himself is, by being united to God: As may be seen by our beloved Lord Christ in our humanity. Which humanity love hath brought up into the highest throne, above all angelical principalities and powers, into the very power of the Deity itself.

But in that I also said, " Its greatness is as great as God," thou art hereby to understand that there is a certain greatness and latitude of heart in love, which is inexpressible; for it enlarges the soul as wide as the whole creation of God. And this shall be truly experienced by thee, beyond all words, when the throne of love shall be set up in thy heart.

Moreover in that I said, " Its virtue is the principle of all principles," hereby it is given thee to understand, that love is the principiating cause of all created beings, both spiritual and corporeal, by virtue whereof the second causes do move and act occasionally according to certain eternal laws from the beginning implanted in the very constitution of things thus originated. This virtue which is in love, is the very life and energy of all the principles of nature, superiour and inferiour: It reaches to all worlds, and to all manner of beings in them contained, they being the workmanship of divine love; and is the first mover, and first moveable both in heaven above and in the earth beneath, and in the water under the earth. And hence there is given to it the name of the Lucid Aleph, or Alpha; by which is expressed the beginning of the alphabet of nature, and of the book of creation and providence, or the divine archetypal book, in which is the light of wisdom, and the source of all lights and forms.

And in that I said, " Its power supports the heavens;" by this thou wilt come to understand that as the heavens, visible and invisible, are originated from this great principle, so are they likewise necessarily sustained by it; and that therefore if this should be but never so little withdrawn, all the lights, glories, beauties, and forms of the heavenly worlds, would presently sink into darkness and chaos.

And whereas I further said, " that it upholds the earth;" this will appear to thee no less evident than the former, and thou shalt perceive it in thyself by daily and hourly experience; forasmuch as the earth without it, even thy own earth also (that is, thy body), would certainly be without form and void. By the power thereof the earth hath been thus long upheld, not-withstanding a foreign usurped power introduced by the folly of sin: And should this but once fail or recede, there could no longer be either vegetation or animation upon it; yea, the very pillars of it be overthrown quite, and the band of union, which is that of attraction or magnetism, called the centripetal power, being broken and dissolved, all must thence run into the utmost disorder, and falling away as into shivers, would be dispersed as loose dust before the wind.

But in that I said, " Its height is higher than the highest heavens;" this thou mayest also understand within thyself: For shouldest thou ascend in spirit through all the orders of angels and heavenly powers, yet the power of love still is undeniably superiour to them all. And as the throne of God, who sits upon the heaven of heavens, is higher than the highest of them, even so must love also be, which fills them all, and comprehends them all.

And whereas I said of the greatness of love, that it is " greater than the very manifestation of the Godhead in the light of the divine essence;" that is also true: For love enters even into that where the Godhead is not manifested in this glorious light, and where God may be said not to dwell. And entering thereinto, love begins to manifest to the soul the light of the Godhead; and thus is the darkness broken through, and the wonders of the new creation successively manifested.

Thus shalt thou be brought to understand really and fundamentally, what is the virtue and power of love, and what the height and greatness thereof is; how that it is indeed the " virtue of all virtues," though it be invisible, and as a nothing in appearance, inasmuch as it is the worker of all things, and a powerful vital energy passing through all virtues and powers natural and supernatural; and the power of all powers, nothing being able to let or obstruct the omnipotence of love, or to resist its invincible penetrating might, which passes through the whole creation of God, inspecting and governing all things.

And in that I said, " It is higher than the highest, and greater than the greatest;" thou mayest hereby perceive as in a glimpse, the supreme height and greatness of omnipotent love, which infinitely transcends all that human sense and reason can reach to. The highest archangels and the greatest powers of heaven, are in comparison of it but as dwarfs. Nothing can be conceived higher and greater in God himself, by the very highest and greatest of his creatures. There is such an infinity in it, as comprehends and surpasses all the divine attributes.

But in that it was also said, " Its greatness is greater than God;" that likewise is very true in the sense wherein it was spoken: For love, as I before observed, can there enter where God dwelleth not, since the Most High God dwelleth not in darkness, but in the light; the hellish darkness being put under his feet. Thus for instance, when our beloved Lord Christ was in hell, hell was not the mansion of God or of Christ; hell was not God, neither was it with God, nor could it be at all with him; hell stood in the darkness and anxiety of nature, and no light of the divine majesty did there enter: God was not there; for he is not in the darkness, or in the anguish; but love was there; and love destroyed death and conquered hell. So also when thou art in anguish or trouble, which is hell within, God is not the anguish or trouble; neither is he in the anguish or trouble; but his love is there, and brings thee out of the anguish and trouble into God, leading thee into the light and joy of his presence. When God hides himself in thee, love is still there, and makes him manifest in thee. Such is the inconceiveable greatness and largeness of love; which will hence appear to thee as great as God above nature, and greater than God in nature, or as considered in his manifestative glory.

Lastly, whereas I also said, " Whosoever finds it, finds nothing and all things; " that is also certain and true. But how finds he nothing? Why, I will tell thee how. He that findeth it, findeth a supernatural supersensual abyss, which hath no ground or byss to stand on, and where there is no place to dwell in; and he findeth also nothing is like unto it, and therefore it may fitly be compared to nothing; for it is deeper than anything, and is as nothing with respect to all things, forasmuch as it is not comprehensible by any of them. And because it is nothing respectively, it is therefore free from all things; and is that only good, which a man cannot express or utter what it is; there being nothing to which it may be compared, to express it by.

But in that I lastly said, " Whosoever finds it, finds all things; " there is nothing can be more true than this assertion. It hath been the beginning of all things; and it ruleth all things. It is also the end of all things; and will thence comprehend all things within its circle. All things are from it, and in it, and by it. If thou findest it, thou comest into that ground from whence all things are proceeded, and wherein they subsist; and thou art in it a KING over all the works of God.

Here the disciple was exceedingly ravished with what his master had so wonderfully and surprisingly declared, and returned his most humble and hearty thanks for that light, which he had been an instrument of conveying to him. But being desirous to hear further concerning these high matters, and to know somewhat more particularly, he requested him, that he would give him leave to wait on him the next day again; and that he would then be pleased to shew him how and where he might find this which was so much beyond all price and value, and whereabout the seat and abode of it might be in human nature; with the entire process of the discovery and bringing it forth to light.

The master said to him: This then we will discourse about at our next conference, as God shall reveal the same to us by his SPIRIT, which is a searcher of all things. And if thou dost remember well what I answered thee in the beginning, thou shalt soon come thereby to understand that hidden mystical wisdom of God, which none of the wise men of the world know; and where the MINE thereof is to be found in thee, shall be given thee from above to discern. Be silent therefore in thy spirit, and watch unto prayer; that when we meet again to-morrow in the love of Christ, thy mind may be disposed for finding that noble pearl, which to the world appears nothing, but which to the children of wisdom is all things.

DIALOGUE II

ARGUMENT

HEREIN is described and set forth the manner of passing the gulf which divides betwixt the two principles or states of heaven and hell: And it is particularly shewn how this transaction is carried on in the soul; what the partition wall therein is, which separates from God.

What the breaking down of this partition wall, and how effected; what the centre of light is, and the pressing into that centre is; what the light of God and the light of nature are; how they are operative in their several spheres, and how to be kept from interfering with each other; with some account of the two wills and their contraposition in the fallen state; of the magical wheel of the will, and how the motion thereof may be regulated; of the eye in the midst thereof, what the right eye is to the soul, and what the left is, but especially what the *single eye* is, and in what manner it is to be obtained; of purification from the contagion of matter; of the destruction of evil, and of the very annihilation of it, by the subsidence of the will from its own something into nothing; of the naked and magical faith, and the attraction thereby of a certain divine substantiality and vestment; how all consists in the will, and proceeds but from *one point*; where that point is placed, and how it may be found out; and which is both the safest and nearest way to attain to the high supersensual state, and the internal kingdom of Christ, according to the true heavenly magia or wisdom.

DISCIPLE.   MASTER.

THE disciple being very earnest to be more fully instructed how he might arrive at the supersensual life; and how, having found all things, he might come to be a king over all God's works; came again to his master the next morning, having watched the night in prayer, that he might be disposed to receive and apprehend the instructions that should be given him by a divine irradiation upon his mind.   And the disciple after a little space of silence, bowed himself, and thus brake forth:

Disciple. O my master! my master! I have now endeavoured to recollect my soul in the presence of God, and to cast myself into that deep where no creature doth nor can dwell; that I might hear the voice of my Lord speaking in me; and be initiated into that high life, whereof I heard yesterday such great and amazing things pronounced.   But, alas! I neither hear nor see as I should: There is still such a partition wall in me which beats back the heavenly sounds in their passage, and obstructs the entrance of that light by which alone divine objects are discoverable, as till this be broken down, I can have

245

but small hopes, yea, even none at all, of arriving at those glorious attainments which you pressed me to, or of entering into that where no creature dwells, and which you call nothing and all things. Wherefore be so kind as to inform me what is required on my part, that this partition which hinders may be broken or removed.

Master. This partition is the creaturely will in thee: And this can be broken by nothing but by the grace of self-denial, which is the entrance into the true following of Christ; and totally removed by nothing but a perfect conformity with the divine will.

Disciple. But how shall I be able to break this creaturely will which is in me, and is at enmity with the divine will? Or, what shall I do to follow Christ in so difficult a path, and not to faint in a continual course of self-denial and resignation to the will of God?

Master. This is not to be done by thyself; but by the light and grace of God received into thy soul, which will, if thou gainsay not, break the darkness that is in thee, and melt down thine own will, which worketh in the darkness and corruption of nature, and bring it into the obedience of Christ, whereby the partition of the creaturely self is removed from betwixt God and thee.

Disciple. I know that I cannot do it of myself: But I would fain learn, how I must receive this divine light and grace into me, which is to do it for me, if I hinder it not my own self. What is then required of me in order to admit this breaker of the partition, and to promote the attainment of the ends of such admission?

Master. There is nothing more required of thee at first, than not to resist this grace, which is manifested in thee; and nothing in the whole process of thy work, but to be obedient and passive to the light of God shining through the darkness of thy creaturely being, which comprehendeth it not, as reaching no higher than the light of nature.

Disciple. But is it not for me to attain, if I can, both the light of God, and the light of the outward nature too: And to make use of them both for the ordering my life wisely and prudently?

Master. It is right, I confess, so to do. And it is indeed a treasure above all earthly treasures, to be possessed of the light of God and nature, operating in their spheres; and to have both the eye of time and eternity at once open together, and yet not to interfere with each other.

Disciple. This is a great satisfaction to me to hear; having been very uneasy about it for some time. But how this can be without interfering with each other, there is the difficulty: Wherefore fain would I know, if it were lawful, the boundaries of the one and the other; and how both the divine and the natural light may in their several spheres respectively act and operate, for the manifestation of the mysteries of God and nature, and for the conduct of my outward and inward life?

Master. That each of these may be preserved distinct in their several spheres, without confounding things heavenly and things earthly, or breaking the golden chain of wisdom, it will be necessary, my child, in the first place to wait for and attend the supernatural and divine light, as that superiour light appointed to govern the day, rising in the true east, which is the centre of paradise; and in great might breaking forth as out of the darkness within thee, through a pillar of fire and thunder-clouds, and thereby also reflecting upon the inferiour light of nature a sort of image of itself, whereby only it can be kept in its due subordination; that which is below being made subservient to that which is above; and that which is without to that which is within. Thus there will be no danger of interfering; but all will go right, and everything abide in its proper sphere.

Disciple. Therefore without reason or the light of nature be sanctified in my soul, and illuminated by this superiour light, as from the central east of the holy light-world, by the eternal and intellectual sun; I perceive there will be always some confusion, and I shall never be able to manage aright either what concerneth time or eternity: But I must always be at a loss, or break the links of wisdom's chain.

Master. It is even so as thou hast said. All is confusion, if thou hast no more but the dim light of nature, or unsanctified and unregenerated reason to guide thee by; and if only the eye of time be opened in thee, which cannot pierce beyond its own limit. Wherefore seek the fountain of light, waiting in the deep ground of thy soul for the rising there of the sun of righteousness, whereby the light of nature in thee, with the properties thereof, will be made to shine seven times brighter than ordinary. For it shall receive the stamp, image, and impression of the super-sensual and supernatural; so that the sensual and rational life will hence be brought into the most perfect order and harmony.

Disciple. But how am I to wait for the rising of this glorious sun, and how am I to seek in the centre, this fountain of light, which may enlighten me throughout, and bring all my properties into perfect harmony? I am in nature, as I said before; and which way shall I pass through nature, and the light thereof, so that I may come into that supernatural and supersensual ground, whence this true light, which is the light of minds, doth arise; and this, without the destruction of my nature, or quenching the light of it, which is my—reason?

Master. Cease but from thine own activity, steadfastly fixing thine eye upon one point, and with a strong purpose relying upon the promised grace of God in Christ, to bring thee out of thy darkness into his marvellous light. For this end gather in all thy thoughts, and by faith press into the centre, laying hold upon the word of God, which is infallible, and which hath called thee. Be thou then obedient to this call; and be silent before the Lord, sitting alone with him in thy inmost and most hidden cell, thy mind being centrally united in itself, and attending his will in the patience of hope. So shall thy light break forth as the morning; and after the redness thereof is passed, the sun himself, which thou waitest for, shall arise unto thee, and under his most healing wings thou shalt greatly rejoice; ascending and descending in his bright and salutiferous beams. Behold this is the true supersensual ground of life.

Disciple. I believe it indeed to be even so. But will not this destroy nature? Will not the light of nature in me be extinguished by this greater light? Or, must not the outward life hence perish, with the earthly body which I carry?

Master. By no means at all. It is true, the evil nature will be destroyed by it; but by the destruction thereof you can be no loser, but very much a gainer. The eternal band of nature is the same afterward as before; and the properties are the same. So that nature hereby is only advanced and meliorated; and the light thereof, or human reason, by being kept within its due bounds, and regulated by a superiour light, is only made useful.

Disciple. Pray therefore let me know how this inferiour light ought to be used by me; how it is to be kept within its due bounds; and after what manner the superiour light doth regulate it and ennoble it.

Master. Know then, my beloved son, that if thou wilt keep the light of nature within its own proper bounds, and make use thereof in just subordination to the light of God; thou must consider that there are in thy soul two wills, an inferiour will, which is for driving thee to things without and below; and a superiour will, which is for drawing to things within and above. These two wills are now set together, as it were back to back, and in a direct contrariety to each other; but in the beginning it was not so. For this contraposition of the soul in these two is no more than the effect of the fallen state; since before that they were placed one under the other, that is, the superiour will above, as the lord, and the inferiour below, as the subject. And thus it ought to have continued. Thou must also further consider, that answering to these two wills there are likewise two eyes in the soul, whereby they are severally directed; forasmuch as these eyes are not united in one single view, but look quite contrary ways at once. They are in a like manner set one against the other, without a common medium to join them. And hence, so long as this double-sightedness doth remain, it is impossible there should be any agreement in the determination of this or that will. This is very plain: And it sheweth the necessity that this malady, arising from the disunion of the rays of vision, be some way remedied and redressed, in order to a true discernment in the mind. Both these eyes therefore must be made to unite by a concentration of rays; there being nothing more dangerous than for the mind to abide thus in the duplicity, and not to seek to arrive at the unity. Thou perceivest, I know, that thou hast two wills in thee, one set against the other, the superiour and the inferiour; and that thou hast also two eyes within, one against another; whereof the one eye may be called the right eye, and the other the left eye. Thou perceivest, too, doubtless, that it is according to the right eye that the wheel of the superiour will is moved; and that it is according to the motion of the left eye that the contrary wheel in the lower is turned about.

Disciple. I perceive this, sir, to be very true; and this it is which causeth a continual combat in me, and createth to me greater anxiety than I am able to express. Nor am I unacquainted with the disease of my own soul, which you have so clearly declared. Alas! I perceive and lament this malady, which so miserably disturbeth my sight; whence I feel such irregular and convulsive motions drawing me on this side and that side. The spirit seeth not as the flesh seeth; neither doth, or can the flesh see, as the spirit seeth. Hence the spirit willeth against the flesh; and the flesh willeth against the spirit in me. This hath been my hard case. And how shall it be remedied? O how may I arrive at the unity of will, and how come into the unity of vision!

Master. Mark now what I say: The right eye looketh forward in thee into eternity. The left eye looketh backward in thee

into time. If now thou sufferest thyself to be always looking
into nature, and the things of time, and to be leading the will,
and to be seeking somewhat for itself in the desire, it will be
impossible for thee ever to arrive at the unity, which thou
wishest for. Remember this; and be upon thy watch. Give
not thy mind leave to enter into, nor to fill itself with, that
which is without thee; neither look thou backward upon thyself;
but quit thyself, and look forward upon Christ. Let not thy
left eye deceive thee, by making continually one representation
after another, and stirring up thereby an earnest longing in the
self-propriety; but let thy right eye command back this left,
and attract it to thee, so that it may not gad abroad into the
wonders and delights of nature. Yea, it is better to pluck it
quite out, and to cast it from thee, than to suffer it to proceed
forth without restraint into nature, and to follow its own lusts:
However, there is for this no necessity, since both eyes may
become very useful, if ordered aright; and both the divine and
natural light may in the soul subsist together, and be of mutual
service to each other. But never shalt thou arrive at the unity
of vision or uniformity of will, but by entering fully into the will
of our Saviour Christ, and therein bringing the eye of time into
the eye of eternity; and then descending by means of this
united through the light of God into the light of nature.

Disciple. So then if I can but enter into the will of my Lord,
and abide therein, I am safe, and may both attain to the light
of God in the spirit of my soul, and see with the eye of God, that
is, the eye of eternity in the eternal ground of my will; and
may also at the same time enjoy the light of this world nevertheless; not degrading, but adorning the light of nature; and
beholding as with the eye of eternity things eternal, so with the
eye of nature things natural, and both contemplating therein
the wonders of God, and sustaining also thereby the life of my
outward vehicle or body.

Master. It is very right. Thou hast well understood; and
thou desirest now to enter into the will of God, and to abide
therein as in the supersensual ground of light and life, where
thou mayest in his light behold both time and eternity, and
bring all the wonders created of God for the exteriour into the
interiour life, and so eternally rejoice in them to the glory of
Christ; the partition of thy creaturely will being broken down,
and the eye of thy spirit simplified in and through the eye of
God manifesting itself in the centre of thy life. Let this be so
now; for it is God's will.

Disciple. But it is very hard to be always looking forwards into eternity; and consequently to attain to this single eye, and simplicity of divine vision. The entrance of a soul naked into the will of God, shutting out all imaginations and desires, and breaking down the strong partition which you mention, is indeed somewhat very terrible and shocking to human nature, as in its present state. O what shall I do, that I may reach this which I so much long for?

Master. My son, let not the eye of nature with the will of the wonders depart from that eye which is introverted into the divine liberty, and into the eternal light of the holy majesty: But let it draw to thee those wonders by union with that heavenly internal eye, which are externally wrought out and manifested in visible nature. For while thou art in the world, and hast an honest employment, thou art certainly by the order of providence obliged to labour in it, and to finish the work given thee, according to thy best ability, without repining in the least; seeking out and manifesting for God's glory, the wonders of nature and art. Since let the nature be what it will, it is all the work and art of God: And let the art also be what it will, it is still God's work; and his art, rather than any art or cunning of man. And all both in art and nature serveth but abundantly to manifest the wonderful works of God; that he for all, and in all, may be glorified. Yea, all serveth, if thou knowest rightly how to use them, but to recollect thee more inwards, and to draw thy spirit into that majestic light, wherein the original patterns and forms of things visible are to be seen. Keep therefore in the centre, and stir not out from the presence of God revealed within thy soul; let the world and the devil make never so great a noise and bustle to draw thee out, mind them not; they cannot hurt thee. It is permitted to the eye of thy reason to seek food, and to thy hands, by their labour, to get food for the terrestrial body: But then this eye ought not with its desire to enter into the food prepared, which would be covetousness; but must in resignation simply bring it before the eye of God in thy spirit, and then thou must seek to place it close to this very eye, without letting it go. Mark this lesson well.

Let the hands or the head be at labour, thy heart ought nevertheless to rest in God. God is a Spirit; dwell in the Spirit, work in the Spirit, pray in the Spirit, and do everything in the Spirit; for remember thou also art a spirit, and thereby created in the image of God: Therefore see thou attract not in thy desire matter unto thee, but as much as possible abstract thyself from all matter whatever; and so, standing in the centre, present thyself as a naked spirit before God, in simplicity and purity; and be sure thy spirit draw in nothing but spirit.

Thou wilt yet be greatly enticed to draw matter, and to gather that which the world calls substance, thereby to have somewhat visible to trust to: But by no means consent to the tempter, nor yield to the lustings of thy flesh against the spirit. For in so doing thou wilt infallibly obscure the divine light in thee; thy spirit will stick in the dark covetous root, and from the fiery source of thy soul will it blaze out in pride and anger; thy will shall be chained in earthliness, and shall sink through the anguish into darkness and materiality; and never shalt thou be able to reach the still liberty, or to stand before the majesty of God. Since this is opening a door for him who reigneth in the corruption of matter, possibly the devil may roar at thee for this refusal; because nothing can vex him worse than such a silent abstraction of the soul, and introversion thereof to the point of rest from all that is worldly and circumferential: But regard him not; neither admit the least dust of that matter into thee which he may pretend any claim to. It will be all darkness to thee, as much matter as is drawn in by the desire of thy will: It will darken God's majesty to thee; and will close the seeing eye, by hiding from thee the light of his beloved countenance. This the serpent longeth to do; but in vain, except thou permittest thy imagination, upon his suggestion, to receive in the alluring matter; else he can never get in. Behold then, if thou desirest to see God's light in thy soul, and be divinely illuminated and conducted, this is the short way that thou art to take; not to let the eye of thy spirit enter into matter, or fill itself with anything whatever, either in heaven or earth; but to let it enter by a naked faith into the light of the majesty; and so receive by pure love the light of God, and attract the divine power into itself, putting on the divine body, and growing up in it to the full maturity of the humanity of Christ.

Disciple. As I said before, so I say again, this is very hard. I conceive indeed well enough that my spirit ought to be free from the contagion of matter, and wholly empty, that it may admit into it the Spirit of God. Also, that this Spirit will not enter, but where the will entereth into nothing, and resigneth itself up in the nakedness of faith, and in the purity of love, to its conduct; feeding magically upon the word of God, and clothing itself thereby with a divine substantiality. But, alas, how hard is it for the will to sink into nothing, to attract nothing, to imagine nothing!

Master. Let it be granted that it is so. Is it not surely worth thy while, and all that thou canst ever do?

Disciple. It is so, I must needs confess.

Master. But perhaps it may not be so hard as at first it appeareth to be; make but the trial, and be in earnest. What is there required of thee but to stand still, and see the salvation of thy God? And couldst thou desire anything less? Where is the hardship in this? Thou hast nothing to care for, nothing to desire in this life, nothing to imagine or attract: Thou needest only cast thy care upon God, who careth for thee, and leave him to dispose of thee according to his good will and pleasure, even as if thou hadst no will at all in thee. For he knoweth what is best; and if thou canst but trust him, he will most certainly do better for thee, than if thou wert left to thine own choice.

Disciple. This I most firmly believe.

Master. If thou believest, then go and do accordingly. All is in the will, as I have shewn thee. When the will imagineth after somewhat, then entereth it into that somewhat, and this somewhat taketh presently the will into itself, and overcloudeth it, so as it can have no light, but must dwell in darkness, unless it return back out of that somewhat into nothing. But when the will imagineth or lusteth after nothing, then it entereth into nothing, where it receiveth the will of God into itself, and so dwelleth in light, and worketh all its works in it.

Disciple. I am now satisfied that the main cause of any one's spiritual blindness, is his letting his will into somewhat, or into that which he hath wrought, of what nature soever it be, good or evil, and his setting his heart and affections upon the work of his own hands or brain; and that when the earthly body perisheth, then the soul must be imprisoned in that very thing which it shall have received and let in; and if the light of God be not in it, being deprived of the light of this world, it cannot but be found in a dark prison.

Master. This is a very precious gate of knowledge; I am glad thou takest it into such consideration. The understanding of the whole Scripture is contained in it; and all that hath been written from the beginning of the world to this day, may be found herein, by him that having entered with his will into nothing, hath there found all things, by finding God; from whom, and to whom, and in whom are all things. By this means

thou shalt come to hear and see God; and after this earthly life
is ended, to see with the eye of eternity all the wonders of God
and of nature, and more particularly those which shall be
wrought by thee in the flesh, or all that the Spirit of God shall
have given thee to labour out for thyself and thy neighbour, or
all that the eye of reason enlightened from above, may at any
time have manifested to thee.   Delay not therefore to enter in
by this gate, which if thou seest in the spirit, as some highly
favoured souls have seen it, thou seest in the supersensual ground
all that God is, and can do; thou seest also therewith, as one
hath said who was taken thereinto, through heaven, hell, and
earth; and through the essence of all essences.   Whosoever
findeth it, hath found all that he can desire.   Here is the virtue
and power of the love of God displayed.   Here is the height and
depth; here is the breadth and length thereof manifested, as
fully as ever the capacity of thy soul can contain.   By this thou
shalt come into that ground out of which all things are originated,
and in which they subsist; and in it thou shalt reign over all
God's works, as a prince of God.

Disciple. Pray tell me, dear master, where dwelleth it in man?

Master. Where man dwelleth not; there hath it its seat in
man.

Disciple. Where is that in a man, where man dwelleth not
in himself?

Master. It is the resigned ground of a soul, to which nothing
cleaveth.

Disciple. Where is the ground in any soul, to which there will
nothing stick?   Or, where is that which abideth and dwelleth
not in something?

Master. It is the centre of rest and motion in the resigned will
of a truly contrite spirit, which is crucified to the world.   This
centre of the will is impenetrable consequently to the world, the
devil, and hell: Nothing in all the world can enter into it, or
adhere to it, though never so many devils should be in the
confederacy against it; because the will is dead with Christ unto
the world, but quickened with him in the centre thereof, after
his blessed image.   Here it is where man dwelleth not; and
where no self abideth, or can abide.

Disciple. O where is this naked ground of the soul void of all
self?   And how shall I come at the hidden centre where God
dwelleth, and not man?   Tell me plainly, loving sir, where it is,
and how it is to be found of me, and entered into?

Master. There where the soul hath slain its own will, and willeth no more anything as from itself, but only as God willeth, and as his Spirit moveth upon the soul, shall this appear: Where the love of self is banished, there dwelleth the love of God. For so much of the soul's own will as is dead unto itself, even so much room hath the will of God, which is his love, taken up in that soul. The reason whereof is this: Where its own will did before sit, there is now nothing; and where nothing is, there it is that the love of God worketh alone.

Disciple. But how shall I comprehend it?

Master. If thou goest about to comprehend it, then it will fly away from thee; but if thou dost surrender thyself wholly up to it, then it will abide with thee, and become the life of thy life, and be natural to thee.

Disciple. And how can this be without dying, or the whole destruction of my will?

Master. Upon this entire surrender and yielding up of thy will, the love of God in thee becometh the life of thy nature; it killeth thee not, but quickeneth thee, who art now dead to thyself in thine own will, according to its proper life, even the life of God. And then thou livest, yet not to thy own will; but thou livest to its will; forasmuch as thy will is henceforth become its will. So then it is no longer thy will, but the will of God; no longer the love of thyself, but the love of God, which moveth and operateth in thee; and then, being thus comprehended in it, thou art dead indeed as to thyself, but art alive unto God. So being dead thou livest, or rather God liveth in thee by his Spirit; and his love is made to thee life from the dead. Never couldst thou, with all thy seeking, have comprehended it; but it hath apprehended thee. Much less couldst thou have comprehended it: But now it hath comprehended thee; and so the treasure of treasures is found.

Disciple. How is it that so few souls do find it, when yet all would be glad enough to have it?

Master. They all seek it in somewhat, and so they find it not: For where there is somewhat for the soul to adhere to, there the soul findeth but that somewhat only, and taketh up its rest therein, until she seeth that it is to be found in nothing, and goeth out of the somewhat into nothing, even into that nothing out of which all things may be made. The soul here saith, " I have nothing, for I am utterly naked and stripped of everything: I can do nothing; for I have no manner of power, but am as water poured out: I am nothing; for all that I am is no more than an image of being, and only God is to me I AM; and so sitting down in my own nothingness, I give glory to the Eternal Being, and will nothing of myself, that so God may will all in me, being unto me my God and all things." Herein now it is that so very few find this most precious treasure in the soul, though every one would so fain have it; and might also have it, were it not for this somewhat in every one which letteth.

Disciple. But if the love should proffer itself to a soul, could not that soul find it, nor lay hold on it, without going for it into nothing?

Master. No verily. Men seek and find not, because they seek it not in the naked ground where it lieth; but in something or other where it never will be, neither can be. They seek it in their own will, and they find it not. They seek it in their self-desire, and they meet not with it. They look for it in an image, or in an opinion, or in affection, or a natural devotion and fervour, and they lose the substance by thus hunting after a shadow. They search for it in something sensible or imaginary, in somewhat which they may have a more peculiar natural inclination for, and adhesion to; and so they miss of what they seek, for want of diving into the supersensual and supernatural ground where the treasure is hid. Now, should the love graciously condescend to proffer itself to such as these, and even to present itself evidently before the eye of their spirit, yet would it find no place in them at all, neither could it be held by them, or remain with them.

Disciple. Why not, if the love should be willing and ready to offer itself, and to stay with them.

Master. Because the imaginariness which is in their own will hath set up itself in the place thereof: And so this imaginariness would have the love in it; but the love fleeth away, for it is its prison. The love may offer itself; but it cannot abide where the self-desire attracteth or imagineth. That will which attracteth nothing, and to which nothing adhereth, is only capable of receiving it; for it dwelleth only in nothing, as I said, and therefore they find it not.

Disciple. If it dwell only in nothing, what is now the office of it in nothing?

Master. The office of the love here is to penetrate incessantly into something; and if it penetrate into, and find a place in something which is standing still and at rest, then its business is to take possession thereof. And when it hath there taken possession, then it rejoiceth therein with its flaming love-fire, even as the sun doth in the visible world. And then the office of it is without intermission to enkindle a fire in this something, which may burn it up; and then with the flames thereof exceedingly to enflame itself, and raise the heat of the love-fire by it, even seven degrees higher.

Disciple. O loving master, how shall I understand this?

Master. If it but once kindle a fire within thee, my son, thou shalt then certainly feel how it consumeth all that which it toucheth; thou shalt feel it in the burning up thyself, and swiftly devouring all egoity, or that which thou callest I and Me, as standing in a separate root, and divided from the Deity, the fountain of thy being. And when this enkindling is made in thee, then the love doth so exceedingly rejoice in thy fire, as thou wouldst not for all the world be out of it; yea, wouldst rather suffer thyself to be killed, than to enter into thy something again. This fire now must grow hotter and hotter, till it shall have perfected its office with respect to thee, and therefore wilt not give over, till it come to the seventh degree. Its flame hence also will be so very great, that it will never leave thee, though it should even cost thee thy temporal life; but it would go with thee in its sweet loving fire in death; and if thou wentest also into hell, it would break hell in pieces also for thy sake. Nothing is more certain than this; for it is stronger than death and hell.

Disciple. Enough, my dearest master, I can no longer endure that anything should divert me from it. But how shall I find the nearest way to it?

Master. Where the way is hardest, there go thou; and what the world casteth away, that take thou up. What the world doth, that do thou not; but in all things walk thou contrary to the world. So thou comest the nearest way to that which thou art seeking.

Disciple. If I should in all things walk contrary to other people, I must needs be in a very unquiet and sad state; and the world would not fail to account me for a madman.

Master. I bid thee not, child, to do harm to any one, thereby to create to thyself any misery or unquietness. This is not what I mean by walking contrary in everything to the world. But because the world, as the world, loveth only deceit and vanity, and walketh in false and treacherous ways; thence, if thou hast a mind to act a clean contrary part to the ways thereof, without any exception or reserve whatsoever, walk thou only in the right way, which is called the way of light, as that of the world is properly the way of darkness. For the right way, even the path of light, is contrary to all the ways of the world.

But whereas thou art afraid of creating to thyself hereby trouble and inquietude, that indeed will be so according to the flesh. In the world thou must have trouble; and thy flesh will not fail to be unquiet, and to give thee occasion of continual repentance. Nevertheless in this very anxiety of soul, arising either from the world or the flesh, the love doth most willingly enkindle itself, and its cheering and conquering fire is but made to blaze forth with greater strength for the destruction of that evil. And whereas thou dost also say, that the world will for this esteem thee mad; it is true the world will be apt enough to censure thee for a madman in walking contrary to it: And thou art not to be surprised if the children thereof laugh at thee, calling thee silly fool. For the way to the love of God is folly to the world, but is wisdom to the children of God. Hence, whenever the world perceiveth this holy fire of love in God's children, it concludeth immediately that they are turned fools, and are besides themselves. But to the children of God, that which is despised of the world is the greatest treasure; yea, so great a treasure it is, as no life can express, nor tongue so much as name what this enflaming, all-conquering love of God is. It is brighter than the sun; it is sweeter than anything that is called sweet; it is stronger than all strength; it is more nutrimental than food; more cheering to the heart than wine, and more pleasant than all the joy and pleasantness of this world. Whosoever obtaineth it, is richer than any monarch on earth; and he who getteth it, is nobler than any emperor can be, and more potent and absolute than all power and authority.

OF HEAVEN AND HELL

A DIALOGUE BETWEEN JUNIUS A SCHOLAR AND THEOPHORUS HIS MASTER

THE scholar asked his master, saying; Whither goeth the soul when the body dieth?

His master answered him; There is no necessity for it to go any whither.

What not! said the inquisitive Junius: Must not the soul leave the body at death, and go either to heaven or hell?

It needs no going forth, replyed the venerable Theophorus: Only the outward mortal life with the body shall separate themselves from the soul. The soul hath heaven and hell within itself before, according as it is written, "The kingdom of God cometh not with observation, neither shall they say, Lo here! or Lo there! For behold the kingdom of God is within you." And which soever of the two, that is, either heaven or hell is manifested in it, in that the soul standeth.

Here Junius said to his master; This is hard to understand. Doth it not enter into heaven or hell, as a man entereth into an house; or as one goeth through an hole or casement, into an unknown place; so goeth it not into another world?

The master spake and said; No. There is verily no such kind of entering in; forasmuch as heaven and hell are everywhere, being universally co-extended.

How is that possible? said the scholar. What, can heaven and hell be here present, where we are now sitting? And if one of them might, can you make me believe that ever both should be here together?

Then spoke the master in this manner: I have said that heaven is everywhere present; and it is true. For God is in heaven; and God is everywhere. I have said also, that hell must be in like manner everywhere; and that is also true. For the wicked one, who is the devil, is in hell; and the whole world, as the apostle hath taught us, lieth in the wicked one, or the evil one; which is as much as to say, not only that the devil is in the world, but also that the world is in the devil; and if in the devil, then in hell too, because he is there. So hell therefore is everywhere, as well as heaven; which is the thing that was to be proved.

The scholar, startled hereat, said, Pray make me to understand this.

To whom the master: Understand then what heaven is: It is but the turning in of the will into the love of God. Wheresoever thou findest God manifesting himself in love, there thou findest heaven, without travelling for it so much as one foot. And by this understand also what hell is, and where it is. I say unto thee, it is but the turning in of the will into the wrath of God. Wheresoever the anger of God doth more or less manifest itself, there certainly is more or less of hell, in whatsoever place it be. So that it is but the turning in of thy will either into his love, or into his anger; and thou art accordingly either in heaven or in hell. Mark it well. And this now cometh to pass in this present life, whereof St. Paul speaking, saith, "Our conversation is in heaven." And the Lord Christ saith also; "My sheep hear my voice, and I know them, and they follow me, and I give them the eternal life; and none shall pluck them out of my hand." Observe, he saith not, I *will* give them, after this life is ended; but I *give* them, that is, now in the time of this life. And what else is this gift of Christ to his followers but an eternity of life; which for certain, can be nowhere but in heaven. And also if Christ be certainly in heaven, and they who follow him in the regeneration are in his hand, then are they where he is, and so cannot be out of heaven: Yea, moreover none shall be able to pluck them out of heaven, because it is he who holdeth them there, and they are in his hand which nothing can resist. All therefore doth consist in the turning in, or entering of the will into heaven, by hearing the voice of Christ, and both knowing him, and following him. And so on the contrary it is also: Understandest thou this?

His scholar said to him; I think, in part, I do. But how cometh this entering of the will into heaven to pass?

The master answered him; This then I will endeavour to satisfy thee in; but thou must be very attentive to what I shall say unto thee. Know then, my son, that when the ground of the will yieldeth up itself to God, then it sinketh out of its own self, and out of and beyond all ground and place, that is or can be imagined, into a certain unknown deep, where God only is manifest, and where he only worketh and willeth. And then it becometh nothing to itself, as to its own working and willing;

and so God worketh and willeth in it. And God dwells in this resigned will; by which the soul is sanctified, and so fitted to come into divine rest. Now in this case when the body breaketh, the soul is so thoroughly penetrated all over with the divine love, and so thoroughly illuminated with the divine light, even as a glowing hot iron is by the fire, by which being penetrated throughout, it loseth its darkness, and becometh bright and shining. Now this is the hand of Christ, where God's love thoroughly inhabiteth the soul, and is in it a shining light, and a new glorious life. And then the soul is in heaven, and is a temple of the Holy Ghost, and is itself the very heaven of God, wherein he dwelleth. Lo, this is the entering of the will into heaven; and thus it cometh to pass.

Be pleased, sir, to proceed, said the scholar, and let me know how it fareth on the other side.

The master said: The godly soul, you see, is in the hand of Christ, that is in heaven, as he himself hath told us; and in what manner this cometh to be so, you have also heard. But the ungodly soul is not willing in this life-time to come into the divine resignation of its will, or to enter into the will of God; but goeth on still in its own lust and desire, in vanity and falsehood, and so entereth into the will of the devil. It receiveth thereupon into itself nothing but wickedness; nothing but lying, pride, covetousness, envy, and wrath; and thereinto it giveth up its will and whole desire. This is the vanity of the will; and this same vanity or vain shadow must also in like manner be manifested in the soul, which hath yielded up itself to be its servant; and must work therein, even as the love of God worketh in the regenerated will, and penetrate it all over, as fire doth iron.

And it is not possible for this soul to come into the rest of God; because God's anger is manifested in it, and worketh in it. Now when the body is parted from this soul, then beginneth the eternal melancholy and despair; because it now findeth that it is become altogether vanity, even a vanity most vexatious to itself, and a distracting fury, and a self-tormenting abomination. Now it perceiveth itself disappointed of everything which it had before fancied, and blind, and naked, and wounded, and hungry, and thirsty; without the least prospect of being ever relieved, or obtaining so much as one drop of the water of eternal life. And it feeleth itself to be a mere devil to itself, and its own vile executioner and tormentor; and is affrighted at its own ugly dark form, appearing as a most hideous and monstrous worm, and fain would flee from itself, if it could, but it cannot, being fast bound with the chains of the dark nature, whereinto it had sunk itself when in the flesh. And so not having learned nor accustomed itself to sink down into the divine grace, and being also strongly possessed with the idea of God, as an angry and jealous God, the poor soul is both afraid and ashamed to bring its will into God, by which deliverance might possibly come to it. The soul is afraid to do it, as fearing to be consumed by so doing, under the apprehension of the Deity as a mere devouring fire. The soul is also ashamed to do it, as being confounded at its own nakedness and monstrosity; and therefore would, if it were possible, hide itself from the majesty of God, and cover its abominable form from his most holy eye, though by casting itself still deeper into the darkness, wherefore then it will not enter into God; nay, it cannot enter with its false will; yea, though it should strive to enter, yet can it not enter into the love, because of the will which hath reigned in it. For such a soul is thereby captivated in the wrath; yea, is itself but mere wrath, having by its false desire, which it had awakened in itself, comprehended and shut up itself therewith, and so transformed itself into the nature and property thereof.

And since also the light of God doth not shine in it, nor the love of God incline it, the soul is moreover a great darkness, and is withal an anxious fire-source, carrying about an hell within itself, and not being able to discern the least glimpse of the light of God, or to feel the least spark of his love. Thus it dwelleth in itself as in hell, and needeth no entering into hell at all, or being carried thither; for in what place soever it may be, so long as it is in itself, it is in the hell. And though it should travel far, and cast itself many hundred thousand leagues from its present place, to be out of hell; yet still would it remain in the hellish source and darkness.

If this be so, how then cometh it, said the scholar to Theophorus, that an heavenly soul doth not in the time of this life perfectly perceive the heavenly light and joy; and the soul which is without God in the world, doth not also here feel hell, as well as hereafter? Why should they not both be perceived and felt as well in this life as in the next, seeing that both of them are in man, and one of them (as you have shewed) worketh in every man?

To whom Theophorus presently returneth this answer: The kingdom of heaven is in the saints operative and manifestative of itself by faith. They who carry God within them, and live by his Spirit, find the kingdom of God in their faith; and they feel the love of God in their faith, by which the will hath given up itself into God, and is made Godlike. In a word, all is transacted within them by faith, which is to them the evidence of the eternal invisibles, and a great manifestation in their spirit of this divine kingdom, which is within them. But their natural life is nevertheless encompassed with flesh and blood; and this standing in a contrariety thereto, and being placed through the Fall in the principle of God's anger, and environed about with the world, which by no means can be reconciled to faith, these faithful souls cannot but be very much exposed to attacks from this world, wherein they are sojourners; neither can they be insensible of their being thus compassed about with flesh and blood, and with this world's vain lust, which ceaseth not continually to penetrate the outward mortal life, and to tempt them manifold ways, even as it did Christ. Whence the world on one side, and the devil on the other, not without the curse of God's anger in flesh and blood, do thoroughly penetrate and sift the life; whereby it cometh to pass that the soul is often in anxiety when these three are all set upon it together, and when hell thus assaulteth the life, and would manifest itself in the soul. But the soul hereupon sinketh down into the hope of the grace of God, and standeth like a beautiful rose in the midst of thorns, until the kingdom of this world shall fall from it in the death of the body: And then the soul first becometh truly manifest in the love of God, and in his kingdom, which is the kingdom of love; having henceforth nothing more to hinder it. But during this life she must walk with Christ in this world; and then Christ delivereth her out of her own hell, by penetrating her with his love throughout, and standing by her in hell, and even changing her hell into heaven.

But in that thou moreover sayest, why do not the souls which are without God feel hell in this world? I answer: They bear it about with them in their wicked consciences, but they know it not; because the world hath put out their eyes, and its deadly cup hath cast them likewise into a sleep, a most fatal sleep. Notwithstanding which it must be owned that the wicked do frequently feel hell within them during the time of this mortal life, though they may not apprehend that it is hell, because of the earthly vanity which cleaveth unto them from without, and the sensible pleasures and amusements wherewith they are intoxicated. And moreover it is to be noted, that the outward life in every such one hath yet the light of the outward nature, which ruleth in that life; and so the pain of hell cannot, so long as that hath the rule, be revealed. But when the body dieth or breaketh away, so as the soul cannot any longer enjoy such temporal pleasure and delight, nor the light of this outward world, which is wholly thereupon extinguished as to it; then the soul stands in an eternal hunger and thirst after such vanities as it was here in love withal, but yet can reach nothing but that false will, which it had impressed in itself while in the body; and wherein it had abounded to its great loss. And now whereas it had too much of its will in this life, and yet was not contented therewith, it hath after this separation by death, as little of it; which createth in it an everlasting thirst after that which it can henceforth never obtain more, and causeth it to be in a perpetual anxious lust after vanity, according to its former impression, and in a continual rage of hunger after those sorts of wickedness and lewdness whereinto it was immersed, being in the flesh. Fain would it do more evil still, but that it hath not either wherein or wherewith to effect the same, left it; and therefore it doth perform this only in itself. All is now internally transacted, as if it were outward; and so the ungodly is tormented by those furies which are in his own mind, and begotten upon himself by himself. For he is verily become his own devil and tormentor; and that by which he sinned here, when the shadow of this world is passed away, abideth still with him in the impression, and is made his prison and his hell. But this hellish hunger and thirst cannot be fully manifested in the soul, till the body which ministered to the soul what it lusted after, and with which the soul was so bewitched, as to doat thereupon, and pursue all its cravings, be stripped off from it.

I perceive then, said Junius to his master, that the soul having played the wanton with the body in all voluptuousness, and served the lusts thereof during this life, retaineth still the very same inclinations and affections which it had before, then when it hath no opportunity nor capacity to satisfy them longer; and that when this cannot be, there is then hell opened in that soul, which had been shut up in it before, by means of the outward life in the body, and of the light of this world. Do I rightly understand?

Theophorus said, It is very rightly understood by you. Go on.

On the other hand (said he) I clearly perceive by what I have heard, that heaven cannot but be in a loving soul, which is possessed of God, and hath subdued thereby the body to the obedience of the spirit in all things, and perfectly immersed itself into the will and love of God. And when the body dieth, and this soul is hence redeemed from the earth, it is now evident to me, that the life of God which was hidden in it, will display itself gloriously, and heaven consequently be then manifested. But notwithstanding, if there be not also a local heaven besides, and a local hell, I am still at a loss where to place no small part of the creation, if not the greatest. For where must all the intellectual inhabitants of it abide?

In their own principle, answered the master, whether it be of light or of darkness. For every created intellectual being remaineth in its deeds and essences, in its wonders and properties, in its life and image; and therein it beholdeth and feeleth God, as who is everywhere, whether it be in the love, or in the wrath.

If it be in the love of God, then beholdeth it God accordingly, and feeleth him as he is love. But if it hath captivated itself in the wrath of God, then it cannot behold God otherwise than in the wrathful nature, nor perceive him otherwise than as an incensed and vindictive spirit. All places are alike to it, if it be in God's love; and if it be not there, every place is hell alike. What place can bound a thought? Or what needeth any understanding spirit to be kept here or there, in order to its happiness or misery? Verily, wheresoever it is, it is in the abyssal world, where there is neither end nor limit. And whither, I pray, should it go? since though it should go a thousand miles off, or a thousand time ten thousand miles, and this ten thousand times over, beyond the bounds of the universe, and into the imaginary spaces above the stars, yet it were then still in the very same point from whence it went out. For God is the place of spirit; if it may be lawful to attribute to him such a name, to the which body hath a relation: And in God there is no limit; both near and afar off is here all one; and be it in his love, or be it in his anger, the abyssal will of the spirit is altogether unconfined. It is swift as thought, passing through all things; it is magical, and nothing corporeal or from without can let it; it dwelleth in its wonders, and they are its house.

Thus it is with every intellectual, whether of the order of angels, or of human souls; and you need not fear but there will be room enough for them all, be they ever so many; and such also as shall best suit them, even according to their election and determination; and which may thence very well be called his own place.

At which, said the scholar; I remember, indeed, that it is

written concerning the great traitor, that he went after death to his own place.

The master here said: The same is true of every soul, when it departeth this mortal life: And it is true in like manner of every angel, or spirit whatsoever; which is necessarily determined by its own choice. As God is everywhere, so also the angels are everywhere; but each one in its own principle, and in its own property, or (if you had rather) in its own place. The same essence of God, which is as a place to spirits, is confessed to be everywhere; but the appropriation, or participation hereof is different to every one, according as each hath attracted magically in the earnestness of the will. The same divine essence which is with the angels of God above, is with us also below: And the same divine nature which is with us, is likewise with them; but after different manners and in different degrees, communicated and participated.

And what I have said here of the divine, is no less to be considered by you in the participation of the diabolical essence and nature, which is the power of darkness, as to the manifold modes, degrees, and appropriations thereof in the false will. In this world there is strife between them: But when this world hath reached in any one the limit, then the principle catcheth that which is its own; and so the soul receiveth companions accordingly, that is, either angels or devils.

To whom the scholar again: Heaven and hell then being in us at strife in the time of this life, and God himself being also thus near unto us, where can angels and devils dwell?

And the master answered him thus: Where thou dost not dwell as to thy self-hood, and to thine own will, there the holy angels dwell with thee, and everywhere all over round about thee. Remember this well. On the contrary, where thou dwellest as to thyself, in self-seeking, and self-will, there to be sure the devils will be with thee, and will take up their abode with thee, and dwell all over thee, and round about thee everywhere. Which God in his mercy prevent.

I understand not this, said the scholar, so perfectly well as I could wish. Be pleased to make it a little more clear to me.

The master then spake: Mark well what I am going to say. Where the will of God in anything willeth, there is God manifested; and in this very manifestation of God, the angels do dwell. But where God in any creature willeth not with the will of that creature, there God is not manifested to it, neither can he be; but dwelleth in himself, without the co-operation thereof, and subjection to him in humility. There God is an unmanifested God to the creature: So the angels dwell not with such an one; for wherever they dwell, there is the glory of God; and they make his glory. What then dwelleth in such a creature as this? God dwelleth not therein; the angels dwell not therein; God willeth not therein, the angels also will not therein. The case is evidently this, in that soul or creature its own will is without God's will, and there the devil dwelleth; and with him all whatever is without God, and without Christ. This is the truth; lay it to heart.

The Scholar. It is possible I may ask several impertinent questions; but I beseech you, good sir, to have patience with me, and to pity my ignorance, if I ask what may appear to you perhaps ridiculous, or may not be at all fit for me to expect an answer to. For I have several questions still to propound to you; but I am ashamed of my own thoughts in this matter.

The Master. Be plain with me, and propose whatever is upon your mind; yea, be not ashamed even to appear ridiculous, so that by querying you may but become wiser.

The scholar thanked his master for this liberty, and said: How far then are heaven and hell asunder?

To whom he answered thus: As far as day and night; or as far as something and nothing. They are in one another, and yet they are at the greatest distance one from the other. Nay, the one of them is as nothing to the other; and yet notwithstanding they cause joy and grief to one another. Heaven is throughout the whole world, and it is also without the world over all, even everywhere that is, or that can be but so much as imagined. It filleth all, it is within all, it is without all, it encompasseth all; without division, without place; working by a divine manifestation, and flowing forth universally, but not going in the least out of itself. For only in itself it worketh, and is revealed, being one, and undivided in all. It appeareth only through the manifestation of God; and never but in itself only: And in that being which cometh into it, or in that wherein it is manifested; there also it is that God is manifested. Because heaven is nothing else but a manifestation or revelation of the Eternal One, wherein all the working and willing is in quiet love.

So in like manner hell also is through the whole world, and dwelleth and worketh but in itself, and in that wherein the foundation of hell is manifested, namely, in self-hood, and in the false will. The visible world hath both in it; and there is no place but heaven and hell may be found or revealed in it.

Now man as to his temporal life, is only of the visible world; and therefore during the time of this life, he seeth not the spiritual world. For the outward world with its substance, is a cover to the spiritual world, even as the body is to the soul. But when the outward man dieth, then the spiritual world, as to the soul, which hath now its covering taken away, is manifested either in the eternal light with the holy angels, or in the eternal darkness, with the devils.

The scholar further queried: What is an angel, or a human soul, that they can be thus manifested either in God's love or anger, either in light or darkness?

To whom Theophorus answered: They come from one and the self-same original: They are little branches of the divine wisdom, of the divine will, sprung from the divine word, and made objects of the divine love. They are out of the ground of eternity, whence light and darkness do spring: Darkness, which consisteth in the receiving of self-desire; and light, which consisteth in willing the same thing with God. For in the conformity of the will with God's will, is heaven; and wheresoever there is this willing with God, there the love of God is undoubtedly in the working, and his light will not fail to manifest itself. But in the self-attraction of the soul's desire, or in the reception of self into the willing of any spirit, angelical or human, the will of God worketh difficultly, and is to that soul or spirit nought but darkness; out of which, notwithstanding, the light may be manifested. And this darkness is the hell of that spirit wherein it is. For heaven and hell are nought else but a manifestation of the divine will either in light or darkness, according to the properties of the spiritual world.[1]

WHAT THE BODY OF MAN IS; AND WHY THE SOUL IS CAPABLE OF RECEIVING GOOD AND EVIL

Scholar. What then is the body of man?

Master. It is the visible world; an image and quintessence, or compound of all that the world is; and the visible world is a manifestation of the inward spiritual world, come out of the eternal light, and out of the eternal darkness, out of the spiritual compaction or connection; and it is also an image or figure of eternity, whereby eternity hath made itself visible; where self-

[1] From the beginning of the Supersensual Life to the reference of this note, was found among the papers of the later editor, in the handwriting of the truely pious and learned Mr. Law, who has so enlarged and elucidated it (as the reader may see by comparing it with the original) that probably he intended it for a separate publication.

will and resigned will, viz. evil and good, work one with the other.

Such a substance is the outward man. For God created man of the outward world, and breathed into him the inward spiritual world for a soul and an intelligent life; and therefore in the things of the outward world man can receive and work evil and good.

OF THE DESTRUCTION OF THE WORLD; OF MAN'S BODY, IN AND
AFTER THE RESURRECTION; WHERE HEAVEN AND HELL
SHALL BE; OF THE LAST JUDGEMENT; AND WHEREFORE
THE STRIFE IN THE CREATURE MUST BE

Scholar. What shall be after this world, when all things perish and come to an end?

Master. The material substance only ceaseth; viz. the four elements, the sun, moon, and stars. And then the inward world will be wholly visible and manifest. But whatsoever hath been wrought by the will or spirit of man in this world's time, whether evil or good. I say, every such work shall there separate itself in a spiritual manner, either into the eternal light, or into the eternal darkness. For that which is born from each will penetrateth and passeth again into that which is like itself. And there the darkness is called hell, and is an eternal forgetting of all good; and the light is called the kingdom of God, and is an eternal joy in and to the saints, who continually glorify and praise God, for having delivered them from the torment of evil.

The last judgement is a kindling of the fire both of God's love and anger, in which the matter of every substance perisheth, and each fire shall attract itself its own, that is, the substance that is like itself: Thus God's fire of love will draw into it whatsoever is born in the love of God, or love-principle, in which also it shall burn after the manner of love, and yield itself into that substance. But the torment will draw into itself what is wrought in the anger of God in darkness, and consume the false substance; and then there will remain only the painful aching will in its own proper nature, image, and figure.

Scholar. With what matter and form shall the human body rise?

Master. It is sown a natural gross and elementary body, which in this life-time is like the outward elements; yet in this gross body there is a subtle power and virtue. As in the earth also there is a subtle good virtue, which is like the sun, and is one and the same with the sun; which also in the beginning of time did spring and proceed out of the divine power and virtue, from whence all the good virtue of the body is likewise derived. This good virtue of the mortal body shall come again and live for ever in a kind of transparent chrystalline material property, in spiritual flesh and blood; as shall return also the good virtue of the earth, for the earth likewise shall become chrystalline, and the divine light shine in everything that hath a being, essence, or substance. And as the gross earth shall perish and never return, so also the gross flesh of man shall perish and not live for ever. But all things must appear before the judgement, and in the judgement be separated by the fire; yea, both the earth, and also the ashes of the human body. For when God shall once move the spiritual world, every spirit shall attract its spiritual substance to itself. A good spirit and soul shall draw to itself its good substance, and an evil one its evil substance. But we must here understand by substance, such a material power and virtue, the essence of which is mere virtue, like a material tincture (such a thing as hath all figures, colours, and virtues in it, and is at the same time transparent), the grossness whereof is perished in all things.

Scholar. Shall we not rise again with our visible bodies, and live in them for ever? See *The Forty Questions of the Soul*, quest. xxi. ver. 12.

Master. When the visible world perisheth, then all that hath come out of it, and hath been external, shall perish with it. There shall remain of the world only the heavenly chrystalline nature and form, and of man also only the spiritual earth; for man shall be then wholly like the spiritual world, which as yet is hidden.

Scholar. Shall there be husband and wife, or children or kindred, in the heavenly life, or shall one associate with another, as they do in this life?

Master. Why art thou so fleshly-minded? There will be neither husband nor wife, but all will be like the angels of God, viz. masculine virgins. There will be neither son nor daughter, brother nor sister, but all of one stock and kindred. For all are but one in Christ, as a tree and its branches are one, though distinct as creatures; but God is all in all. Indeed, there will be spiritual knowledge of what every one hath been, and done, but no possessing or enjoying, or desire of possessing earthly things, or enjoying fleshly relations any more.

Scholar. Shall they all have that eternal joy and glorification alike?

Master. The Scripture saith, " Such as the people is, such is their God." And in another place, " With the holy thou art holy, and with the perverse thou art perverse." And St. Paul saith, " In the resurrection one shall differ from another in glory, as do the sun, moon, and stars." Therefore know, that the blessed shall indeed all enjoy the divine working in and upon them; but their virtue, and illumination or glory, shall be very different, according as they have been endued in this life with different measures and degrees of power and virtue in their painful working. For the painful working of the creature in this life-time is the opening and begetting of divine power, by which that power is made moveable and operative. Now those who have wrought with Christ in this life-time, and not in the lust of the flesh, shall have great power and transcendent glorification in and upon them. But others, who have only expected, and relied upon, an imputed satisfaction, and in the meanwhile have served their belly-god, and yet at last have turned, and obtained grace; those, I say, shall not attain to so high a degree of power and illumination. So that there will be as great a difference of degrees between them, as is between the sun, moon, and stars; or between the flowers of the field in their varieties of beauty, power, and virtue.

Scholar. How shall the world be judged, and by whom?

Master. Jesus Christ, that " word of God which became man," shall by the power of his divine stirring or motion separate from himself all that belongeth not to him, and shall wholly manifest his kingdom in the place or space where this world now is; for the separating motion worketh all over the universe, through all at once.

Scholar. Whither shall the devils and all the damned be thrown, when the place of this world is become the kingdom of Christ, and such as shall be glorified? Shall they be cast out of the place of this world? Or shall Christ have, and manifest his dominion, out of the sphere or place of this world?

Master. Hell shall remain in the place or sphere of this world everywhere, but hidden to the kingdom of heaven, as the night is hidden in and to the day. " The light shall shine for ever in the darkness, but the darkness can never comprehend, or reach it." And the light is the kingdom of Christ; but the darkness is hell, wherein the devils and the wicked dwell; and thus they shall be suppressed by the kingdom of Christ, and made his footstool, viz. a reproach.

Scholar. How shall all people and nations be brought to judgement?

Master. The eternal word of God, out of which every spiritual creaturely life hath proceeded, will move itself at that hour, according to love and anger, in every life which is come out of the eternity, and will draw every creature before the judgement of Christ, to be sentenced by this motion of the world. The life will then be manifested in all its works, and every soul shall see and feel its judgement and sentence in itself. For the judgement is, indeed, immediately at the departure of the body, manifested in and to every soul: And the last judgement is but a return of the spiritual body, and a separation of the world, when the evil shall be separated from the good, in the substance of the world, and of the human body, and everything enter into its eternal receptacle. And thus is it a manifestation of the mystery of God in every substance and life.

Scholar. How will the sentence be pronounced?

Master. Here consider the words of Christ. " He will say to those on his right hand, Come, ye blessed of my Father, inherit the kingdom prepared for you from the foundation of the world. For I was hungry, and ye gave me meat; I was thirsty, and ye gave me drink; I was a stranger, and ye took me in; naked, and ye clothed me. I was sick, and ye visited me, in prison, and ye came unto me.

" Then shall they answer him, saying, Lord, when saw we thee hungry, thirsty, a stranger, naked, sick, or in prison, and ministered thus unto thee?

" Then shall the King answer and say unto them; Inasmuch as ye have done it unto one of the least of these my brethren, ye have done it unto me.

" And unto the wicked on his left hand he will say, Depart from me, ye cursed, into everlasting fire, prepared for the devil and his angels. For I was hungry, thirsty, a stranger, naked, sick, and in prison, and ye ministered not unto me.

" And they shall also answer him, and say, When did we see thee thus, and ministered not unto thee?

" And he will answer them, Verily I say unto you, inasmuch as ye have not done it unto one of the least of these, ye did it not to me.

" And these shall depart into everlasting punishment, but the righteous into life eternal."

Scholar. Loving master, pray tell me why Christ saith, " What you have done to the least of these, you have done to me; and what you have not done to them, neither have you done it to me." And how doth a man this so, as that he doth it to Christ himself!

Master. Christ dwelleth really and essentially in the faith of those that wholly yield up themselves to him, and giveth them his flesh for food, and his blood for drink; and thus possesseth the ground of their faith, according to the interior or inward man. And a Christian is called a branch of the vine Christ, and a Christian, because Christ dwelleth spiritually in him; therefore whatsoever good any shall do to such a Christian in his bodily necessities, it is done to Christ himself, who dwelleth in him. For such a Christian is not his own, but is wholly resigned to Christ, and become his peculiar possession, and consequently the good deed is done to Christ himself. Therefore also, whosoever shall withhold their help from such a needy Christian, and forbear to serve him in his necessity, they thrust Christ away from themselves, and despise him in his members. When a poor person that belongeth thus to Christ, asketh anything of thee, and thou deniest it him in his necessity, thou deniest it to Christ himself. And whatsoever hurt any shall do to such a Christian, they do it to Christ himself. When any mock, scorn, revile, reject, or thrust away such a one, they do all that to Christ; but he that receiveth him, giveth him meat and drink, or apparel, and assisteth him in his necessities, doth it likewise to Christ, and to a fellow-member of his own body. Nay, he doth it to himself if he be a Christian; for we are all one in Christ, as a tree and its branches are.

Scholar. How then will those subsist in the day of that fierce judgement, who afflict and vex the poor and distressed, and deprive them of their very sweat; necessitating and constraining them by force to submit to their wills, and trampling upon them as their footstools, only that they themselves may live in pomp and power, and spend the fruits of this poor people's sweat and labour in voluptuousness, pride, and vanity?

Master. Christ suffereth in the persecution of his members. Therefore all the wrong that such hard exactors do to the poor wretches under their control, is done to Christ himself; and falleth under his severe sentence and judgement: And besides that, they help the devil to augment his kingdom; for by such oppression of the poor they draw them off from Christ, and make them seek unlawful ways to fill their bellies. Nay, they work for, and with the devil himself, doing the very same thing which he doth; who, without intermission, opposeth the kingdom of

Christ, which consisteth only in love. All these oppressors, if they do not turn with their whole hearts to Christ, and minister to, or serve him, must go into hell-fire, which is fed and kept alive by nothing else but such mere self, as that which they have exercised over the poor here.

Scholar. But how will it fare with those, and how will they be able to stand that severe trial, who in this time do so fiercely contend about the kingdom of Christ, and slander, revile, and persecute one another for their religion, as they do?

Master. All such have not yet known Christ; and they are but as a type or figure of heaven and hell, striving with each other for the victory.

All rising, swelling pride, which contendeth about opinions, is an image of self. And whosoever hath not faith and humility, nor liveth in the spirit of Christ, which is love, is only armed with the anger of God, and helpeth forward the victory of the imaginary self, that is, the kingdom of darkness, and the anger of God. For at the day of judgement all self shall be given to the darkness, as shall also all the unprofitable contentions of men; in which they seek not after love, but merely after their imaginary self, that they may exalt themselves by exalting and establishing their opinions; stirring up princes to wars for the sake of the same, and by that means occasioning the desolation of whole countries of people. All such things belong to the judgement, which will separate the false from the true; and then all images or opinions shall cease, and all the children of God shall dwell for ever in the love of Christ, and that in them.

All whosoever in this time of strife, namely, from the Fall to the Resurrection, are not zealous in the spirit of Christ, and desirous to promote peace and love, but seek and strive for themselves only, are of the devil, and belong to the pit of darkness, and must consequently be separated from Christ. For in heaven all serve God their Creator in humble love.

Scholar. Wherefore then doth God suffer such strife and contention to be in this time?

Master. The life itself standeth in strife, that it may be made manifest, sensible, and palpable, and that the wisdom may be made separable and known.

The strife also constituteth the eternal joy of the victory. For there will arise great praise and thanksgiving in the saints from the experimental sense and knowledge that Christ in them hath overcome darkness, and all the self of nature, and that they are at length totally delivered from the strife; at which they shall rejoice eternally, when they shall know how the wicked are recompenced. And therefore God suffereth all souls to stand in a free-will, that the eternal dominion both of love and anger, of light and of darkness, may be made manifest and known; and that every life might cause and find its own sentence in itself. For that which is now a strife and pain to the saints in their wretched warfare here, shall in the end be turned into great joy to them; and that which hath been a joy and pleasure to ungodly persons in this world, shall afterwards be turned into eternal torment and shame to them. Therefore the joy of the saints must arise to them out of death, as the light ariseth out of a candle by the destruction and consumption of it in its fire; that so the life may be freed from the painfulness of nature, and possess another world.

And as the light hath quite another property than the fire hath, for it giveth and yieldeth itself forth; whereas the fire draweth in and consumeth itself; so the holy life of meekness springeth forth through the death of self-will, and then God's will of love only ruleth, and doth all in all. For thus the Eternal One hath attained feeling and separability, and brought itself forth again with the feeling, through death in great joyfulness; that there might be an eternal delight in the infinite unity, and an eternal cause of joy; and therefore that which was before painfulness, must now be the ground and cause of this motion or stirring to the manifestation of all things. And herein lieth the mystery of the hidden wisdom of God.

" Every one that asketh receiveth, every one that seeketh findeth; and to every one that knocketh it shall be opened. The grace of our Lord Jesus Christ, and the love of God, and the communion of the Holy Ghost, be with us all. Amen."

Heb. xii. 22, 23, 24.

" Thank ye the Lord, for ye are now come to Mount Zion, to the city of the living God, to the heavenly Jerusalem, to the innumerable company of angels, and to the general assembly and church of the first born, who are written in heaven.

" And to God the Judge of all; and to the spirits of just men made perfect; and to Jesus the mediator of the new covenant.

" And to the blood of sprinkling, that speaketh better things than that of Abel. Amen.

" Praise, glory, and thanksgiving; honour, wisdom and power, be unto him that sitteth on the throne, to our God, and the Lamb for ever and ever. Amen."

A DISCOURSE

BETWEEN

A SOUL HUNGRY AND THIRSTY

AFTER

THE FOUNTAIN OF LIFE, THE SWEET LOVE OF JESUS CHRIST,

AND

A SOUL ENLIGHTENED.

SHEWING

Which Way one Soul should seek after and comfort another, and bring it by Means of its Knowledge into the Paths of Christ's Pilgrimage, and faithfully warn it of the thorny Way of the World, which leadeth the fallen Soul that naturally walketh therein, into the Abyss or Pit of Hell.

Composed by a Soul that loveth all who are the Children of Jesus Christ under the Cross.

THE WAY FROM DARKNESS TO TRUE ILLUMINATION

THERE was a poor soul that had wandered out of paradise, and come into the kingdom of this world; where the devil met with it, and said to it, " Whither dost thou go, thou soul that art half blind? "

The Soul said : I would see and speculate into the creatures of the world, which the Creator hath made.

The Devil said : How wilt thou see and speculate into them, when thou canst not know their essence and property? Thou wilt look upon their outside only, as upon a graven image, and canst not know them throughly.

The Soul said : How may I come to know their essence and property?

The Devil said : Thine eyes would be opened to see them throughly, if thou didst but eat of that from whence the creatures themselves are come to be good and evil. Thou wouldst then be as God himself is, and know what the creature is.

The Soul said : I am now a noble and holy creature; but if I should do so, the Creator hath said, that I should die.

The Devil said : No, thou shouldst not die at all; but thy eyes would be opened, and thou wouldst be as God himself, and be master of good and evil. Also, thou shouldst be mighty, powerful, and very great, as I am; all the subtilty that is in the creatures would be made known to thee.

The Soul said : If I had the knowledge of nature and of the creatures, I would then rule the whole world as I listed.

The Devil said : The whole ground of that knowledge lieth in thee. Do but turn thy will and desire from God or goodness into nature and the creatures, and then there will arise in thee a lust to taste; and so thou mayest eat of the Tree of Knowledge of Good and Evil, and by that means come to know all things.

The Soul said : Well then, I will eat of the Tree of Knowledge of Good and Evil, that I may rule all things by my own power; and be of myself a lord on earth, and do what I will, as God himself doth.

The Devil said : I am the prince of this world; and if thou wouldst rule on earth, thou must turn thy lust towards my image, or desire to be like me, that thou mayest get the cunning, wit, reason, and subtilty, that my image hath.

Thus did the devil present to the soul the Vulcan in the Mercury (the power that is in the fiery root of the creature), that is, the fiery wheel of essence or substance, in the form of a serpent. Upon which,

The Soul said : Behold, this is the power which can do all things.—What must I do to get it?

The Devil said : Thou thyself art also such a fiery Mercury. If thou dost break thy will off from God, and bring it into this power and skill, then thy hidden ground will be manifested in thee, and thou mayest work in the same manner. But thou must eat of that fruit, wherein each of the four elements in itself ruleth over the other, and is in strife; the heat striving against the cold, and the cold against the heat; and so all the properties of nature work feelingly. And then thou wilt instantly be as the fiery wheel is, and so bring all things into thine own power, and possess them as thine own.

The Soul did so, and what happened thereupon

Now when the soul broke its will thus off from God, and brought it into the Mercury, or the fiery will (which is the root of life and power), there presently arose in it a lust to eat of the Tree of Knowledge of Good and Evil; and the soul did eat thereof. Which as soon as it had done, Vulcan (or the artificer in the fire) instantly kindled the fiery wheel of its substance, and thereupon all the properties of nature awoke in the soul and exercised each its own lust and desire.

First arose the lust of pride; a desire to be great, mighty, and powerful; to bring all things under subjection to it, and so to be lord itself without control; despising all humility and equality, as esteeming itself the only prudent, witty, and cunning one, and accounting everything folly that is not according to its own humour and liking.

Secondly arose the lust of covetousness; a desire of getting, which would draw all things to itself, into its own possession. For when the lust of pride had turned away the will from God, then the life of the soul would not trust God any further, but would take care for itself; and therefore brought its desire into the creatures, viz. into the earth, metals, trees, and other creatures. Thus the kindled fiery life became hungry and covetous, when it had broken itself off from the unity, love, and meekness of God, and attracted to itself the four elements and their essence, and brought itself into the condition of the beasts; and so the life became dark, empty, and wrathful; and the heavenly virtues and colours went out, like a candle extinguished.

Thirdly, there awoke in this fiery life the stinging thorny lust of envy; a hellish poison, a property which all devils have, and a torment which makes the life a mere enmity to God, and to all creatures. Which envy raged furiously in the desire of covetousness, as a venomous sting doth in the body. Envy cannot endure, but hateth and would hurt or destroy that which covetousness cannot draw to itself, by which hellish passion the noble love of the soul is smothered.

Fourthly, there awoke in this fiery life a torment like fire, viz. anger; which would murther and remove out of the way all who would not be subject to pride. Thus the ground and foundation of hell, which is called the anger of God, was wholly manifested in this soul. Whereby it lost the fair paradise of God and the kingdom of heaven, and became such a worm as the fiery serpent was, which the devil presented to it in his own image and likeness. And so the soul began to rule on earth in a bestial manner, and did all things according to the will of the devil; living in mere pride, covetousness, envy, and anger, having no longer any true love towards God. But there arose in the stead thereof an evil bestial love of filthy lechery, wantonness, and vanity, and there was no purity left in the heart; for the soul had forsaken paradise, and taken the earth into its possession. Its mind was wholly bent upon cunning knowledge, subtilty, and getting together a multitude of earthly things. No righteousness nor virtue remained in it at all; but whatsoever evil and wrong it committed, it covered all cunningly and subtilly under the cloak of its power and authority by law, and called it by the name of right and justice, and accounted it good.

The Devil came to the Soul

Upon this the devil drew near to the soul, and brought it on from one vice to another, for he had taken it captive in his essence, and set joy and pleasure before it therein, saying thus to it: Behold, now thou art powerful, mighty, and noble, endeavour to be greater, richer, and more powerful still. Display thy knowledge, wit, and subtilty, that every one may fear thee, and stand in awe of thee, and that thou mayest be respected, and get a great name in the world.

The Soul did so

The soul did as the devil counselled it, and yet knew not that its counsellor was the devil; but thought it was guided by its own knowledge, wit, and understanding, and that it did very well and right all the while.

Jesus Christ met with the Soul

The soul going on in this course of life, our dear and loving Lord Jesus Christ, who was come into this world with the love and wrath of God, to destroy the works of the devil, and to execute judgement upon all ungodly deeds, on a time met with it, and spake by a strong power, viz. by his passion and death, into it, and destroyed the works of the devil in it, and discovered to it the way to his grace, and shone upon it with his mercy, calling it to return and repent; and promising that he would then deliver it from that monstrous deformed shape or image which it had gotten, and bring it into paradise again.

How Christ wrought in the Soul

Now when the spark of the love of God, or the divine light, was accordingly manifested in the soul, it presently saw itself with its will and works to be in hell, in the wrath of God, and found that it was a misshapen ugly monster in the divine presence and the kingdom of heaven; at which it was so affrighted, that it fell into the greatest anguish possible, for the judgement of God was manifested in it.

What Christ said

Upon this the Lord Christ spake into it with the voice of his grace, and said, " Repent and forsake vanity, and thou shalt attain my grace."

What the Soul said

Then the soul in its ugly misshapen image, with the defiled coat of vanity, went before God, and entreated for grace and the pardon of its sins, and came to be strongly persuaded in itself, that the satisfaction and atonement of our Lord Jesus Christ did belong to it. But the evil properties of the serpent, formed in the astral spirit, or reason of the outward man, would not suffer the will of the soul to come before God, but brought their lusts and inclinations thereinto. For those evil properties would not die to their own lusts, nor leave the world, for they were come out of the world, and therefore they feared the reproach of it, in case they should forsake their worldly honour and glory.

But the poor soul turned its countenance towards God, and desired grace from him, even that he would bestow his love upon it.

The Devil came to it again

But when the devil saw that the soul thus prayed to God, and would enter into repentance, he drew near to it, and thrust the inclinations of the earthly properties into its prayers, and disturbed its good thoughts and desires which pressed forward towards God, and drew them back again to earthly things that they might have no access to him.

The Soul sighed

The central will of the soul indeed sighed after God, but the thoughts arising in the mind, that it should penetrate into him, were distracted, scattered, and destroyed, so that they could not reach the power of God. At which the poor soul was still more affrighted, and began to pray more earnestly. But the devil with his desire took hold of the mercurial kindled fiery wheel of life, and awakened the evil properties, so that evil or false inclinations arose in the soul, and went into that thing wherein they had taken most pleasure and delight before.

The poor soul would very fain go forward to God with its will, and therefore used all its endeavours; but its thoughts continually fled away from God into earthly things, and would not go to him.

Upon this the soul sighed and bewailed itself to God; but was as if it were quite forsaken by him, and cast out from his presence. It could not get so much as one look of grace, but was in mere anguish, fear, and terror, and dreaded every moment that the wrath and severe judgement of God would be manifested in it, and that the devil would take hold of it and have it. And thereupon fell into such great heaviness and sorrow, that it became weary of all the temporal things, which before were its chief joy and happiness.

The earthly natural will indeed desired those things still, but the soul would willingly leave them altogether, and desired to die to all temporal lust and joy whatsoever, and longed only after its first native country, from whence it originally came. But found itself to be far from thence, in great distress and want, and knew not what to do, yet resolved to enter into itself, and try to pray more earnestly.

The Devil's Opposition

But the devil opposed it, and withheld it so that it could not bring itself into any greater fervency of repentance.

He awakened the earthly lusts in its heart, that they might still keep their evil nature and false right therein, and set them at variance with the new-born will and desire of the soul. For they would not die to their own will and light, but would still maintain their temporal pleasures, and so kept the poor soul captive in their evil desires, that it could not stir, though it sighed and longed never so much after the grace of God. For whensoever it prayed, or offered to press forward towards God, then the lusts of the flesh swallowed up the rays and ejaculations that went forth from it, and brought them away from God into earthly thoughts, that it might not partake of divine strength. Which caused the poor soul to think itself forsaken of God, not knowing that he was so near it, and did thus attract it. Also the devil got access to it, and entered into the fiery Mercury, or fiery wheel of its life, and mingled his desires with the earthly lusts of the flesh, and tempted the poor soul; saying to it in the earthly thoughts, " Why dost thou pray? Dost thou think that God knoweth thee or regardeth thee? Consider but what thoughts thou hast in his presence; are they not altogether evil? Thou hast no faith or belief in God at all; how then should he hear thee? He heareth thee not, leave off; why wilt thou needlessly torment and vex thyself? Thou hast time enough to repent at leisure. Wilt thou be mad? Do but look upon the world, I pray thee, a little; doth it not live in jollity and mirth? yet it will be saved well enough for all that. Hath not Christ paid the ransom and satisfied for all men? Thou needest only persuade and comfort thyself that it is done for thee, and then thou shalt be saved. Thou canst not possibly in this world come to any feeling of God; therefore leave off, and take care for thy body, and look after temporal glory. What dost thou suppose will become of thee, if thou turn to be so stupid and melancholy? Thou wilt be the scorn of everybody, and they will laugh at thy folly; and so thou wilt spend thy days in mere sorrow and heaviness, which is pleasing neither to God nor nature. I pray thee, look upon the beauty of the world; for God hath created and placed thee in it, to be a lord over all creatures, and to rule them. Gather store of temporal goods beforehand, that thou mayest not be beholden to the world, or stand in need hereafter. And when old age cometh, or that thou growest near thy end, then prepare thyself for repentance. God will save thee, and receive thee into the heavenly mansions then. There is no need of such ado in vexing, bewailing, and stirring up thyself, as thou makest."

The Condition of the Soul

In these and the like thoughts the soul was ensnared by the devil, and brought into the lusts of the flesh, and earthly desires; and so bound as it were with fetters and strong chains, that it did not know what to do. It looked back a little into the world and the pleasures thereof, but still felt in itself a hunger after divine grace, and would always rather enter into repentance, and favour with God. For the hand of God had touched and bruised it, and therefore it could rest nowhere; but always sighed in itself after sorrow for the sins it had committed, and would fain be rid of them. Yet could not get true repentance, or even the knowledge of sin, though it had a mighty hunger and longing desire after such penitential sorrow.

The soul being thus heavy and sad, and finding no remedy or rest, began to cast about where it might find a fit place to perform true repentance in, where it might be free from business, cares, and the hinderances of the world; and also by what means it might win the favour of God. And at length purposed to betake itself to some private solitary place, and give over all worldly employments and temporal things; and hoped, that by being bountiful and pitiful to the poor, it should obtain God's mercy. Thus did it devise all kinds of ways to get rest, and gain the love, favour, and grace of God again. But all would not do; for its worldly business still followed it in the lusts of the flesh, and it was ensnared in the net of the devil now, as well as before, and could not attain rest. And though for a little while it was somewhat cheered with earthly things, yet presently it fell to be as sad and heavy again, as it was before. The truth was, it felt the awakened wrath of God in itself, but knew not how that came to pass, nor what it ailed. For many times great trouble and terror fell upon it, which made it comfortless, sick, and faint with very fear; so mightily did the first bruising it with the ray or influence of the stirring of grace work upon it. And yet it knew not that Christ was in the wrath and severe justice of God, and fought therein with Satan that spirit of error, which was incorporated in soul and body; nor understood that the hunger and desire to turn and repent came from Christ himself, by which it was drawn in this manner; neither did it know what hindered that it could not yet attain to divine feeling. It knew not that itself was a monster, and did bear the image of the serpent, in which the devil had such power and access to it, and had confounded all its good desires, thoughts, and motions, and brought them away from God and goodness; concerning which Christ himself said, "The devil snatcheth the word out of their hearts, lest they should believe and be saved."

An enlightened and regenerate Soul met the distressed Soul

By the providence of God, an enlightened and regenerate soul met this poor afflicted and distressed soul, and said, "What ailest thou, thou distressed soul, that thou art so restless and troubled?"

The distressed Soul answered

The Creator hath hid his countenance from me, so that I cannot come to his rest; therefore I am thus troubled, and know not what I shall do to get his loving-kindness again. For great cliffs and rocks lie in my way to his grace, so that I cannot come to him. Though I sigh and long after him never so much, yet I am kept back, that I cannot partake of his power, virtue, and strength.

The enlightened Soul said

Thou bearest the monstrous shape of the devil, and art clothed therewith; in which, being his own property or principle, he hath access or power of entrance into thee, and thereby keepeth thy will from penetrating into God. For if thy will might penetrate into God, it would be anointed with the highest power and strength of God, in the resurrection of our Lord Jesus Christ; and that unction would break in pieces the monster which thou carriest about thee; and thy first image of paradise would revive in the centre; which would destroy the devil's power therein, and thou wouldst become an angel again. And because the devil envieth thee this happiness, he holdeth thee captive in his desire in the lusts of the flesh; from which if thou art not delivered, thou wilt be separated from God, and canst never enter into our society.

The distressed Soul terrified

At this speech the poor distressed soul was so terrified and amazed, that it could not speak one word more. When it found that it stood in the form and condition of the serpent, which separated it from God; and that the devil was so nigh it in that condition, who injected evil thoughts into the will of the soul, and had so much power over it thereby, that it was near damnation, and sticking fast in the abyss or bottomless pit of hell, in the anger of God; it would have even despaired of divine mercy; but that the power, virtue, and strength of the first stirring of the grace of God, which had before bruised the soul, upheld and preserved it from total despair. But still it wrestled in itself between hope and doubt; whatsoever hope built up, that doubt threw down again. And thus was it agitated with such continual disquiet, that at last the world and all the glory thereof became loathsome to it, neither would it enjoy worldly pleasures any more; and yet for all this, could it not come to rest.

The enlightened Soul came again, and spoke to the troubled Soul

On a time the enlightened soul came again to this soul, and finding it still in so great trouble, anguish, and grief of mind, said to it:

What dost thou? Wilt thou destroy thyself in thy anguish and sorrow? Why dost torment thyself in thy own power and will, who art but a worm, seeing thy torment increaseth thereby more and more? Yea, if thou shouldst sink thyself down to the bottom of the sea, or couldst fly to the uttermost coasts of the morning, or raise thyself above the stars, yet thou wouldst not be released. For the more thou grievest, tormentest, and troublest thyself, the more painful thy nature will be; and yet thou wilt not be able to come to rest. For thy power is quite lost; and as a dry stick burnt to a coal cannot grow green and spring afresh by its own power, nor get sap to flourish again with other trees and plants; so neither canst thou reach the place of God by thy own power and strength, and transform thyself into that angelical image which thou hadst at first. For in respect to God thou art withered and dry, like a dead plant that hath lost its sap and strength, and so art become a dry tormenting hunger. Thy properties are like heat and cold, which continually strive one against the other, and can never unite.

The distressed Soul said

What then shall I do to bud forth again, and recover the first life, wherein I was at rest before I became an image?

The enlightened Soul said

Thou shalt do nothing at all but forsake thy own will, viz.
that which thou callest I, or thyself. By which means all thy
evil properties will grow weak, faint, and ready to die; and then
thou wilt sink down again into that one thing, from which
thou art originally sprung. For now thou liest captive in the
creatures; but if thy will forsaketh them, the creatures, with
their evil inclinations, will die in thee, which at present stay and
hinder thee, that thou canst not come to God. But if thou
takest this course, thy God will meet thee with his infinite love,
which he hath manifested in Christ Jesus in the humanity, or
human nature. And that will impart sap, life, and vigour to
thee; whereby thou mayest bud, spring, flourish again, and
rejoice in the living God, as a branch growing on his true vine.
And so thou wilt at length recover the image of God, and be
delivered from the image or condition of the serpent: Then
shalt thou come to be my brother, and have fellowship with the
angels.

The poor Soul said

How can I forsake my will, so that the creatures which lodge
therein may die, seeing I must be in the world, and also have
need of it as long as I live?

The enlightened Soul said

Now thou hast worldly power and riches, which thou possessest
as thy own, to do what thou wilt with, and regardest not how
thou gettest or usest the same; employing them in the service
and indulgence of thy carnal and vain desires. Nay, though
thou seest the poor and needy wretch, who wanteth thy help,
and is thy brother, yet thou helpest him not, but layest heavy
burdens upon him, by requiring more of him than his abilities
will bear, or his necessities afford; and oppressest him, by
forcing him to spend his labour and sweat for thee, and the
gratification of thy voluptuous will. Thou art moreover proud,
and insultest over him, and behavest roughly and sternly to
him, exalting thyself above him, and making small account of
him in respect of thyself. Then that poor oppressed brother of
thine cometh, and complaineth with sighs towards God, that he
cannot reap the benefit of his labour and pains, but is forced
by thee to live in misery. By which sighings and groanings of
his he raiseth up the wrath of God in thee; which maketh thy
flame and unquietness still the greater. These are the creatures

which thou art in love with, and hast broken thyself off from God for their sakes, and brought thy love into them, or them into thy love, so that they live therein. Thou nourishest and keepest them by continually receiving them into thy desire, for they live in and by thy receiving them into thy mind; because thou thereby bringest the lust of thy life into them. They are but unclean, filthy, and evil births, and issues of the bestial nature, which yet, by thy receiving them in thy lust or desire, have gotten an image, and formed themselves in thee. And that image is a beast with four heads: First, Pride. Secondly, Covetousness. Thirdly, Envy. Fourthly, Anger. And in these four properties the foundation of hell consisteth, which thou carriest in thee and about thee. It is imprinted and engraven in thee, and thou art wholly taken captive thereby. For these properties live in thy natural life; and thereby thou art severed from God, neither canst thou ever come to him, unless thou so forsake these evil creatures that they may die in thee.

But since thou desirest me to tell thee how to forsake thy own perverse creaturely will, that the creatures might die, and that yet thou mightest live with them in the world. I must assure thee that there is but one way to do it, which is narrow and straight, and will be very hard and irksome to thee at the beginning, but afterwards thou wilt walk in it cheerfully.

Thou must seriously consider, that in the course of this worldly life thou walkest in the anger of God and in the foundation of hell; and that this is not thy true native country; but that a Christian should, and must live in Christ, and in his walking truely follow him; and that he cannot be a Christian, unless the spirit and power of Christ so live in him, that he becometh wholly subject to it. Now seeing the kingdom of Christ is not of this world, but in heaven, therefore thou must always be in a continual ascension towards heaven, if thou wilt follow Christ; though thy body must dwell among the creatures and use them.

The narrow way to which perpetual ascension into heaven and imitation of Christ is this: Thou must despair of all thy own power and strength, for in and by thy own power thou canst not reach the gates of God; and firmly purpose and resolve wholly to give thyself up to the mercy of God, and to sink down with thy whole mind and reason into the passion and death of our Lord Jesus Christ, always desiring to persevere in the same, and to die from all thy creatures therein. Also thou must resolve to watch and guard thy mind, thoughts, and inclinations that they admit no evil into them, neither must thou suffer thyself to be held fast by temporal honour or profit. Thou must resolve likewise to put away from thee all unrighteousness, and whatsoever else may hinder the freedom of thy motion and progress. Thy will must be wholly pure, and fixed in a firm resolution never to return to its old idols any more, but that thou wilt that very instant leave them, and separate thy mind from them, and enter into the sincere way of truth and righteousness, according to the plain and full doctrine of Christ. And as thou dost thus purpose to forsake the enemies of thine own inward nature, so thou must also forgive all thy outward enemies, and resolve to meet them with thy love; that there may be left no creature, person, or thing at all able to take hold of thy will and captivate it; but that it may be sincere, and purged from all creatures. Nay further; if it should be required, thou must be willing and ready to forsake all thy temporal honour and profit for Christ's sake, and regard nothing that is earthly so as to set thy heart and affections upon it; but esteem thyself in whatsoever state, degree, and condition thou art, as to worldly rank or riches, to be but a servant of God and of thy fellow-Christians; or as a steward in the office wherein thy Lord hath placed thee. All arrogance and self-exaltation must be humbled, brought low, and so annihilated that nothing of thine own or of any other creature may stay in thy will to bring thy thoughts or imagination to be set upon it.

Thou must also firmly impress it on thy mind, that thou shalt certainly partake of the promised grace in the merit of Jesus Christ, viz. of his outflowing love, which indeed is already in thee, and which will deliver thee from thy creatures, and enlighten thy will, and kindle it with the flame of love, whereby thou shalt have victory over the devil. Not as if thou couldst will or do anything in thine own strength, but only enter into the suffering and resurrection of Jesus Christ, and take them to thyself, and with them assault and break in pieces the kingdom of the devil in thee, and mortify thy creatures. Thou must resolve to enter into this way this very hour, and never to depart from it, but willingly to submit thyself to God in all thy endeavours and doings, that he may do with thee what he pleaseth.

When thy will is thus prepared and resolved, it hath then broken through its own creatures, and is sincere in the presence of God, and clothed with the merits of Jesus Christ. It may then freely go to the Father with the Prodigal Son, and fall down in his presence and pour forth its prayers; and putting forth all its strength in this divine work, confess its sins and disobedience; and how far it hath departed from God. This must be done not with bare words, but with all its strength, which indeed amounteth only to a strong purpose and resolution; for the soul of itself hath no strength or power to effect any good work.

Now when thou art thus ready, and that thy Heavenly Father shall see thy coming and returning to him in such repentance and humility, he will inwardly speak to thee, and say in thee, "Behold, this is my son which I had lost, he was dead and is alive again." And he will come to meet thee in thy mind with the grace and love of Jesus Christ, and embrace thee with the beams of his love, and kiss thee with his Spirit and strength; and then thou shalt receive grace to pour out thy confession before him, and to pray powerfully. This indeed is the right place where thou must wrestle in the light of his countenance. And if thou standest resolutely here, and shrinkest not back, thou shalt see or feel great wonders. For thou shalt find Christ in thee assaulting hell, and crushing thy beasts in pieces, and that a great tumult and misery will arise in thee; also thy secret undiscovered sins will then first awake, and labour to separate thee from God, and to keep thee back. Thus shalt thou truely find and feel how death and life fight one against the other, and shalt understand by what passeth within thyself, what heaven and hell are. At all which be not moved, but stand firm and shrink not; for at length all thy creatures will grow faint, weak, and ready to die; and then thy will shall wax stronger, and be able to subdue and keep down the evil inclinations. So shall thy will and mind ascend into heaven every day, and thy creatures gradually die away. Thou wilt get a mind wholly new, and begin to be a new creature, and getting rid of the bestial deformity, recover the divine image. Thus shalt thou be delivered from thy present anguish, and return to thy original rest.

The poor Soul's Practice

Then the poor soul began to practise this course with such earnestness, that it conceived it should get the victory presently; but it found that the gates of heaven were shut against it in its own strength and power, and it was, as it were, rejected and forsaken by God, and received not so much as one look or glimpse of grace from him. Upon which it said to itself, "Surely thou hast not sincerely submitted thyself to God. Desire nothing at all of him, but only submit thyself to his judgement and condemnation, that he may kill thy evil inclinations. Sink down into him beyond the limits of nature and creature, and submit thyself to him, that he may do with thee what he will, for thou art not worthy to speak to him." Accordingly the soul took a resolution to sink down, and to forsake its own will; and when it had done so, there fell upon it presently the greatest repentance that could be for the sins it had committed; and it bewailed bitterly its ugly shape, and was truely and deeply sorry that the evil creatures did dwell in it. And because of its sorrow it could not speak one word more in the presence of God, but in its repentance did consider the bitter passion and death of Jesus Christ, viz. what great anguish and torment he had suffered for its sake, in order to deliver it out of its anguish, and change it into the image of God. In which consideration it wholly sunk down, and did nothing but complain of its ignorance and negligence, and that it had not been thankful to its Redeemer, nor once considered the great love he had shewn to it, but had idly spent its time, and not at all regarded how it might come to partake of his purchased and proffered grace; but instead thereof had formed in itself the images and figures of earthly things, with the vain lusts and pleasures of the world. Whereby it had gotten such bestial inclinations, that now it must lie captive in great misery, and for very shame dared not lift up its eyes to God, who hid the light of his countenance from it, and would not so much as look upon it. And as it was thus sighing and crying, it was drawn into the abyss or pit of horror, and laid it as it were at the gates of hell, there to perish. Upon which the poor troubled soul was, as it were, bereft of sense, and wholly forsaken, so that it in a manner forgot all its doings, and would willingly yield itself to death, and cease to be a creature. Accordingly it did yield itself to death, and desired nothing else but to die and perish in the death of its Redeemer Jesus Christ, who had suffered such torments and death for its sake. And in this perishing it began to sigh and pray in itself very inwardly to the divine goodness, and to sink down into the mere mercy of God.

Upon this there suddenly appeared unto it the amiable countenance of the love of God, which penetrated through it as a great light, and made it exceedingly joyful. It then began to pray aright, and to thank the Most High for such grace, and to rejoice abundantly, that it was delivered from the death and anguish of hell. Now it tasted of the sweetness of God, and of his promised truth; and now all the evil spirits which had harassed it before, and kept it back from the grace, love, and inward presence of God, were forced to depart from it. The " wedding of the Lamb " was now kept and solemnised, that is, the noble Sophia espoused or betrothed herself to the soul; and the seal-ring of Christ's victory was impressed into its essence, and it was received to be a child and heir of God again.

When this was done, the soul became very joyful, and began to work in this new power, and to celebrate with praise the wonders of God, and thought thenceforth to walk continually in the same light, strength, and joy. But it was soon assaulted; from without, by the shame and reproach of the world, and from within, by great temptation, so that it began to doubt whether its ground was truely from God, and whether it had really partaken of his grace. For the accuser Satan went to it, and would fain lead it out of this course, and make it doubtful whether it was the true way; whispering thus to it inwardly, " This happy change in thy spirit is not from God, but only from thine own imagination." Also the divine light retired in the soul, and shone but in the inward ground, as fire raked up in embers, so that reason was perplexed, and thought itself forsaken, and the soul knew not what had happened to itself, nor whether it had really and truely tasted of the heavenly gift or not. Yet it could not leave off struggling; for the burning fire of love was sown in it, which had raised in it a vehement and continual hunger and thirst after the divine sweetness. So at length it began to pray aright, and to humble itself in the presence of God, and to examine and try its evil inclinations and thoughts, and to put them away. By which means the will of reason was broken, and the evil inclinations inherent in it were killed, and extirpated more and more. This process was very severe and painful to the nature of the body, for it made it faint and weak, as if it had been very sick; and yet it was no natural sickness that it had, but only the melancholy of its earthly nature, feeling and lamenting the destruction of its evil lusts.

Now when the earthly reason found itself thus forsaken, and the poor soul saw that it was despised outwardly, and derided by the world, because it would walk no longer in the way of wickedness and vanity; and also that it was inwardly assaulted by the accuser Satan, who mocked it, and continually set before it the beauty, riches, and glory of the world, and called it a fool for not embracing them; it began to think and say thus within itself: " O eternal God! What shall I now do to come to rest? "

The enlightened Soul met it again, and spoke to it

While it was in this consideration, the enlightened soul met with it again, and said, "What ailest thou, my brother, that thou art so heavy and sad?"

The distressed Soul said

I have followed thy counsel, and thereby attained a ray, or emanation of the divine sweetness, but it is gone from me again, and I am now deserted. Moreover I have outwardly very great trials and afflictions in the world; for all my good friends forsake and scorn me; and am also inwardly assaulted with anguish, and doubt, and know not what to do.

The enlightened Soul said

Now I like thee very well; for now our beloved Lord Jesus Christ is performing that pilgrimage or process on earth with thee and in thee, which he did himself when he was in this world, who was continually reviled, despised, and evil spoken of, and had nothing of his own in it; and now thou bearest his mark or badge. But do not wonder at it, or think it strange; for it must be so, in order that thou mayest be tried, refined, and purified. In this anguish and distress thou wilt necessarily hunger and cry after deliverance; and by such hunger and prayer thou wilt attract grace to thee both from within and from without. For thou must grow from above and from beneath to be the image of God again. Just as a young plant is agitated by the wind, and must stand its ground in heat and cold, drawing strength and virtue to it from above and from beneath by that agitation, and must endure many a tempest, and undergo much danger before it can come to be a tree, and bring forth fruit. For through that agitation the virtue of the sun moveth in the plant, whereby its wild properties come to be penetrated and tinctured with the solar virtue, and grow thereby.

And this is the time wherein thou must play the part of a valiant soldier in the spirit of Christ, and co-operate thyself therewith. For now the Eternal Father by his fiery power begetteth his son in thee, who changeth the fire of the Father, namely, the first principle, or wrathful property of the soul, into the flame of love, so that out of fire and light (viz. wrath and love) there cometh to be one essence, being, or substance, which is the true temple of God. And now thou shalt bud forth out of the vine Christ, in the vineyard of God, and bring forth

fruit in thy life, and by assisting and instructing others, shew forth thy love in abundance, as a good tree.   For paradise must thus spring up again in thee, through the wrath of God, and hell be changed into heaven in thee.   Therefore be not dismayed at the temptations of the devil, who seeketh and striveth for the kingdom which he once had in thee; but, having now lost it, must be confounded, and depart from thee.   And he covereth thee outwardly with the shame and reproach of the world, that his own shame may not be known, and that thou mayest be hidden to the world.   For with thy new birth or regenerated nature thou art in the divine harmony in heaven.   Be patient, therefore, and wait upon the Lord; and whatsoever shall befall thee, take it all from his hands, as intended by him for thy highest good.   And so the enlightened soul departed from it.

The distressed Soul's Course

The distressed soul began its course now under the patient suffering of Christ, and depending solely upon the strength and power of God in it, entered into hope.   Thenceforth it grew stronger every day, and its evil inclinations died more and more in it.   So that it arrived at length to a high state or degree of grace; and the gates of the divine revelation, and the kingdom of heaven, were opened to, and manifested in it.

And thus the soul through repentance, faith, and prayer, returned to its original and true rest, and became a right and beloved child of God again; to which may he of his infinite mercy help us all.   Amen.

THE TEMPLE PRESS, PRINTERS, LETCHWORTH

EVERYMAN,
I WILL GO WITH
THEE,
& BE THY GVIDE
IN THY MOST NEED
TO GO BY THY SIDE